PABLO ESCOBAR

PABLO ESCOBAR

MY FATHER

Juan Pablo Escobar

Translated by Andrea Rosenberg

Thomas Dunne Books
St. Martin's Griffin
New York

THOMAS DUNNE BOOKS.
An imprint of St. Martin's Press.

www.thomasdunnebooks.com
www.stmartins.com

Designed by Donna Sinisgalli Noetzel

The Library of Congress has cataloged the hardcover edition as follows:

Names: Santos, Marroquín, Sebastián, Juan, author.
Title: Pablo Escobar, my father / Juan Pablo Escobar ; translated from the Spanish by Andrea Rosenberg.
Other titles: Pablo Escobar, mi padre. English
Description: New York : Thomas Dunne Books, 2016.
Identifiers: LCCN 2016013863 | ISBN 9781250104625 (hardcover) | ISBN 9781250104632 (ebook)
Subjects: LCSH: Escobar, Pablo. | Santos, Marroquín, Sebastián, Juan. | Escobar, Pablo—Family. | Drug dealers—Colombia—Biography. | Drug traffic—Colombia—History—20th century. | BISAC: BIOGRAPHY & AUTOBIOGRAPHY / Criminals & Outlaws. | TRUE CRIME / Organized Crime.
Classification: LCC HV5805.E82 M3513 2016 | DDC 363.45092 [B]—dc23
LC record available at https://lccn.loc.gov/2016013863

ISBN 978-1-250-14502-4 (trade paperback)

Our books may be purchased in bulk for promotional, educational, or business use. Please contact your local bookseller or the Macmillan Corporate and Premium Sales Department at 1-800-221-7945, extension 5442, or by email at MacmillanSpecialMarkets@macmillan.com.

First published under the title *Pablo Escobar: Mi Padre* in Colombia by Editorial Planeta Colombiana, S.A.

First St. Martin's Griffin Edition: August 2017

5 7 9 11 13 14 12 10 8 6

To my son, who gives me the strength and
energy to be a good man.

To my unconditionally beloved, companion
in all my adventures.

To my brave mother.

To my cherished sister.

To my dear family.

And to those few friends who overcame fear.

Contents

Introduction   1

1. Betrayal   5

2. Where Did the Money Go?   16

3. My Father's Origins   28

4. The Renault Coke   53

5. Papá Narco   59

6. Excess   79

7. Nápoles: Dreams and Nightmares   83

8. MAS Mayhem   103

9. Politics: His Biggest Mistake   111

10. Better a Grave in Colombia   124

11. Barbarity   154

12. Tales from La Catedral   205

13. Worry When I Tie My Sneakers   238

14. Peace with the Cartels   288

Epilogue: Two Decades in Exile   322

Acknowledgments   *355*

PABLO ESCOBAR

Introduction

I stayed silent for more than twenty years as I pieced my life back together in exile. There is a time for everything, and this book, like its author, required a period of maturation, self-reflection, and humility. Only after that was I ready to sit down and write these stories.

From the day I was born till the day he died, my father was my friend, my guide, my teacher, and my trusted adviser. While he was still alive, I sometimes pleaded with him to write his real story, but he refused: "Grégory,"* he'd say, "you've got to finish making history before you can write it."

After he died, I swore to avenge my father's death, but I broke that promise within ten minutes. All of us have the right to change, and for more than two decades I have been living a life guided by clear rules of tolerance, peaceful coexistence, dialogue, forgiveness, justice, and reconciliation.

This book does not point fingers. Instead, it offers reflections on how Colombia and its politics function, and on why Colombia produces people like my father. I have a great deal of respect for life,

---

* This was my father's affectionate nickname for me. We used to watch a lot of movies about Grigori Rasputin, the Russian mystic and faith healer who had tremendous influence over the family of Nicholas II, the last czar of Russia.

and it is from that place that I have written this book. I have no hidden agenda, unlike most who have written about my father.

Nor is this book the absolute truth. It is a quest, an attempt to get closer to my father's life. It is a personal, intimate investigation. It is the rediscovery of a man, with all of his virtues but also with all of his faults. Most of these anecdotes are ones he told me as we huddled around bonfires on the long, chilly nights of the last year of his life. Others he left me in writing when it seemed that his enemies were very close to killing us all.

I wasn't always by my father's side; I don't know all his stories. Anyone who claims to know them all is lying. I learned the stories contained in this book long after the events had taken place. My father never consulted with me nor with anyone else about any of his decisions. He was a man who made up his own mind.

My journey to learn more of my father's story led me to people who had been in hiding for years, who only now were ready to participate. Their contributions have added much-needed clarity to my own memories and research. Most of all, though, they help ensure that these demons will never be passed down to subsequent generations.

Many "truths" about my father are known only partially—or not known at all. And so telling his story involves great risk because it must be recounted with an enormous sense of responsibility, as much of the terrible things that have been said about him sadly seem to be quite accurate. This is a deeply personal exploration of the inner world of a human being who, in addition to being my father, headed up the most notorious Mafia organization in human history.

I wish to publicly ask my father's victims, every single one of them, for forgiveness. I am anguished by the devastation they experienced in the face of an unparalleled, indiscriminate violence that affected so many innocent people. I want them to know that today I seek to honor each of their memories, with all my heart.

This book will be written with tears, but without bitterness. Not out of a desire to condemn or to seek vengeance, and without offering excuses to promote violence or attempt to justify wrongdoing. The reader will be surprised by the contents of the first chapters, in which I reveal for the first time the deep rift that yawns between me and my father's side of the family. After twenty-one years of quarrels with them, I am convinced that a number actively contributed to the final events that resulted in my father's death.

It is no exaggeration to say that we have been treated more harshly by my father's family than by his worst enemies. My actions toward them were always born out of love and an unconditional respect for the value of family, which must be held on to even in the chaos of war and especially in the hardship of poverty. God and my father both know that I, more than anyone, wished fiercely to believe that this painful family tragedy was only a nightmare. I am grateful to my father for his brutal honesty; it has been my fate to have to see him clearly, to face the man he was without justifying his actions in the least.

When I asked for forgiveness in the documentary *Sins of My Father*, the children of the assassinated politicians Luis Carlos Galán and Rodrigo Lara Bonilla told me, "You are a victim too." My reply to that remains unchanged: if I am a victim, I am merely the last one on a long list of Colombians. My father was responsible for his fate, for his actions, for his life choices as a father, as an individual, and—at the same time—as the criminal who inflicted on Colombia and, indeed, on the whole world, deep wounds that are still being felt. I dream that one day those wounds might heal and become sources of good, so that nobody dares to repeat this story but learns from it instead.

I was not a blindly loyal son. I questioned my father's violent tactics while he was alive, and I repeatedly pleaded with him to abandon his hatred, to put down his arms, to find nonviolent solutions to his problems.

1

Betrayal

In the Residencias Tequendama apartment hotel on December 3, 1993, after the trip to bury my father in Medellín, our firm intention was to live as normal a life as circumstances allowed. For my mother, my sister Manuela, and me, the past twenty-four hours had been the most dramatic of our lives. Not only did we have to endure the agonizing pain of losing the head of the family in such a violent manner, but the funeral had been even more traumatic.

A few hours after Ana Montes, the national director of the attorney general's office, personally confirmed to us that my father had died, we had called the Campos de Paz cemetery in Medellín. They refused to perform the funeral service, and we might have had a similar experience with Jardines de Montesacro, except that relatives of our lawyer at the time, Francisco Fernández, owned the cemetery. My grandmother Hermilda had two lots there, and we decided to use them to bury my father and Álvaro de Jesús Agudelo, known as "Lemon," the bodyguard who was with him when he died.

After assessing the risks of attending the funeral, for the first time we defied one of my father's old orders: "When I die, don't go to the funeral; something could happen to you there." He'd insisted that we shouldn't bring him flowers or visit his grave either. But my mother said she'd go to Medellín "against Pablo's wishes."

"Well, then we'll all go, and if they kill us, so be it," I said, and we rented a small plane to travel to Medellín with two bodyguards assigned by the attorney general's office.

After landing at Olaya Herrera Airport and being besieged by dozens of journalists, who even risked their lives by swarming onto the runway while the plane was still moving, Manuela and my mother were ushered into a red SUV and my girlfriend Andrea and I into a black one.

When we arrived at Jardines de Montesacro, I was pleasantly surprised to see how many people had shown up for the funeral. It was a testament to the love that the lower classes felt for my father, and I was touched to hear the same chant they used when he would inaugurate athletic fields or health clinics in poor areas: "Pablo! Pablo! Pablo!"

In an instant, dozens of people surrounded our SUV and began pounding on it as we headed to the site where my father was to be buried. One of the bodyguards asked if I was planning to get out, but since I knew that we might be in danger, we retreated to the cemetery's office to wait for my mother and sister. I remembered my father's warning and decided the wisest move was to take a step back.

A few minutes after we entered the office, a secretary came in, panicked and in tears. Someone had just called to announce an attack. We ran out of there and got into the black SUV again, where we stayed until the funeral was over. I was right there, just thirty yards away, but I couldn't attend the service, couldn't say good-bye to my father.

ON DECEMBER 19, 1993, TWO WEEKS AFTER MY FATHER'S DEATH, we received a call from Medellín: an assassination attempt had been made on my uncle Roberto Escobar in the Itagüí maximum-security prison.

At the time we were still sequestered under heavy guard on the twenty-ninth floor of Residencias Tequendama in Bogotá. Worried, we tried to find out what had happened, but nobody could tell us anything. The television news reported that Roberto had opened an envelope from the Office of the Inspector General and it had exploded, resulting in serious injuries to his eyes and abdomen. The next day, my aunts called and told us that the Clínica Las Vegas, where he'd been taken for emergency treatment, lacked the ophthalmology equipment needed to operate. And as if that weren't enough, there were also rumors that an armed commando was planning to finish him off in his sickbed.

My family decided to move Roberto to the central military hospital in Bogotá, which not only was better equipped but also offered security. My mother paid three thousand dollars to rent an ambulance plane, and once we'd confirmed that Roberto had arrived at the hospital, we decided to visit him with my uncle Fernando, my mother's brother.

As we left the hotel, we were unnerved to discover that the agents from the Technical Investigation Corps (CTI), the division of the attorney general's office that had been protecting us since late November, had been replaced that day, without previous notice, by agents from SIJIN, the police's criminal investigation unit. I didn't say anything to my uncle, but I sensed that something bad was about to happen. In other areas of the building, managing other aspects of our security, were agents from the Central Directorate of the Judicial Police and Intelligence (DIJIN) and the Administrative Department of Security (DAS). Outside, the Colombian army was responsible for our safety.

A couple of hours after we arrived at the hospital, a doctor requested authorization from one of Roberto's family members to remove both of his eyes, which had been badly damaged in the explosion. We refused to sign and asked the specialist to do whatever he could to preserve Roberto's sight, no matter the cost, even if the chances of success were vanishingly small. We even offered to fly in the best ophthalmologist from wherever he might be located.

Hours later, not yet conscious, Roberto came out of surgery and was moved to a room where a guard from the National Penitentiary and Prison Institute was on duty. Roberto's face, abdomen, and left hand were bandaged.

We waited patiently until he began to wake up. Still groggy from the sedation, he said he could see shades of light and darkness but was unable to make out shapes.

When I saw he'd recovered a bit, I told him I was feeling anxious. If they'd made an attempt on Roberto's life after my father's death, then my mother, my sister, and I were surely next. I desperately asked him if my father had a helicopter hidden somewhere that we might be able to use to make an escape. Over the course of our conversation, which was frequently interrupted by nurses and doctors making their rounds, I repeatedly asked Roberto what we could do to survive the threat posed by my father's enemies.

He was silent for a few moments and then instructed me to grab a pencil and paper.

"Write this down, Juan Pablo: 'AAA.' Take it to the U.S. embassy. Ask them for help, and tell them I sent you."

As I put the paper in my pocket, Roberto's surgeon entered and informed us he was optimistic, that he'd done everything he could to save my uncle's eyes. We thanked the doctor and motioned to leave, but he told me that I had to stay at the hospital.

"What do you mean? Why?"

"Your security detail hasn't arrived," he said.

The doctor's words made me paranoid because if he'd been in surgery all this time, he had no reason to know what was going on with our security.

"I'm a free man, Doctor. Or am I being detained here?" I said.

"In any event, I'm leaving. I think someone's plotting to kill me today. They switched out the CTI agents who were guarding us."

"You're under our protection here, not under arrest. We are responsible for your safety at this military hospital, and we can deliver you only to government security forces," he said.

"The people who are responsible for my safety out there are the same ones who are coming to kill me," I insisted. "So you can either help me out by authorizing me to leave the hospital, or I'll have to make a run for it. I'm not getting in a car with the very people who are after me."

The doctor must have seen the fear on my face. He quietly agreed to sign the order, and Fernando and I furtively returned to Residencias Tequendama, deciding to visit the embassy the next day.

We got up early and headed to the room where the agents charged with our security were staying. I said hello to the agent known as "A1" and told him we needed an escort to the U.S. embassy.

"Why are you going there?" he demanded to know.

"I don't have to tell you that. Are you going to give us protection, or do I have to call the attorney general and tell him you've refused?" I replied.

"I don't have enough men to escort you there at the moment," A1 said, irritated.

"How is that possible, when a twenty-four-hour security detail of some forty government agents and vehicles has been assigned to protect us?"

"You can go if you want, but I'm not going to protect you. And you'll need to sign a piece of paper waiving our protection," he said.

"Bring it, and I'll sign it."

The agent went into another room to look for something to write on, and we seized the moment to rush downstairs and hail a taxi to the U.S. embassy. It was eight in the morning, and at that hour there was a long line of people waiting to get in so they could apply for an American visa.

I was very nervous as I pushed past the waiting people, explaining that I wasn't there for a visa. When I reached the booth by the entrance, I took out the paper with the triple A and held it up against the dark, bulletproof glass. In an instant, four muscular men appeared and started to photograph us. I didn't say a word, and soon one of them approached and instructed me to follow him.

They didn't ask my name or for ID, didn't search me or even make me go through the metal detector. Roberto's triple A was obviously some sort of safe-conduct signal. I was scared. Maybe that's why it didn't occur to me to wonder what sort of contact my father's brother had with the U.S. government.

I was about to take a seat in a waiting room when an older man with nearly white hair and a serious expression appeared. "I'm Joe Toft, director of the DEA for Latin America. Come with me." He took me to a nearby office and asked me straightaway why I'd come to the embassy.

"I'm here to ask for help because they're killing my whole family. My uncle Roberto told me to tell you he sent me."

"My government can't guarantee you any kind of assistance," Toft said in a dry, distant tone. "The most I can do is recommend that a judge in the United States assess the possibility of offering you residence in my country in exchange for your cooperation."

"What sort of cooperation? I'm not legally an adult yet," I replied, only seventeen at the time.

"You can help us a great deal . . . with information."

"Information? About what?"

"About your father's files."

"When you killed him, you killed those files."

"I don't understand," said the official.

"The day you collaborated in my father's death. . . . His files were in his head, and he's dead. He stored it all in his memory. The only thing he kept on paper was information about the license plates and addresses of his enemies from the Cali Cartel, and the Colombian police have had those materials for a while now."

"Well, the judge is the one who decides whether you'll be allowed to go to the United States, so you'll have to convince him."

"Then we have nothing more to discuss, sir. I'm leaving now. Thank you very much," I told the DEA director, who tersely said good-bye and handed me a business card. "If you remember anything, don't hesitate to call me."

I was full of questions as I left the U.S. embassy. My surprising encounter with the head of the DEA in Latin America hadn't improved our precarious situation, but it had revealed something we hadn't known before: my uncle Roberto's high-level contacts with the Americans, the same people who just three weeks earlier had offered five million dollars for my father's capture, the same ones who'd sent their massive war machine to Colombia to help hunt him.

It was hard for me to believe that my father's own brother might be working with his number-one enemy. But the possibility gave rise to other doubts, and I soon wondered whether Roberto, the U.S. government, and the Los Pepes vigilante group (named for its members' shared claim of being "persecuted by Pablo Escobar") might have formed an alliance to bring my father down. It wasn't such a crazy theory. It made us reevaluate events we previously hadn't given much thought.

Back when we'd been in hiding with my father in a country house in the hilly Belén area of Medellín, Roberto's son, my cousin Nicolás Escobar Urquijo, had been kidnapped. On the afternoon of May 18, 1993, he'd been snatched and taken to the roadside restaurant Catíos between the villages of Caldas and Amagá in the Antioquia region.

We assumed the worst because at the time, in their zeal to find my father, Los Pepes had already attacked a number of family members on both my father's and my mother's sides. Fortunately, the scare ended within a few hours. At around ten that night, the kidnappers released Nicolás, unharmed, near Medellín's Inter-Continental Hotel.

In hiding, we had less and less contact with the rest of the family, so Nicolás's kidnapping was eventually forgotten, though my father and I did wonder how he'd gotten out of it alive. In the dynamics of that war between my father and Los Pepes and everyone else who wanted to take him down, a kidnapping was basically a death sentence. How had Nicolás been saved? What had Los Pepes received in exchange for his release only a few hours after abducting him? It seemed likely that Roberto had decided to make a deal with my father's enemies in exchange for his son's life.

I got confirmation of that alliance in August 1994, eight months after my visit to the U.S. embassy. My mother, my sister Manuela, Andrea, and I went to see what little remained of our family's Nápoles estate, which had been left in ruins since my father had gone into hiding. The attorney general's office had given us permission to go there so my mother could meet with a powerful local drug lord to transfer some of my father's real estate holdings. On one of those afternoons, as we were walking along the estate's old landing strip, we received a call from my paternal aunt Alba Marina Escobar, who told us she had to meet with us that night to discuss an urgent matter.

We immediately agreed because in our family, the use of the word "urgent" meant that someone's life was in danger. She arrived at the estate that same night, without any luggage. We met her in the estate manager's house, the only building that had survived the ravages of war. The government agents who were guarding us waited outside, and we headed to the dining room, where my aunt ate a bowl of stew. She was going to tell us something only my mother and I could know about.

"I've got a message for you from Roberto," she went on.

"What's going on?" I inquired anxiously.

"He's excited because there's a chance they might give you all visas for the United States."

"That's wonderful. How did he manage that?" we asked, and the expression on her face grew serious.

"They're not going to give them to you right away. There's something that has to be done first," she said. Her tone made me uneasy. "It's simple. Roberto was talking with the DEA, and they asked him a favor in exchange for visas for all of you. All you have to do is write a book about whatever topic you want, as long as the book mentions your father and Vladimiro Montesinos, Fujimori's head of intelligence services in Peru. Also, in the book you have to say that you saw Fujimori here at the Nápoles estate, talking with your father, and that Montesinos showed up on a plane. It doesn't matter what's in the rest of the book. . . ."

"That's not actually such good news, Auntie," I interrupted.

"What do you mean? Don't you want the visas?"

"It's one thing for the DEA to ask us to say something that's true and something I'm comfortable saying, but it's something else for them to ask me to lie to further their devious ends."

"Yes, Marina," my mother broke in, "what they're asking for is really quite tricky. How are we supposed to justify saying things that aren't true?"

"Who cares? Don't you want the visas? You don't know Montesinos and Fujimori, so what does it matter if you say those things? What you want is to live in peace. These people have sent word that the DEA would be very grateful to you and that nobody would bother you in the United States from that moment on. They're also offering you the possibility of taking money there with you and using it without any interference from the government."

"Marina, I don't want to get myself tangled up in new problems by saying things that aren't true," my mother said.

"Poor Roberto, he's moving heaven and earth to try to help you, and the first opportunity he gets you, the two of you say no."

In a huff, Alba Marina left Nápoles that night. A few days after that meeting, back in Bogotá, I received a phone call from grandmother Hermilda, who was in New York with Alba Marina. After explaining that she'd traveled there for a bit of sightseeing, she asked me if I wanted her to bring me anything from the city. Naively, without recognizing the significance of the fact that my grandmother was in the United States, I asked her to buy a few bottles of a cologne that weren't available in Colombia.

Once I hung up, I felt unsettled. How could my grandmother be in the United States less than a year after my father's death, when as far as I knew the visas of all members of the Escobar and Henao families had been canceled? This was only the latest in a series of events in which my relatives appeared to have murky ties to my father's enemies. But, distracted by the struggle to merely stay alive, we let time pass without exploring those suspicions further.

Several years later, living in exile in Argentina, we'd be shocked by a TV news report that the president of Peru, Alberto Fujimori, had fled to Japan and sent his resignation by fax. A week prior, *Cambio* magazine had published an interview in which Roberto claimed that my father had given a million dollars to Fujimori's first presidential campaign in 1989. He also stated that the money had been sent through Vladimiro Montesinos, who, he said, had visited the Nápoles estate a number of times. My uncle added that Fujimori had promised that when he became president, he would make it easier for my father to traffic drugs out of Peru. At the end of the interview, Roberto noted that he had no proof of any of the allegations he was making because, he claimed, the cartel hadn't left a trail of its illegal activities.

A few weeks later, Roberto Escobar's *My Brother Pablo* hit the bookstores. The 186-page book, published by Quintero Editores, "re-created" my father's relationship with Montesinos and Fujimori.

In two chapters, Roberto described Montesinos's visit to Nápoles, his trafficking of cocaine with my father, the delivery of a million dollars for Fujimori's campaign, the new president's grateful phone calls to my father, and the offer of cooperation in exchange for the economic assistance my father provided. At the end, a sentence caught my eye: "Montesinos knows that I know it. And Fujimori knows that I know it. That's why the two of them fell from power." Roberto alleged that he had been present for things that my mother and I had never heard of, let alone witnessed.

I don't know if Roberto's book is the one my aunt suggested we write to get visas to the United States. All I know about the matter I discovered by chance in the winter of 2003, when I received a phone call from a foreign journalist to whom I'd occasionally expressed my suspicions.

"I have to tell you something that just happened to me, and it can't wait till tomorrow!" the journalist said.

"Go on, what happened?"

"I just had dinner here in Washington with two former DEA agents who participated in the hunt for your father. I was meeting with them to talk about the possibility of having you and them come on a show about Pablo's life and death for American television."

"OK, but what happened?" I repeated.

"They know a lot about the subject, and I got the chance to bring up your theory about your uncle's betrayal. And it's true! I couldn't believe it when they confirmed that he'd been an active collaborator in your father's death."

I'd been right. How else could you explain that we were the only members of Pablo Escobar's family living in exile?

2

Where Did the Money Go?

After my father's funeral, we realized that the peace we'd been seeking after my father's death was fleeting and that very soon we'd be plunged into the hectic daily existence that awaited us. In addition to our deep sorrow at what had happened to my father, being surrounded by secret agents and dozens of journalists lying in wait indicated that our confinement in that hotel in downtown Bogotá was going to be tumultuous.

At the same time, our lack of money started to cause problems for us almost immediately. My father was dead, and we had no one to turn to for help.

We'd been staying in that upscale hotel in Bogotá since November 29, and to reduce the risks around us we'd rented the entire twenty-ninth floor even though we occupied only five rooms. Our financial predicament became more dire in mid-December, when the hotel sent us the first bill for lodging and food, which, to our surprise, also included the tab for the government's security team. It was an astronomical sum thanks to the large quantities of food and drink they'd ordered. They consumed shrimp, lobster, shell-fish stew, and pricy cuts of meat, as well as all sorts of hard alcohol, especially whiskey, seeming to have deliberately chosen the most expensive items on the menu.

We paid the bill, but our money worries continued to grow,

with no solution in sight. One day, my aunts Alba Marina and Luz María; Luz María's husband, Leonardo; and their three children, Leonardo, Mary Luz, and Sara, came to the hotel. Though we hadn't seen each other for months and weren't really close, we were glad for the visit. My little sister finally had someone to play dolls with—after having spent almost a year indoors without being allowed to look out a window, without knowing where she was, and without an explanation for why she was always surrounded by more than twenty men armed to the teeth.

We sat down at the dining table, and after describing what we'd been through in the last few weeks, my mother mentioned her concern over how little money we had. We discussed the matter for a long time, and the compassion and generosity that Alba Marina exhibited made me think that she was the right person to help. I needed her to retrieve an unknown amount of cash that my father had hidden in two stashes at the property we called "the blue house." It was time to go get it so we could have a bit of financial breathing room.

As I moved to a seat next to her, I remembered that the apartment we were staying in was still being monitored by the authorities, who had not only bugged our phones but probably also installed microphones throughout the place. I had searched for them many times, dismantling lamps, telephones, furniture, and all sorts of other objects. I had even poked around for them in the electrical outlets, but in doing so I'd caused a short circuit that had knocked out the electricity to the whole floor.

I decided to whisper my secret in her ear. First I put on the television and turned the volume way up. Then I told her.

One night during our period of suffocating confinement in the blue house, my father decided to take stock of his finances. When everybody was sleeping, he took me to two different hiding places he'd had built in the house. He showed me the boxes where cash was hidden and said that, apart from him and now me, the only other person who knew about them was his man "Fatty." Then he added that my mother and sister and, most of all, his siblings must never learn that secret. According to my father, the two caches had enough money to win the war and get us back on our feet. Therefore, we had to manage it carefully. He also told me that a while back he'd sent six million dollars to his brother Roberto: three for Roberto's expenses while in prison and the other three for him to keep for us in case we needed it. If something happened to my father, Roberto had specific instructions to give us the money.

Once my account was over, I got right to the point:

"Auntie, would you be willing to go to Medellín to get the money that's stashed in those two hiding places? We don't have anyone else we can ask, and there's no way we can go."

Alba Marina had a reputation for being tough, and she immediately agreed. So I revealed the exact locations of the hiding places in the blue house—one in the living room near the fireplace and another in the clothes-drying courtyard behind a thick wall—and told her not to say anything to anybody; to go there alone, at night, preferably using someone else's car; to take a very indirect route to the house; and to keep an eye on her rearview mirrors to make sure she wasn't being followed. Finally, I wrote a letter to Fatty authorizing my aunt to remove the boxes of money.

After I'd given the instructions, I asked her if she was scared.

"I won't be intimidated. I'll go after that money wherever it is," she said firmly.

My aunt returned three days later, and when she walked into the hotel room, she wasn't looking so positive. My first thought was that something had gone wrong. I asked for the keys to one of the empty rooms on the floor and met with her alone.

"Juan Pablo, there was only a little bit of money at the blue house, that's it," she said all in a rush.

I was silent for a few minutes, disconcerted. I didn't doubt her story and directed my rage against Fatty, the guard, who'd probably stolen the caches.

A flood of questions remained after the money's disappearance, but we had to keep quiet because we didn't have a way to contest my aunt's version of events. I'd never dared to doubt her, since on several occasions I'd noticed that she was loyal to my father.

All in all, money-related matters were far from being settled.

In mid-March 1994, three months after we moved into Residencias Tequendama, we rented a large, two-story apartment in the Santa Ana neighborhood to reduce costs. Not only were we running out of money but we were also still in danger, so at all times we had a security detail of agents from DIJIN, SIJIN, the DAS, and the CTI.

Without the stashes from the blue house, our situation became urgent, so we decided to ask my aunt and uncle for the three million dollars that my father had given Roberto to hold for us.

We assumed they'd already spent a good bit of the money. When we requested it, we got an explanation fairly quickly. It came in the form of my grandmother Hermilda and my father's siblings Gloria, Alba Marina, Luz María, and Argemiro, who visited the Santa Ana apartment one afternoon. To keep the guards on the first floor from overhearing our conversation, we gathered in my mother's room on the second floor.

They pulled out several sheets of paper that had been torn out of a notebook, as if we were dealing with the accounts of a small neighborhood shop. The papers listed the expenses of the last few months: three hundred thousand dollars to furnish my aunt Gloria's new apartment, forty thousand for a taxi for Gloria as a business investment, and countless outlays of money for my grandfather Abel, for the butler's wages, for car repair, and to buy a car to replace one that had been confiscated, among many other things.

It was as if, with this list, they sought to justify the way Roberto had squandered three-quarters of the money that my father had entrusted to his care.

Roberto was willing to honor only the amount that remained. Irritated, I questioned the expenses, which seemed to me utterly profligate, focusing in on the astounding cost of my aunt Gloria's furniture. She got flustered and asked me if she didn't have the right to replace the things she'd lost in the war. Despite her tantrum, I knew the accounts had to have been cooked. It wasn't plausible that the furniture was worth more than the apartment itself. Alba Marina backed her up and said that Roberto hadn't frittered the money away.

I told them I wasn't convinced by their neat numbers, and the meeting with my grandmother and my father's siblings ended on sour terms. It was clear we weren't going to get the money back.

As I pondered what to do, my mind shifted gears. For weeks now we'd been receiving threats from at least thirty men in prison who'd worked for my father and had been set adrift in the wake of his death. I knew that the only way to get Roberto to let go of that money was to force him to give it to the prisoners.

According to my calculations, the money would be enough for them for a year. That was a commitment we thought we owed the people who'd joined my father in his war and were now serving long sentences as a result. My father always used to say that you can't just abandon people to their fate in prison: that was when they needed help the most. Whenever his men told him, "Boss, they got so-and-so," he'd send lawyers to defend the man and make sure the family received some money. That's how my father treated every single one of the people who fell while helping him carry out his misdeeds. So to avoid more problems from the prisons, we asked Roberto to use the remaining money to aid those men and their families.

But the entire business was born under a bad star. Distributing that money turned out to be a whole new headache for us, and eventually a breaking point in our increasingly strained relations with my relatives.

Weeks after the turbulent meeting, we got news from some of the prisons that we found quite worrying. One account suggested that my grandmother Hermilda had visited a number of the men and claimed that Roberto was the one providing the money.

I knew I had to send letters to the prisons to tell my father's men the truth.

Soon, though, despite my efforts, we again started having problems because the men had stopped receiving money from Roberto. Several of them complained that they had no way to feed or protect their families and pointed out that they'd given everything for "the Boss," accusing us of being ungrateful. Roberto must have blamed us. Uneasy, I called Roberto, and he had no compunction in telling me that the money had lasted only five months.

The message from the prisons contained a veiled threat, so I sent a reply explaining that the money they'd been getting had been not from my uncle but from my father: "All of your salaries, your lawyers, and your meals have been paid for so far with my father's money, not Roberto's, let's make that quite clear. . . . It is not our fault that Roberto has spent all of that money. When they told us the money was gone, they told us my aunt Gloria had spent it, but it was never clear to us where that money actually went."

Roberto must have found out what was going on, as a few days after I sent my letter, he wrote a note to my mother for Mother's Day. The handwritten letter clearly attempted to use the assassination attempt he'd survived back in December to justify his behavior. "Tata," he said, using my mother's nickname, "I'm not the same man I was before. I'm quite depressed about what I'm going through. Though I've gotten a little better, it's been five months of suffering, with what happened to my brother and then my own near-death experience. Don't listen to all the gossip, there are so many people who do not love us. I have a lot to talk to you about, but I'm really depressed about my situation."

Reports of the family squabble over financial support for the prisoners reached the ears of Iván Urdinola, one of the capos from the Norte del Valle Cartel, whom my mother had met with a couple of times at Bogotá's La Modelo prison as the Colombian cartels attempted to restore order following my father's death. On his personal letterhead, Urdinola sent my mother a note in which his tone was cordial but commanding: "Señora, I am sending this letter to request that you please clear up your misunderstandings with the Escobar family. It's not Pablo's men's fault that Roberto doesn't have the money. Please help them out—that's what we're all here for, and you are the closest to this matter as the new head of the family. You will continue to have problems as long as this matter goes unresolved."

But that wasn't the end of it. On the morning of August 19, 1994, I was lying in bed when a fax came in that left me cold. It was a letter signed by several of the men who'd worked for my father and were now being held at the Itagüí maximum-security prison, and it contained serious accusations against Roberto:

"Doña Victoria, a warm greeting to you and please give our regards to your children, Juancho and Manuela, as well. We are sending this letter to clear up certain rumors being spread by Señor Roberto Escobar. We are notifying you because we realized what he was trying to do by sending his sister Gloria to throw your son under the bus.

"We wish to notify you that Roberto has said that unless certain statements are retracted, he will keep this going. We want to make our position quite clear: none of us is willing to participate in this game of deceit and abuse. We don't want conflict with anybody; what we want is to live in peace.

"If he goes through with this, it's on his own and at his own risk because none of us are going to participate in the least. We were firm with him, and we will be firm with you as well."

The message was signed by many of my father's men: Giovanni Lopera, known as "the Supermodel," along with "Comanche," "Mystery," "Tato" Avendaño, "the Claw," "Polystyrene," "Fatty" Lambas, Valentín de Jesús Taborda, and William Cárdenas.

After reading the names of the men who had signed the message, I was worried, so I decided to tell Gustavo De Greiff, the attorney general of Colombia, to stymie any possible setup by my uncle. I had no option but to put a stop to Roberto's deceit and dodge the rocks he was throwing at me. De Greiff met me along with our lawyer, Fernández, and I expressed my concern that there was a plan afoot to get me thrown in prison. I also informed him that two of the prisoners in Itagüí who had not signed the letter—Juan Urquijo and "Ñeris"—had joined forces with Roberto and were attempting to collect on my father's supposed drug-trafficking-related debts. Roberto hadn't expected us to have the ability or courage to stand up to him.

We'd barely gotten out of this difficulty when something else happened to prove the accuracy of the old saying that lies stand on one leg, and the truth on two.

At eleven o'clock one night in September 1994, a SIJIN agent called up from the street at the Santa Ana apartment and said that a man who identified himself as Fatty had just arrived and wanted to see me, but he refused to give his identification number and real name, as was required of anyone who wanted to talk to us.

The officer was strict in adhering to this rule, which didn't surprise me. We knew that wherever we were—whether it was back in the Altos apartment building in Medellín or in Residencias Tequendama or now Santa Ana in Bogotá—the people protecting us were also doing intelligence work to find out who had it in for us and who was on our side.

The true surprise was that the man in question was none other than the one who'd been guarding my father's money, the one I'd accused of stealing the cash hidden in the blue house. "If he's got the nerve to show up at this hour of night, I'm going to ask him about the missing money," I said to myself. After a brief argument, I managed to persuade the officer to allow Fatty to come up without showing any identification, with the understanding that it was at my own risk.

When he reached the door, Fatty hugged me and started to cry. "Juancho, my brother," he said, "it's so good to see you."

I couldn't mask my shock: the man's embrace and tears seemed sincere. What's more, he was dressed the same as ever, in his ordinary clothing and battered tennis shoes. He didn't look in the least like someone who just a few months earlier had stolen a cache of money. Plus, why would he come visit us when that money should have set him up for life?

Looking him up and down with suspicion and warily listening to his account of life since my father and the rest of the family had left the blue house in November 1993, I concluded that he was still the loyal man we'd known.

After we chatted for a few minutes on the second-floor balcony, where nobody could hear us, I decided it was time to ask him about the missing money.

"Fatty, tell me what happened with the stash at the blue house. Did you let my aunt in? What happened to the money?"

"Juancho, I let your aunt in on your instructions. When she gave me the message, we went to the two locations and removed the boxes, and I helped her put them in the back of the SUV she'd brought. I never heard from her again. I just came to say hello, to hear how you were doing, because I'm very fond of you all. I am ready to help however I can."

"Well, she claims there was only a little money," I told him.

"That's a lie! I helped her load all that money into the SUV. It was so full of money that the back of the vehicle was riding lower to the ground. I swear, your aunt took everything," he said, almost in tears. "If you want, I'll stay here while you call her, and I'll say it to her face."

IN HIS WILL, MY FATHER HAD LEFT A PERCENTAGE OF HIS ESTATE to the Escobar Gavirias, and we'd informed them immediately after his death, prepared to comply with his wishes to a tee. In the document, he indicated that 50 percent of his estate should go to my mother as his conjugal partner, 37.5 percent to me (Manuela had not yet been born when he wrote his will), and the remaining 12.5 percent, referred to as the "freely disposable portion," to my grandparents Hermilda and Abel, my father's siblings, and one of his aunts.

The will clearly stipulated the percentages of each bequest, but my father only had thirty thousand dollars in stocks and a 1977 Mercedes-Benz in his name—and that had all been confiscated. My father had acquired a large quantity of real estate and other assets, but they weren't deeded in his name. Some were in my and Manuela's names, but those had already been seized by the attorney general's office.

It wasn't easy settling my father's inheritance with his family, but after a couple of meetings in which they tried to take more, they finally relented. The Escobar Gavirias ended up receiving a large number of properties that were not under legal constraint. These included rural estates, lots in Medellín, the blue house in Las Palmas, an apartment near the army base of the Fourth Brigade, and the house in the Los Colores neighborhood that my father had purchased as a newlywed and which my aunt Gloria had claimed, saying that he'd given it to her as a gift.

We were left with the Mónaco, Dallas, and Ovni buildings in Medellín and the Nápoles estate in Puerto Triunfo. Though they were currently in the possession of the attorney general's office, we hoped that we might be able to recover them. Members of various cartels and paramilitary groups who had fought the war against my father had been demanding reparation for the costs he caused them—and calling for my head. In the months to come we'd have to face some of the most powerful and dangerous leaders in the country to bargain for our lives with money we didn't have.

By the summer of 1994, we would manage to make peace with the cartels and leave everything having to do with my Escobar relatives behind, moving first to Mozambique and then to Buenos Aires and starting over with very little to our name (and new identities). But conflict with my father's family over money would rear its ugly head again when my grandfather and then grandmother passed away, and my father's relatives refused to give Manuela and me our inheritances. It would take until 2014 for everything to be resolved.

I remember one proceeding in which the judge set up an inquiry with my mother and me and refused to allow us to give the interview at the Colombian consulate in Buenos Aires. Instead, we had to travel to Medellín. I was worried that my father's family would find out the exact place and time of our appointment in court. Frightened, I requested assistance and protection from relatives and friends, who loaned me an armored car and four bodyguards.

The meeting began much later than scheduled because the judge arrived late. Some of my aunts and uncles were represented by the lawyer Magdalena Vallejo, who opened the meeting and asked questions clearly intended to confuse me. But I shut her down with a response I'd prepared some time earlier: "Regardless of your questions, the fact is that none of my father's siblings have fulfilled their responsibilities. They have kept all of the assets and left us nothing." After I provided the same answer to five questions in a row, the lawyer, visibly exasperated, gave up. Before bringing the meeting to a close, the court asked if I wanted to add anything.

I looked at Magdalena and told her that I didn't understand why she was so angry with me when she knew that my little sister and I were the ones being wronged.

"Juan Pablo, it's not the 1980s. Your family isn't in charge anymore. I have plenty of friends and acquaintances in positions of power who will protect me," she replied.

I told the court I wished to add something else on the record: "I want it to be quite clear that I am ashamed to have to turn to the judicial system to remind my father's siblings that Pablo Emilio Escobar Gaviria existed and was their brother and their sole benefactor. Not a single member of my paternal family ever made a living on his own. All of them, without exception, have what they have today because of my father, not through their own efforts. Colombia hasn't forgotten who Pablo Escobar was, but his own family has."

3

My Father's Origins

Sweetheart, are you ready to spend your life taking meals to Pablo in prison?"

"Yes, Mother, I am."

This short conversation between Victoria Eugenia Henao Vallejo and her mother, Leonor, in 1973 sealed the fate of the beautiful, tall, studious girl who just a few years later would become my mother.

Leonor, who was known as Nora to her family, asked her thirteen-year-old daughter this question as a last resort. She had all but given up on being able to put a stop to Victoria's engagement to Pablo Emilio Escobar Gaviria, a badly dressed womanizer eleven years the girl's senior, short in stature, without an established occupation, and who made no secret of his criminal tendencies.

My grandmother Nora would have liked for Victoria to marry someone powerful from a more respectable family. Not Pablo Escobar.

THE ESCOBAR AND HENAO FAMILIES BOTH CAME TO THE NEWLY built La Paz neighborhood in 1964 but didn't meet until several years later. At the time, that rural area in the town of Envigado, on the outskirts of Medellín, was reachable only by a long, narrow stretch of unpaved road.

In January of that year, the Land Loans Institute—a now defunct government agency that developed housing for low-income families—granted the Escobars a house during the last of the three construction phases of the new community, which was composed of cookie-cutter, single-story homes, all with gray roofs and small yards full of brightly colored flowers but no electricity or running water.

Hermilda and Abel Escobar's arrival in the neighborhood with their seven children marked the end of a long journey that had begun two decades earlier when Hermilda was assigned as an elementary school teacher in El Tablazo, a cold, misty little village in eastern Antioquia surrounded by vast fields of blackberries, tree tomatoes, and a stunning variety of flowers. After a few months, Abel, who lived four miles from the school with his parents on a farm in the upper part of El Tablazo, came to admire Hermilda's dignified bearing, sophistication, and enterprising spirit. The smitten farmer proposed, and she immediately accepted. They were married on March 4, 1946, and she resigned from her teaching post, in accordance with the cultural norms of the day, and moved in with her husband and parents-in-law.

Ten months later, on January 13, 1947, my uncle Roberto was born, and on December 1, 1949, my father followed, named after his grandfather: Pablo Emilio.

In April 2014, I returned to El Tablazo for research and visited my grandfather Abel's farm, which is still standing, if noticeably dilapidated. Even so, the passage of time has not entirely erased the mark that my paternal family left on the place. To the right of the front entrance is my father's room, six by eight feet. The wooden door is the same, but I was struck most by the color of the walls, which, despite the grime and deterioration, are still clearly the light-blue color he'd preferred throughout his life.

My grandmother threw herself into taking care of the family, but it quickly became evident that the farm wasn't productive enough. Abel had no choice but to seek employment with his neighbor, the renowned Antioquian political leader Joaquín Vallejo Arbeláez, who hired my grandfather to run his estate, El Tesoro.

My grandparents moved to Vallejo's estate, and the boss became their guardian angel. My grandmother Hermilda, who loved reminiscing, once told me that when they came to live at the estate, Vallejo had made it clear that Abel was the manager and that under no circumstances was Hermilda to work. According to my grandmother, Vallejo was so good to them that they asked him to be Pablo's godfather. Vallejo gladly accepted, and on December 4, 1949, he and his wife, Nelly, attended the baptism ceremony at the San Nicolás church in Rionegro.

But still the financial difficulties persisted, and the daily hardships drove my grandmother, against Abel's wishes, to ask to be reinstated as a teacher in any town in the Antioquia Department. The bureaucrats accepted her request, but they punished her for being married, sending her to a school in the southwestern village of Titiribí.

It was customary at the time for teachers to live on the school grounds, so the Escobar Gaviria family moved into a small house next to the school. While Hermilda taught, Abel tried to find work as a farmhand, painter, or gardener, without success. Soon the long arm of partisan violence that had erupted in Colombia in April 1948 with the assassination of the Liberal leader Jorge Eliécer Gaitán reached them even in that isolated, inhospitable place.

It was 1952; the conflict between the Conservative and Liberal parties was raging, and my grandparents and their family were forced to hide several times when bandits armed with machetes came looking to kill them. In those years, they had to change schools at least four times as they fled the violence. After Titiribí, they moved to Girardota and two other villages. Danger became an ordinary part of life.

Many years later, one weekend at the Nápoles estate, my grandmother would sit several of her grandchildren down by the swimming pool and relate details of that awful period in which they'd lived so close to death. Still distressed by the memory, she'd recount how one cold, rainy night four bandits wielding machetes had come looking for them, and they'd had to lock themselves up in one of the classrooms to keep the bandits from coming in and cutting off their heads, which was common at the time. Terrified, my grandmother told her husband and children to stay absolutely silent and not to get up or look out the window because she could see the killers' shadows on the wall. At that moment, when everything seemed lost, my grandmother had entrusted their lives to the only religious image in the place: a portrait of the Holy Child of Atocha. In a whisper, she promised to build a church in His honor if He saved them that night.

They'd all survived, and thereafter my grandmother would become a devotee of the Holy Child of Atocha, carrying His image around with her and even arranging an altar to Him in her room. She'd fulfill her promise to build a church in His name many years later on one of the parcels of land my father bought for his free social housing project, Medellín Without Slums. My father would finance the construction, and my grandmother would breathe easier knowing that she had followed through on the promise that had saved her life all those years ago.

THE CONSTANT ANXIETY FINALLY ENDED WHEN ANTIOQUIA'S education ministry transferred my grandmother to the Guayabito School near Rionegro, an old building with two classrooms, a bathroom, and one large room that housed my grandparents and their children—who now numbered six, as Gloria, Argemiro, Alba Marina, and Luz María had been born during the stints at the various rural schools.

Roberto and Pablo attended their first two years of elementary school with their mother in Guayabito, but since the school went up only to fourth grade, they had to transfer to a larger school in the city of Rionegro. The brothers enrolled at the Julio Sanín School, but it was far away, a two-hour walk there and back on an unpaved road that the boys often made without shoes. It pained my grandmother to see her sons' hardship, so she decided to save up enough money to buy a bicycle. It was a relief. In the mornings when they left for school, Roberto would pedal while Pablo sat on the cargo rack. Soon, after Roberto complained about how heavy Pablo was, my grandmother managed to buy a second bicycle.

Roberto took up bicycle racing, and the two brothers challenged each other to races. Roberto became increasingly furious because, though he trained hard every day, Pablo, who was much lazier, won them all. For Roberto, this seemingly harmless competition reinforced a deep resentment toward Pablo that would become all the more acute later on, when Pablo would beat Roberto once more: in the race to see which one of them would become a millionaire first.

As the rivalry between the brothers grew, Pablo spent more and more time with his cousin Gustavo Gaviria, who came to visit on weekends.

The Escobar Gavirias' lives took an unexpected turn when Hermilda—once more against Abel's wishes—managed to get herself transferred to a school in Medellín. Convinced that her now seven children could only be educated in the big city, she had pulled every string available to her.

The family moved into the large, comfortable home of my great-grandmother Inés—Hermilda's mother—in Medellín's Francisco Antonio Zea neighborhood, where Inés owned a successful dye factory. My grandmother started teaching in the school in the low-income Enciso neighborhood, high up on a hill.

The Escobar Gavirias had finally arrived in Medellín, but their journey was far from over. Over the next two years, my grandmother was transferred to the Caracas and San Bernardita schools in other parts of the city, and the family moved several times. Finally, in the mid-1960s, they put down roots in La Paz. Their house had three bedrooms, a bathroom, a combined living and dining room, a kitchen, and a courtyard. They crammed themselves as best as they could into two of the bedrooms, and in the third, at the front of the house, my grandfather Abel set up a small shop that went under a few months later for lack of customers.

Pablo, always ready to exploit any opportunity, moved into that space, which he painted light blue, like his room in El Tablazo. He set up a small library with two of the wooden shelves from my grandfather's failed business, on which he meticulously arranged a few books on politics, his collection of *Reader's Digest*, and texts by the communist leaders Lenin and Mao. In a corner of his makeshift library, he displayed a real human skull.

My father once told me the story of that skull. "Grégory, one day I decided to challenge my fears, and the best way to do that was to sneak into a cemetery at midnight and steal a skull from a grave," he said. "Nobody spotted me, and nothing happened to me. After I cleaned it, I painted it and put it on my desk as a paperweight."

My father was nearly fifteen when they moved to La Paz, and soon thereafter he spent afternoons studying at the Liceo de Antioquia, which was a half-hour bus ride away.

At night he met up with "Rasputin," the Toro brothers, the Maya brothers, and "Rodriguito" at La Iguana ice cream shop, where they drank coffee and jotted their thoughts down in a little notebook.

They were very close friends. They started the neighborhood Boy Scouts troop together, earned money organizing the first home dances, cut lawns on Saturdays, and went camping on the weekends on a nearby hill. They became enthusiastic patrons of the Colombia de Envigado cinema, where they went two or three times a week to see James Bond movies, Mexican films, and Westerns.

The boys teased one another a lot, and they all had to endure it. My father set only one condition: they couldn't call him *midget* or *shorty.* He hated feeling short and always wished he was taller than his five feet six inches.

Then politics entered their lives. The boys, especially my father, were already aware of Fidel Castro's revolution in Cuba and the January 1961 assassination of Congolese anticolonialist leader Patrice Lumumba. My father had become particularly interested in Lumumba's life story.

Back then, the upheaval around the world was reflected in public universities across most of Colombia, and the students organized massive street protests. My father attended one of these demonstrations at the University of Antioquia, and when he met up with his friends that night at La Iguana, he told them, "I'm going to start a revolution really soon, but it'll be for me."

My father was furious about the way the police had repressed the student protests, and after that, every time a police car came through the neighborhood, he'd throw rocks at it and call them "fucking pigs."

My father had started spending a lot of time with his cousin Gustavo Gaviria, who now attended the same high school. Roberto, meanwhile, had gone all in on bike racing and competed in national and regional trials; he also had a couple of wins in Italy and Costa Rica. His winnings didn't cover his expenses, but he managed to find a sponsor, the Mora Brothers electronics store.

Though my father avoided talking about the subject, a number of discussions that we had toward the end of his life revealed that his criminal career began the day he figured out how to forge his school's high school diplomas.

To pull off the fraud, my father and Gustavo managed to get their hands on the keys to the faculty lounge and secretly made copies of them with a mold made of modeling clay. From the lounge they stole blank diplomas, which at the time were issued with the school's seal, and had a copy of the seal made. They also learned to imitate the professors' handwriting so they could insert the final grades and the necessary signatures. And so dozens of young people graduated from the Liceo de Antioquia without ever having set foot inside its walls.

They got another use out of those keys too. For a while, they were able to sell students the answers to exams for the more difficult classes, such as math and chemistry. But when students started earning unusually high grades in those subjects, the school administrators became suspicious and modified future tests.

Still, by now there was a little money in Pablo Escobar's pockets, and that was enough to encourage him to continue with his misdeeds, which were still fairly minor.

Around the same time that my father and Gustavo were selling the fake diplomas, they would also steal oranges from an orchard a few streets over in La Paz and sell them in the market or door-to-door around the neighborhood. On other occasions they'd walk through a store in the upper part of the neighborhood and pretend to bump into a display of oranges; the fruits would fall and roll downhill, where the boys would pick them up and, later that night, sell them back to the very storeowner from whom the fruits had been pilfered.

It was also at this time that the *Reader's Digest* collection on my father's shelves began to expand. The reason? He convinced the neighborhood kids to steal copies from their parents for him. That way, he got the latest issues. He was such a smooth talker that he was even able to rent them out to the neighbors to read over the weekend.

My father and his friends became bolder in their crimes, and one day they stole the Cadillac belonging to the bishop of Medellín, who was attending a groundbreaking in the neighborhood. One of the boys studied at the National Training Service and knew how to hotwire a car. Once it was running, they went joyriding through the nearby villages. When they got home, they saw the neighborhood was swarming with police searching for the vehicle, so they drove to an area between La Paz and El Dorado—a neighborhood along the road to Envigado—and abandoned the car.

With the money he saved up, Pablo took a first step toward success and bought a 1961 gray Vespa motorcycle, which made him the neighborhood lady's man overnight. The girls discovered a young man who was romantic, talkative, and attentive, even if not exactly a snappy dresser. He didn't care whether his clothes matched, and he liked to roll up his sleeves and leave his shirts untucked. Sometimes he'd wear a white wool poncho similar to the one he would wear years later when he arrived at the La Catedral prison. He loved that motorcycle, but money was still scarce, so he owned only four shirts, two pairs of jeans, and a pair of loafers.

During this period, Pablo adopted four habits that persisted for the rest of his life. First, he left his shirt unbuttoned down to the middle of his chest. No higher, no lower. It's funny: over the years I've seen dozens of photos of my father, and in all of them, without exception, his shirt is unbuttoned to his preferred spot. Second, he cut his own hair. He didn't like barbers, never went to a barbershop, and permitted my mother to cut his hair only a few times. She used to beg him to have his hair cut professionally, but he never gave in and trimmed his own hair with scissors. Third, he always used the same kind of comb to tidy his hair. It was a small tortoiseshell comb that he kept handy in his shirt pocket. My father's tendency to tidy his hair frequently throughout the day was perhaps one of his few displays of vanity. On a normal day he'd pull out that comb at least ten times. He was so attached to it that years later, in his time of opulence and excess, he'd have five hundred of them brought down from the United States. And fourth, he took extraordinarily long showers. Because he went to school in the afternoon and stayed out late at night with his friends, he generally woke up after ten in the morning. He'd then spend up to three hours in the shower. This routine didn't change even in the worst period, when he was living on the run and his enemies were at the door. The simple act of brushing his teeth took him at least forty-five minutes, always with a Pro children's toothbrush.

I once teased him about how much time he spent brushing his teeth, and he replied, "Son, as a fugitive I don't have the luxury of being able to go to the dentist. You do."

Even as my father and Gustavo became more involved in dirty dealings, my grandmother Hermilda persuaded Pablo to take the entrance exam for the accounting program at the Latin American Autonomous University, a Catholic university in Medellín. He passed easily, but he dropped out halfway through the first semester because he was fed up with his family's financial distress. Instead, my father dedicated himself full time to hanging out with his friends and spending hours at La Iguana ice cream shop, where watching the neighborhood girls walk by became more interesting than talking about politics.

Music began to occupy an important place in his day-to-day life. It was 1970, and Pablo loved the cheerful, infectious rhythms of Billo's Caracas Boys, Los Graduados, and the newly formed Fruko y sus Tesos; he also enjoyed listening to Piero, Joan Manuel Serrat, Camilo Sesto, Julio Iglesias, Miguel Bosé, Raphael, Sandro, Elio Roca, Nino Bravo, and his idol, Leonardo Favio. But there was one song, which he heard one night at La Iguana, that for many years was special to him: "En Casa de Irene," a pop song by the Italian singer Gian Franco Pagliaro.

La Paz continued to grow, and the youths of Medellín would come to the neighborhood for its famous weekend garage parties and twenty-four-hour ice cream shops.

But the festivities soon gave way to problems. Pablo was infuriated by the way young men would show up in their fancy cars and expensive clothes and dance with the neighborhood girls. Even when he wasn't dating any of them, he was outraged that the "pretty boys" of Medellín were cozying up to the young women of La Paz. Pablo's gang would throw rocks at the visitors' cars, and the confrontations generally ended in brawls as each group would occupy a corner and hurl chairs, bottles, and other objects at the other.

A number of these fights were with the notorious 11 Crew, led by Jorge Tulio Garcés, a wealthy young man who would show up like a Don Juan to pick up girls in his convertible. Things came to a head one night when Jorge Tulio crashed a *quinceañera* party. Pablo angrily went up to him and said, "You rich little son-of-a-bitch, you think because you have a car you can pick up all the *mamacitas* in the neighborhood?" That was the last straw. A scuffle broke out that ended when Jorge Tulio punched Pablo in the nose and knocked him down.

Not long afterward, Pablo got into it with Julio Gaviria, a man who would go dancing in La Paz but always overdid it with the liquor. One night, Gaviria made a fuss when a girl refused to dance with him at a party. Without thinking, Pablo pulled out a small five-chamber revolver and shot him in the foot. Gaviria reported him to the police, and for the first time a warrant was issued for my father's arrest. He went to jail, though only for a short time because Gaviria soon dropped the charges.

To make sure the incident hadn't put him on the radar of criminal investigation agencies, on June 2, 1970, Pablo went to the Medellín offices of the DAS and applied for a background check, which they issued to him relatively quickly. Because such documents were difficult to obtain, once he had it, on the last page he wrote, "If found, please call Pablo Escobar at 762976."

Pablo was spending most of his time with his cousin Gustavo at this point, always looking to do some business or pull off a crime to get money in his pocket. One time they robbed a truck loaded with Rexona and Sanit K bath soaps, which they sold at half price to the local stores. With the money they got for the soap, they immediately traded the Vespa in for another Italian motorcycle, a 1962 Lambretta, license plate A-1653, which they frequently used to take out the local girls.

Still, they constantly were in need of money, so one day they decided to start selling gravestones. It was a lucrative business because Gustavo's father owned a tile factory, and they were able to achieve a good profit margin.

The two went on the Lambretta to visit clients in the villages around Medellín, carrying stones with them as samples. Of course, they soon figured out that it would be easier just to buy the tombstones from the village gravedigger, who almost certainly stole them from the cemetery at night and fixed them up to look new again. Between the stones from the factory and the used ones they brought to be recarved with the names of the newly deceased, it didn't take long for rumors to start circulating. There was so much gossip about it that once, after the death of a close friend of the family, Pablo offered the widow a gravestone, and she rejected it. Though she didn't say anything at the time, she later commented that she wouldn't put a stolen stone on her husband's grave.

Pablo and Gustavo eventually gave up the tombstone business because the profits weren't high enough. My father was always searching for better options. One night he said something as they were leaving La Iguana that a number of his friends would never forget. In a solemn, determined voice, he told them, "If I haven't earned a million pesos by the time I'm thirty, I'll kill myself."

Determined to reach that goal as soon as possible, he and Gustavo started robbing the cinema box offices in downtown Medellín. They hit the El Cid, La Playa, Teatro Avenida, Odeón, and Lido movie theaters, holding them up at gunpoint and making off with the money.

Then they moved on to stealing cars, for which they had a number of different methods. One was to take new vehicles that had only recently left the dealership. Their accomplice was a paperwork processor at a dealership who provided them with legal documents and made a copy of the car key for my father. When the unfortunate owner picked up the new car, they'd follow him to his house, wait for him to park and enter his home, and drive off in it a few minutes later.

Sometimes they'd take the plates from cars that had been declared totaled by insurance companies and swap them onto the new cars. First my father and Gustavo would buy wrecked cars and take them to a body shop, where the mechanic would strip off the license plates. Then they'd put the old plates on the new cars so that the cars would not be traced to stolen property.

But the two also used some strategies that were so simple that they'd make you laugh if they weren't against the law. For example, my father once saw a man stranded on the side of the road, asked him what had happened, and offered to repair the car. Then he said he had to get behind the wheel to start it up and told the poor owner to push. When the car started, Pablo took off.

My father and Gustavo used the money from the car thefts to buy a noisy 1955 Studebaker, dark blue with a white roof, which expanded their neighborhood fan club. They'd go out with girls on the weekends and take trips with their gang of friends.

A number of my father's buddies recall a long trip they took to the village of Piendamó in the Cauca Department to see if rumors that the Virgin had appeared to a little girl there were true. It was May 1971, and the whole country was in a tizzy about the supposed miracle. My grandmother Hermilda was excited about the trip and asked Pablo to bring back some holy water.

It was a long way to Piendamó, and Pablo dutifully filled a bottle with water near the spot where the girl had supposedly had her vision. But on the way back, when they had reached Minas, outside Medellín, the Studebaker overheated, and they had to pour that water into the radiator. My father filled the bottle again with river water and gave it to my grandmother, who believed it to be holy.

A few days later, my father and Gustavo got a temporary contract from the Carvajal company to distribute three thousand phone books in Envigado and collect the ones from the previous year. They soon earned praise for the speed with which they completed their work, but that's because nobody realized they were passing out the directories without even looking at the addresses.

With income their top priority, they also decided to rip out half the pages of the old phone books and sell them to a recycler. They earned more money for that than they did for distributing the new ones, but they only managed to keep the job for twelve days, as Carvajal soon discovered that the stacks of old phone books were falling over because they were missing half their pages.

CRIME HAD BECOME AN EVERYDAY AFFAIR FOR MY FATHER AND Gustavo, and they now owned the Studebaker and two Lambretta motorcycles.

The cousins' successful business pursuits had gradually made a difference, and eventually Pablo had enough money to open up his first savings account at the Banco Industrial Colombiano. In February 1973, he made his first deposit of 1,160 pesos (50 dollars at the time). In November he deposited 114,062 pesos (4,740 dollars). He was quickly becoming a wealthy man.

At the end of that year, my father first spotted a tall, slender, pretty girl with long legs in the neighborhood. Her name was Victoria Eugenia Henao Vallejo, she was thirteen years old, she went to school at El Carmelo in the nearby village of Sabaneta, and she was the sixth of eight siblings: five girls and three boys.

The Henaos were the wealthiest family in La Paz. Nora, the mother, had a successful store where she sold fabric for school uniforms, shirts, pants, electronics, school supplies, and lotions that she brought from the distant duty-free zone of Maicao, on the border with Venezuela. Carlos Emilio, the father, delivered guava jelly in a spotless, late-'50s Ford pickup truck. The sweets were produced by the La Piñata company, so the Henao daughters were known in the neighborhood as "the piñatas."

My father was twenty-four years old, eleven years older than Victoria, but he was intrigued. A few days later he found out that her best friend was a girl named Yolanda, and then he tracked down Yolanda for her help in asking Victoria out.

The strategy worked, and my future parents started seeing each other in secret, though they made quite an odd couple. She was taller than he and had a slim figure from swimming a thousand yards every week and frequently skating. At the time my parents had no idea that what they had embarked upon would become an intense relationship full of ups and downs—maybe more downs than ups—that would end only with his death twenty years later.

At first they'd meet on Saturdays, from seven to nine at night, with the help of Yolanda and my father's gang of friends. They didn't see each other during the week because, so he told her, he traveled for business. She was still completely unaware that her suitor was on a bad path.

Yolanda, the go-between in the relationship, soon acquired a tough opponent: Nora, Victoria's mother, who was very angry to learn that her daughter was going out with Pablo Escobar—eleven years older, from a bad family, of undetermined occupation, a womanizer, and a delinquent in the making. Her father and her brother Mario were no more supportive, even though Mario actually knew Pablo quite well.

The relationship progressed despite the opposition of my grandmother Nora, who threw every obstacle she could at them. For example, she imposed a curfew on Victoria and would allow her to go to local parties only if her brothers were going too. But Pablo wasn't about to give up and showered the girl with gifts, which she received through Yolanda. The first was a brand-name watch that he used to wear, and then a ring with pearls and turquoise that he bought in a Medellín jewelry store for 1,600 pesos, a fortune at the time.

But Nora didn't relent, and her doubts about her daughter's beau continued to percolate.

"Sweetheart, there's no need to get all dolled up since you're just dating a driver," she'd say.

"Tell him to leave the poncho at home. He can't come here looking like that," said my grandfather Carlos.

"You'd better show my daughter respect. You're not getting past that door," Nora once told Pablo when he dropped Victoria off at the house after they went out one Saturday afternoon.

Despite the challenges, the relationship deepened, and they started seeing each other more often. Pablo offered to teach Victoria how to drive his mustard-yellow Renault 4, which he had gotten for the Studebaker. And so, of course, he took her to incredibly dangerous places, with cliffs and drop-offs, and they always ended up going up the Vía Las Palmas to the restaurant El Peñasco, which offered an impressive and romantic view of Medellín.

I never thought to ask my mother why she fell in love with my father—enough to forgive everything he did—until just now, as I was finishing this book. After thinking about it a while, she replied:

"Because of his naughty smile, the way he looked at me. I fell in love because he was so romantic. He was a poet with me, very thoughtful. He wooed me with romantic music, gave me LP records all the time. He was affectionate and sweet. A great seducer. A nature lover. I fell in love with his desire to help people and his compassion for their hardship. When we were dating, we used to drive to the places where he dreamed of building universities and schools for the poor. I can't think of a single time he ever said anything cruel to me or mistreated me. From beginning to end, he was always a gentleman with me."

The budding romance was interrupted in the second half of 1974, when the police stopped my father in a stolen Renault 4. They booked him in the La Ladera prison, where he met a man who would be formative to his burgeoning criminal career: Alberto Prieto, the great contraband boss of the era, known as "the Godfather." Prieto, my father's cellmate, was a powerful figure who'd made an enormous fortune smuggling whiskey, cigarettes, electronics, and other products into Colombia from the border zone of Urabá to sell throughout Medellín and other areas of the country. But he also had contacts with Antioquia's political elites and bragged about his relationships with legislators and judges in Bogotá.

Pablo was incarcerated for two months. In that time, he became friends with the Godfather and learned how his business worked. My father never talked about it with me, but I later found out that the Godfather had arranged for the evidence from the stolen Renault 4 case to disappear, so the judge had no choice but to dismiss the proceedings and release him from La Ladera.

Weeks later, my father met up with the Godfather—now out of prison—and the older man offered him a job guarding the caravans of trucks that transported goods from Urabá. My father accepted on the condition that his cousin Gustavo could work with him. Very soon, the two became famous among the smugglers for their courage and ruthlessness. On one notorious occasion, the police stopped five trucks departing Urabá loaded with Marlboro cigarettes, and my father and Gustavo traveled there and managed to get the trucks back in less than twenty-four hours.

The Godfather's world, my father and Gustavo realized, was one in which misdemeanors didn't exist and death was commonplace. In this murky, increasingly high-pressure environment, my father committed a murder—the first of his life. Though people tell several versions of these events, those who were closest to the action have shared this one with me: my father and my uncle Mario agreed to participate in a scam in which a man with the last name of Sanín would "kidnap himself" on a farm near Envigado so that Sanín's brother, a millionaire smuggler, would pay the ransom. While my father went to collect the ransom, Mario would stay with the supposed abductee. Unluckily for them, though, the police arrived on the scene after some neighbors reported strange activity. Sanín immediately told the officers he'd been kidnapped and that Mario, who was with him, was one of the culprits. My uncle went to prison for nine months, and my father refused to forgive the deception. One night he trailed Sanín to a building in Medellín, and when the man entered the garage, my father shot and killed him. That was probably the first motorcycle drive-by in Medellín history.

In the meantime, the Godfather, pleased with my father and Gustavo's work protecting his smuggling operations, gave them another responsibility: escorting a caravan of thirty-five vehicles loaded with goods from Urabá's port of Turbo to Medellín. Thanks to Pablo and Gustavo's cunning, the Godfather's shipment arrived safely after passing without incident through numerous checkpoints set up by the police, the navy, and Antioquia's customs officials.

By that point, my mother was becoming unhappy with my father's frequent absences. He would disappear for several days and return with a gift and no further explanation. She noticed that he was bringing wool blankets woven with a pattern of four tigers, handmade by indigenous artisans in Ecuador. But my mother was unaware that Pablo had discovered the business that would quickly make him a millionaire: cocaine trafficking.

According to several people who were close to him at the time, it was through my father's relationship with the Godfather that he recognized that some of the estates in the nearby villages of Caldas, La Estrella, Guarne, and San Cristóbal had small facilities where they processed a paste brought from Ecuador, Peru, and Bolivia and turned it into a white powder called cocaine.

My father immediately tracked down Atelio González, an associate of the Godfather who was getting on in years, and asked him how he could become involved in the business. González told my father he ran one of those facilities, known as a "kitchen," where they mixed the imported paste with a few chemicals, including ether and acetone, and then heated it to high temperatures to dry it. The end result was cocaine.

My father was fascinated and soon learned that the three people who owned the kitchens flew totally under the radar and sold the cocaine to buyers who came in from the United States. As soon as he understood the broad strokes of the business, he and Gustavo took their first road trip to the Ecuadorian port of Guayaquil, where they bought their first five *cosos,* as kilos of coca paste were called. To avoid being caught at the border checkpoint on the Rumichaca International Bridge, they'd built a hiding place above the gas tank of my father's Renault 4.

Atelio González processed the five kilos of coca paste and produced a kilo of cocaine, which they sold to a buyer for six thousand dollars. From then on, my father and Gustavo gave up stealing cars, delivering phone books, and the long smuggling trips from Urabá. They'd officially entered the narco world.

TRUE TO FORM, IT DIDN'T TAKE LONG FOR PABLO AND GUSTAVO to set up their own kitchen on a nearby farm and appoint my uncle Mario (who still opposed the relationship between Pablo and his sister Victoria) to run it. They also found someone to sell them the chemical supplies they needed, which they sometimes hid in the laboratories of the La Paz school with the help of a teacher there—who also happened to be my father's sister, Alba Marina.

The cousins made frequent trips south to the Ecuadorian province of La Loja, on the border with Peru, where they met several coca paste distributors and went into partnership with Jorge Galeano, a fellow Antioquian who was just getting into the business. Together they brought back larger and larger quantities of coca paste, always by land. Small loads were occasionally confiscated when they crossed the border.

My father's cocaine business slowly grew, and his financial circumstances were improving. In 1975, having already processed and sold a significant amount of cocaine, my father made good—and then some—on his old dream of getting rich before he was thirty. He was twenty-six when he asked friends from his gang to accompany him to the Banco Industrial Colombiano in the town of Sabaneta to deposit a check for not one million, but one hundred million pesos (US$3,225,000).

Still, my mother's family remained fiercely opposed to their romance. My grandmother Nora didn't think Pablo was the right man for her daughter, objecting to their meetings and trying hard to persuade Victoria to break up with him. Despite her family's disapproval, on the whole things were going well between Pablo and Victoria, though she was often angered by his unexpected trips and the excuses he always had at the ready to hide his real activities. When my mother turned fifteen in September 1975, they had a big fight because my father had disappeared for a week and spoiled a celebration that was important to her. She later learned he'd gone to Ecuador. Eventually, though, something happened that cemented their relationship for good.

One Saturday afternoon in late March 1976, my father told Victoria he was going on a long trip and made a date to say good-bye at the El Paso ice cream shop near her home. She asked my grandmother's permission, but Nora told her not to go, to let him leave. Anxious to see him, my mother sneaked out and told him what had happened. My father was outraged that Victoria's stubborn mother wouldn't even allow her daughter to say good-bye when he was going to be away for several months. He decided to go for broke, telling Victoria they couldn't go on like that and suggesting they run away to Pasto, a city in southern Colombia, to get married.

Without hesitation, my mother agreed, and they went to spend the night in the home of Gustavo and his wife, who had no problem providing them a place to stay.

As they hid at Gustavo's house, the pair learned that my uncle Mario was furious and looking for my father so he could kill him for corrupting the "little girl," as he referred to his sister. So they moved on to Pasto immediately. To get there, however, their only option was to fly to Cali and wait for a connection there.

Meanwhile, the neighborhood of La Paz was in an uproar. Desperate, the Henaos harassed every household until someone finally revealed that the fugitives had traveled to Cali and had to wait there for six hours till they could leave for Pasto. My grandmother Nora called her mother, Lola, who lived near the cathedral in Palmira, and asked her to go to Cali and prevent them from leaving. Alfredo and Rigoberto, two of my father's best friends, had already left for Cali in a truck, also hoping to catch Pablo and Victoria. When they reached the airport, they found my great-grandmother with the couple and witnessed the moment Pablo convinced her that he wanted to marry my mother.

My father was so convincing that my great-grandmother instructed them to come with her to Palmira, as she was certain Pablo could persuade the bishop there to marry them. She had close connections among the clergy, so it wasn't hard to get the church's authorization.

Victoria and Pablo were married without pomp and circumstance. My mother must have been wearing the same green army pants and orange-and-beige sweater—the clothes she was wearing when she'd run away from home—for days. Always the jokesters, Pablo's friends Alfredo and Rigoberto gave them their sole wedding present, a card offering heartfelt condolences: "For the regrettable mistake you've just made."

The newlyweds spent their week-long honeymoon in my great-grandmother's house before returning to La Paz, where they lived for a few months in a small room in the house my father had loaned my aunt Alba Marina when she'd gotten married not long before. My mother knew that my father loved fried plantains, and whenever she could she prepared the dish just the way he liked: cut into little cubes and scrambled with eggs and scallions. She served it with white rice, grilled meat, and beet salad, his favorite. All accompanied by a glass of cold milk and a thick *arepa*, a cornmeal cake.

Though my mother is reluctant to discuss the subject, it would be impossible not to mention my father's numerous infidelities, which began only a few weeks after their wedding. She'd hear rumors of his affairs and suffer in silence, and he'd deftly soothe her by insisting she was the love of his life, that their marriage would last forever, and that she should ignore spiteful, envious people who wanted only to tear them apart.

In a way, this prophecy was lived out. My father and mother were together until death did them part, but he never stopped cheating on her. One of his first affairs was with the principal of the local high school. After that, for a few months he was seeing a pretty, dark-haired, young woman, the widow of a notorious thief. When my mother once left a networking gala at the InterContinental Hotel early, my aunt had to slap my father for dancing rather closely with the wife of one of his employees. For my father, seducing women was a sort of challenge, and he never missed an opportunity.

The relative tranquility that reigned in my father's household was shattered on June 7, 1976, when one of his employees called to inform him that agents from the DAS had found the shipment of coca paste they were bringing by truck from Ecuador. When he reassured my father that the detectives were open to receiving money in exchange for letting the shipment through to Medellín, my father accepted the deal.

At five o'clock the next morning, my father got word that the

DAS agents were waiting for him at an ice cream shop at La Mayorista, Medellín's wholesale market, where they would collect the money. My father called my uncle Mario to go with him, who in turn called Gustavo and arranged to meet at the appointed location. Before entering the place, still in the car, my father counted out the five thousand dollars he intended to use to buy their silence.

But it was all a trap. Far from accepting a bribe, the agents intended to capture the whole gang and confiscate the nineteen pounds of coca paste hidden inside the truck's spare tire. They waited for my father to offer them the money and then announced that he, Mario, Gustavo, and the two truck drivers were under arrest for drug trafficking and attempted bribery.

They were immediately carted off to the DAS holding cells in Medellín, where they spent the night; the next morning they were transferred to the Bellavista prison in the town of Bello, north of Medellín. In the booking records, my father was given the ID number 128482. He is smiling in his mugshot, perhaps because he was certain his stay in jail would be brief. But the first few days in prison were hard on him, Mario, and Gustavo, as there was a rumor circulating that they were undercover officers looking for information about the various gangs that held sway in different areas of the prison. Things got so bad that someone even warned them they were going to be assaulted one night.

Everything suddenly changed when one of the prisoners, whom my father did not know, told the others that Pablo, Mario, and Gustavo weren't snitches and to leave them alone. They obeyed, and the danger evaporated. The unexpected benefactor turned out to be Jorge "Blackie" Pabón, a fellow prisoner serving a short sentence who definitely had heard of my father. The two of them maintained a close relationship after that, and years later Pabón would play a key role in the cartels.

Though conditions improved for my father, Mario, and Gustavo after Blackie Pabón's intervention, Bellavista was a hostile, dangerous prison. It was there, in that fetid, crowded place, that my mother learned that she was pregnant. On a visiting day, accompanied by Gustavo's wife and my aunt Alba Marina, she started throwing up while they were in line to enter the prison. My father was overjoyed at the news of his wife's pregnancy, but his extended incarceration and financial limitations forced my mother to leave the house in the Los Colores neighborhood and return to her parents' home.

Driven to despair by his confinement and the tough conditions at Bellavista, my father asked his lawyer to do whatever it took—even bribery—to get him transferred to another prison. The attorney's efforts were effective, and a few days later he, Gustavo, and Mario were taken to an estate in the town of Itagüí that served as the Yarumito prison. Life there improved substantially, as my mother and grandmother visited daily with breakfast and lunch. Even so, my father wasn't willing to remain a prisoner, and one day he escaped Yarumito and hid at a neighbor's house in La Paz. He'd made his getaway during a prisoner soccer match by enlisting the help of some of the players, whom he'd asked to keep kicking the ball farther and farther so he could go after it.

Things were very different in Colombia back then. The prison warden simply called up my grandmother to inform her Pablo had escaped and asked her to convince him to return, reassuring her there would be no repercussions. A couple of hours later, Pablo called Hermilda's house, and she told him not to make my mother, who was three months pregnant and must have weighed just ninety pounds, suffer any longer. My father then contacted my mother, who begged him to turn himself in immediately. He gave in and appeared at the prison that same night.

Despite the good conditions at Yarumito, my father was worried. The judge on the case, Mariela Espinosa, seemed determined to convict them all because the evidence was overwhelming. So he and the lawyer agreed to make a crucial play: to request that the trial be moved to the city of Pasto, on the border with Ecuador,

where the coca paste had been purchased and the DAS had inter-
cepted the truck. The motion was granted, and the prisoners
were to be transferred immediately to the Pasto prison. Right as
my mother was arriving to visit them at Yarumito, my father was
being led out in handcuffs. He was happy to see her, but his face
grew dark with rage when a police officer struck her with the butt
of his rifle to move her out of the way.

Over the next few weeks, my mother and grandmother traveled regularly to Pasto. It was easy for the prisoners to bribe the
guards, who treated them well. They even let my father go to the
Morasurco, the city's most famous hotel, where he'd spend weekends with my mother.

The situation began to be resolved in August 1976, when a Pasto
judge released Mario and Gustavo. In November, after he'd spent
five months in prison, the charges against my father were dropped,
and he returned home. But his arrest would have consequences. He
had appeared for the first time in police records, and Bogotá's *El
Espectador* newspaper had also revealed his identity. There was no
turning back from his career as a criminal now, and he knew it.

4

The Renault Coke

The amateurs to watch out for are Lucio Bernal of Bogotá and Pablo Escobar, Gustavo Gaviria, and Juan Yepes, all from Medellín. Drivers like Pablo Escobar are on the rise. Escobar is in second, with 13 points," Bogotá's *El Tiempo* newspaper reported on one of the races for the Renault Cup in the International Autodrome in early 1979.

My father and Gustavo's penchant for high-speed racing had developed a year prior, when they'd already amassed a good bit of money through drug trafficking and were looking for other ways to amuse themselves. At first my father had competed in motocross races on the Furesa track near SOFASA, the Renault assembly plant in Envigado. He had some success and ranked highly, but a dramatic crash left him with injuries that took several months to heal.

Cars awoke a great passion for speed in my father. When he heard the public announcement that the traditional Renault Cup, held at the speedway every year, would admit amateur racers, not just professionals, he became determined to enter, and Gustavo wasn't about to be left behind.

The requirement for the new category of drivers was fairly simple: an original Renault 4, whose engine and suspension could be altered according to authorized specifications. Other modifications were the competitor's choice.

Excited, my father and Gustavo purchased ten Renault 4s with 1,000cc engines and handed them off to an engineer who had worked at the SOFASA assembly plant so he could make the changes they wanted. The engineer installed a safety cage inside each car and a special muffler for high speeds, scraped each engine's cylinder head, and altered the camshafts.

The cars were ready for competition. My father and Gustavo were sponsored by Bicicletas El Osito, a bicycle manufacturer, and the Depósitos Cundinamarca bank. My father's car was number 70, and Gustavo's was 71. Jorge Luis Ochoa Vásquez, another member of the Medellín Cartel, sponsored the Las Margaritas team, with four vehicles. He didn't race, but his younger brother, Fabio, did.

My father and Gustavo took the championship so seriously that a year before the first race they sent two of their employees to Bogotá to finalize all the details. They bought a van and filled it with replacement parts for their Renault 4s, hired an engineer and five mechanics to take care of the cars for the next year, and paid a huge sum for enough room in the pits to hold not only the mechanics and the cars but also a good portion of the family.

But something was still missing: accommodations. My father rented the entire top floor of the Hilton Hotel and paid a year in advance. It was completely unnecessary and over the top since, with the exception of just six weekends a year, those rooms were usually empty.

Feeling cheeky now that he was a race car driver, my father made a joke: the Renault Cup should be called the Renault Coke instead. And he wasn't wrong. That year, besides Pablo and Gustavo, several other drug runners from Medellín and Cali were also racing.

The first race was scheduled for Sunday, February 25, 1979, but my father and Gustavo traveled down by helicopter the previous Monday to prepare their cars and have their medical checkups. In a briefcase, my father brought two hundred million pesos in cash as pocket money to cover the expenses during their stay.

The outcome of my father's physical wasn't good. The encephalogram revealed that he wasn't fit enough to drive race cars. But being who he was, someone used to solving every problem with money, he bribed the doctors to alter the exam results and authorize the issuance of his license so he could compete.

The atmosphere before the start of the Renault Cup was festive, and the stands at the racetrack were completely full. There was a lot of buzz about the Las Margaritas team, which arrived with a new bus that had a mechanic's shop in the rear and a large, well-equipped office in the front. According to the reporters covering the event, such a thing had never before been seen in Colombian racing.

My father went out onto the track wearing garish orange overalls; Gustavo was wearing red ones. In their first race, the two amateurs proved their driving abilities but came in only third and fourth, respectively. Even so, the next day's papers were full of praise, and experts claimed that the Antioquian drivers had really ramped up the competition.

My father, Gustavo, and the whole family went out that evening to eat at the Las Margaritas restaurant, owned by Fabio Ochoa, Sr., not far from the racetrack. There they spotted a modestly dressed man in a hat sitting alone. They'd never seen him before, and it turned out to be Gonzalo Rodríguez Gacha, who visited the area every weekend to sell horses.

In the next few Renault Cup races, some of which also took place in Cali and Medellín, my father and Gustavo would arrive on Saturday by helicopter and fly back home on Monday morning.

Throughout the Cup, my father and Gustavo were among the top drivers in the standings—my father even reached second place—but they ended up facing off against two excellent drivers who kept them from taking the lead: Álvaro Mejía, sponsored by

Cali's Roldanautos, and Lucio Bernal, sponsored by Bogotá's Supercar-Hertz. Mejía and Bernal's battle for first place would go on to the very end of the championship in November 1979, despite my father's efforts to beat them. At first he spent a lot of money, hiring two automobile engineers who tried unsuccessfully to improve his car. He even offered them extra money for every pound of weight they managed to strip off his vehicle. When someone mentioned that a Renault engineer in France had designed engines for competing in similar races, he ordered three. But that didn't work either.

My father ended up coming in fourth place and Gustavo, ninth. Disappointed, neither of them wanted to have anything more to do with racing.

As could be expected, my father and Gustavo's racing careers generated plenty of colorful anecdotes.

First: because of their extravagant enthusiasm, they bought two luxurious, very fast Porsche 911SCs, one of which had belonged to the prominent Brazilian race car driver Emerson Fittipaldi. My father ordered his painted white and red and gave it the number 21; Gustavo's was 23.

Second: one Sunday evening, back at the Hilton after a race, they had gone up to their rooms on the top floor. One of the team mechanics threw an empty bottle out a window and hit the shoulder of a bodyguard who happened to be accompanying President Julio César Turbay Ayala at the time. The head of state's security forces ran upstairs to investigate and found more than forty people engaged in a wild party. To keep things from getting out of control, Turbay's bodyguards escorted everyone who wasn't a hotel guest from the premises.

Third: on a different evening, the renowned musician and pianist Jimmy Salcedo came to the Hilton to speak with my father, accompanied by one of the dancers from the group Las Superno- tas. The beautiful woman told him she wanted to race at the track and asked him to be her sponsor, but the matter never went any further because my father retired shortly after the championship.

Fourth: the Renault Cup was moved to Cali one weekend, and my father and his whole team stayed at the InterContinental, where they happened to run into the Spanish crooner Julio Iglesias. When my father learned that Iglesias was scheduled to perform at the Los Años Locos nightclub that Saturday night, he purchased more than one hundred tickets and invited his competitors to the show.

In his brief career as a race car driver, my father met several people who would later play vital roles in his life, his business deal- ings, and his wars.

Gonzalo Rodríguez Gacha, the solitary horse trader, was known as "the Mexican." He would become my father's main partner in cocaine trafficking a few months later, and together they would wage war against the Colombian government.

Ricardo "Razor" Londoño, an experienced driver who raced that year in a Dodge Alpine—and was also the first Colombian to compete in the Formula One World Championship—would be re- sponsible for fulfilling my father's vehicular fancies through an import/export company he set up in Miami.

Héctor Roldán—sponsor of the Roldanautos team, whose main driver, Álvaro Mejía, won the 1979 Renault Cup for amateurs— became close friends with my father during the competition in Bogotá. He owned a car dealership in Cali and, according to people close to my father, was a powerful drug trafficker in western Colombia. When my mother didn't come to Bogotá to watch my father race, Roldán would bring beautiful women to my father's hotel room. Later, he would do the same at our Nápoles estate, where Roldán was a frequent guest.

Years after, when my sister was born, my father decided to name Roldán her godfather, but my mother objected, outraged, as she knew the two of them were going out with women all the time.

"If you choose Roldán, I'll refuse to get the baby baptized, and when she grows up she can decide who she wants to be her godfather," my mother had threatened.

My father relented and instead named Juan Yepes Flórez, whom my father had raced with in the Renault Cup. They'd nicknamed him "John Lada" because he was one of the first importers of Russian Lada 4x4s, which hit the Colombian market in 1977. A retired soldier, he was young, handsome, polite, friendly with everybody, and always smiling.

5

Papá Narco

On several occasions I asked my father about the size of his fortune, as I'd often heard people say he was one of the richest men in the world. He always gave me the same reply: "At a certain point I had so much money that I lost count. Once I knew I was a money-making machine, I stopped worrying about counting it."

I'm used to seeing astronomical figures associated with my father's supposed wealth. *Forbes* magazine once claimed that he had $3 billion, though nobody from that publication ever reached out to him to confirm the number. Elsewhere I read the wildly exaggerated sum of $25 billion. I am sure that if I ventured to give a figure, I, too, would be simply guessing.

Drug trafficking gave my father everything—and also took everything from him. Even his life. And so I am frankly skeptical of the long-term prospects of such a business, as it inevitably devolves into a violent struggle for power. That was all the lesson I needed.

I can't claim to know all the details of my father's drug-trafficking activities, nor do I intend to offer an exhaustive account of his cocaine trafficking empire. My aim is to reflect on the way he and a handful of drug runners took advantage of that quiet moment before the business became so wildly and recklessly dangerous—before anyone in the United States, much less in Colombia or the rest of the world, had any idea of the reach that the cocaine trade was going to have.

RETURNING TO MEDELLÍN AFTER HIS RELEASE FROM THE PASTO prison in early November 1976, my father had gotten off the bus wearing the same beige shoes he'd been wearing when he was arrested for the first and last time in his life for cocaine trafficking. On his way to my grandmother Hermilda's house in the La Paz neighborhood, he ran into my mother's relative, Alfredo Astado. Greeting him with a warm hug, he asked Alfredo for a coin to make a call from a nearby pay phone. He spoke to someone in code and hung up two minutes later.

At his mother's house once more, he tossed his backpack on a sofa and sat down to rest for a bit. He was exhausted after the long trip from southern Colombia, though my aunts and uncles and their friends from the neighborhood who stopped by noted an odd determination in his face.

Two hours later, a man dropped off a new Toyota SUV and two hundred thousand dollars in cash. Nobody ever learned who they were from, but they assumed the vehicle and the money were somehow related to the earlier phone call. The gifts confirmed that his five months in jail hadn't altered his goal of becoming insanely wealthy—even if by illegal means. He seemed even more energetic than before, and that afternoon, after communicating with his contact in Loja, Ecuador, he sent one of his workers down there to buy coca paste. The following day, he was informed that the police in the town of La Virginia, in the neighboring Department of Risaralda, had stopped the vehicle at a checkpoint and found the cash hidden in the air conditioning system. My father and Gustavo rushed there, paid a fat bribe, and reclaimed the vehicle and the money.

Undaunted, my father and Gustavo decided to travel to Ecuador for the coca paste themselves. This time they didn't run into any problems. The trip would prove to be crucial, as they were able to make contact with some of the traffickers my father had met in the Pasto prison, who helped them find better providers and smuggling routes to bring the coca paste to Colombia.

Over the course of their frequent trips back and forth to Ecuador, they established a system that allowed them to regularly transport increasingly large shipments of coca paste. They hired a colonel in the Ecuadorian army to head the project and paid him well. The colonel made an arrangement between the sellers in Loja and a dozen day laborers who would carry up to twenty kilos of alkaloid hidden inside hollowed-out blocks of wood. Hoisting the wood onto their shoulders, they would trek through the jungle for fifteen or twenty hours straight till they reached the San Miguel River, on the Ecuador–Colombia border, where my father's men would meet them. The blocks of wood were then transported nearly six hundred miles in small trucks to the kitchens my father and Gustavo had already set up on small farms in the Colombian countryside near the villages of Guarne, Marinilla, and El Santuario in eastern Antioquia.

That precarious period when my father and Gustavo had to hide their coca-processing chemicals in La Paz's neighborhood school labs was behind them. Everything was now under control. All that was left was to connect with the final link in the chain of drug trafficking: consumers, who had remained elusive because my father and Gustavo were focused on selling processed coca paste to drug runners from the United States who came to Medellín to buy it.

Since my father's release from prison, my parents had been forced to split up and stay in different relatives' houses. Tired of never being able to be with my mother, who was about to give birth to me, my father rented an apartment next to La Candelaria, a large supermarket in an area of Medellín known as Castropol. And so my father left his family's home in La Paz, thirteen years after he'd arrived there in poverty, just as broke as ever.

My parents didn't have much money at that point because the drug trade is a high-risk business where you can be rich one day and lose it all the next. And my father hadn't made it yet. Still, he was sure that he was on the right path, even if he barely had enough money to cover rent.

Some major cocaine deal must have come through, however, because a few weeks after they moved, an expensive Porsche Carrera convertible appeared at their apartment. My mother still didn't have a car, though Pablo and Gustavo sometimes loaned her a red Toyota pickup.

I was born into that world on February 24, 1977, in the Rosario clinic in Medellín's Boston neighborhood. My mother was only fifteen, and a woman named Sofía would be my nanny from then on.

Eventually, power was within my father's reach, and he bought a sprawling house in the affluent Provenza neighborhood in El Poblado. After a few months, my father moved the rest of his family out of La Paz. He gave my grandmother Hermilda a house in the Estadio neighborhood and placed his sisters in apartments nearby. He would later move his sisters closer to our house in El Poblado, which was then one of Medellín's up-and-coming areas. My grandfather Abel had already returned to his farm in El Tablazo, and my uncles Roberto and Fernando were living in the city of Manizales and working for Bicicletas El Osito, the bicycle manufacturing company that would later sponsor Pablo's and Gustavo's attempt at the Renault Cup.

The cousins' illegal dealings were going so well that Pablo and Gustavo stopped meeting in the neighborhood ice cream shops; instead, my father planned to set up an office at our house. When my uncle Mario Henao advised that he shouldn't mix his family life with business, however, my father moved to an office near the El Poblado church. In time, he and Gustavo acquired another, much larger office next to the Oviedo shopping center, in the recently constructed Torre La Vega building; he and Gustavo purchased the fourth floor and managed their affairs from there.

My father's ability to buy property in the best areas of Medellín was indisputable evidence that he was beginning to amass a huge fortune. And he wasn't the only one. Many other narcos were also taking advantage of the lack of awareness of the cocaine trade in Colombia and the United States. Governments and officials hadn't realized that a lucrative business was developing in far-off South America that even forty years later remains profitable and continues to grow at an exponential rate.

At the time, cocaine was all the rage in U.S. social circles. In its May 1977 edition—three months after my birth—*Newsweek* magazine noted that at fashionable parties among the celebrity crowd in Los Angeles and New York, it was common to pass around a silver tray of cocaine along with expensive beluga caviar and Dom Perignon champagne. Due to the infrastructure they'd built by mid-1977, it didn't take my father and Gustavo long to set up their own smuggling routes to transport cocaine to the United States, where oversight of the ports and airports was less than comprehensive. The officials' naivety made the traffickers' work easier since there was no need to go to great lengths to hide the drugs. There were no x-ray machines or drug-sniffing dogs or agents or thorough searches. A simple false-bottomed suitcase was enough to export a lot of drugs without fear of detection. There were also no specific laws about drug trafficking, and it was treated as a type of smuggling. The demonization and criminalization of the trade would come later.

MY FATHER ONCE TOLD ME THAT HE AND GUSTAVO DID A PRACTICE run to test-ship a hundred kilos of cocaine in a twin-engine Piper Seneca plane. It arrived at Opa Locka Airport, a private airport in the heart of Miami used exclusively by wealthy Americans, without a hitch. When they heard that the shipment had made it safely, my father and Gustavo threw a huge party at Kevin's, a Medellín nightclub, with plenty of alcohol and beautiful women to go around.

They were staring into a gold mine. A kilo of processed cocaine that cost them two hundred thousand pesos (about five thousand dollars at the time) in Colombia had a final cost, with shipping and security factored in, of six thousand dollars. Selling it to individual buyers on the street, a wholesale distributor like my father could bring in twenty thousand dollars per kilo in southern Florida—twenty-five or even thirty thousand dollars in New York.

Despite this extraordinary profitability, what my father brought in was small compared to the amount earned by American resellers—only about ten percent of the ultimate value of each kilo. The dealers added aspirin, lime, ground glass, talcum powder, or any other white powder to his product. That way, they could get three or four kilos out of a single kilo of pure cocaine. Those kilos, sold by the gram, would generate earnings of up to two hundred thousand dollars each.

The business began to expand rapidly, and my father and Gustavo found powerful providers in the Upper Huallaga Valley in northern Peru, where one of the largest coca paste production centers on the continent was forming.

New players entered the scene, and my father and Gustavo were able to stop using day laborers to walk many hours to transport a few kilos. Experienced pilots transformed the dynamics of drug trafficking. They were the missing ingredient that would make my father's operation the biggest one around.

The duo set up a sort of airlift between secret runways in the Monzón and Campanilla regions in Peru's Upper Huallaga Valley, and they built other runways in Colombia's Magdalena Medio and eastern Antioquia regions. Huge shipments of coca paste started coming in two or three times a week after passing unimpeded through the skies of at least four countries. My father and Gustavo's success attracted the attention of other drug trafficking opera-tions, small and large alike, who were interested in doing business. One of these was run by Fidel Castaño, who showed up at my father's office one day with his brother, Carlos, a young man of average height with starry eyes.

Fidel told my father and Gustavo that he had contacts in the vast coca leaf plantations in Santa Cruz de la Sierra, Bolivia, where they produced huge quantities of coca paste. Business-wise, the men hit it off immediately and started bringing in loads of three to five hundred kilos by plane to an airstrip on an estate in Obando, north of the Cauca Valley. The drug was picked up there in one or more vehicles and transported to the kitchens in Antioquia.

That's how my father's relationship with the Castaño brothers started. For a long time it was a good one. Fidel even told my father one of his most closely guarded secrets: that one of his main US contacts for selling drugs was the famous crooner Frank Sinatra.

As I mentioned earlier, at the time the United States was wide open because no one charged with overseeing the country's air-ports, highways, and ports was on the lookout for cocaine. Drug traffickers from Colombia and other nations took advantage of the minimal regulation and fanned out across the United States, flood-ing it with the drug.

The Medellín Cartel, which was headed by my father and also included Gonzalo Rodríguez Gacha, "the Mexican"; Gerardo "Kiko" Moncada; Fernando Galeano; Elkin Correa; and many others, took control of southern Florida and the neighboring states. The Cali dons—mainly the Rodríguez brothers, Pacho Herrera, and Chepe Santacruz—went to New York, the Big Apple. The market was so vast and profitable that the two cartels never clashed. For years they maintained a remarkably close and cooperative rela-tionship that would only end because of matters unrelated to the cocaine trade.

Because they'd already successfully landed a shipment there, for more than a year Miami's Opa Locka Airport was my father's favorite drug-trafficking destination. Small executive jets—loaded at first with one hundred or one hundred and twenty kilos, and later with three or four hundred—landed there two or three times a week after first stopping over in Barranquilla on Colombia's northern coast, and Port-au-Prince, Haiti's poverty-stricken capital city. The pilots presented these flight plans to officials, claiming the trips were to transport tourists who were looking for sunshine and shopping centers. Later, Carlos Lehder would join the lucrative business with the use of his famous private island in the Bahamas, which had a landing strip.

During that golden age, a lot of cocaine also traveled by boat. Ships left the Caribbean ports of Necoclí and Turbo and arrived in Miami, where they weren't searched because their cargo of bananas was perfectly packed and didn't appear at all suspicious—but in fact they'd have up to eight hundred kilos of cocaine stashed in the hold. The Mafia called that well-known trafficking route "the banana route."

After arriving in the United States, the cocaine was transported to houses in residential areas such as Kendall and Boca Raton, where my father's men hid it in underground caches to be picked up by local distributors, who paid in cash. The method these distributors used to spread the drug throughout Miami and nearby cities such as Fort Lauderdale, Pompano Beach, and West Palm Beach was simple: they called their customers on the phone and arranged to meet in quiet public places. Business couldn't have been going better; the drug was selling like hotcakes.

Around that time, my father started traveling to Miami on commercial flights and would check in to the luxurious Omni Hotel as the head of the Fredonian Petroleum Company. The company name was my father's idea of a joke: there's not a drop of petroleum in the Antioquian village of Fredonia. He would rent out an entire floor of the hotel and receive visits from all sorts of U.S. traffickers, holding parties that lasted till dawn and featured thirty or forty beautiful women hired from the city's best nightclubs.

The next morning, after a night of excess, my father's clients would pay for their cocaine and then receive the keys to new cars that were parked in the hotel garage. In the trunks they would find the "merch" in perfect condition: Diamante, Esmeralda (Diamond, Emerald). My father and Gustavo had branded their cocaine shipments with the names of those two precious stones, and a seal with an image of the gems would be stamped on each kilo package. The Mexican used the brand "Reina" (Queen), and his product became quite popular among U.S. buyers for its purity.

For a long time, Diamante, Esmeralda, and Reina were symbols of guaranteed quality. Eventually my father's product would begin to get a bad reputation due to its low purity and clumsy packaging. Once a distributor—a dangerous American mobster—even rejected a shipment. There was much chatter about that incident among my father's men, as it was the first time a kilo had been returned to its country of origin. My father once told me that he used to sell low-quality cocaine because—from his conman perspective—the consumers were addicts who couldn't tell the difference between good coke and bad. Kiko Moncada, on the other hand, made sure to provide only a high-quality product, with neat packaging that looked like it belonged on a supermarket shelf.

Back then there was also little oversight of international wire transfers, and my father received hundreds of millions of dollars through official channels, using third-party front men to open bank accounts. Just imagine the famous movie *Scarface*, in which mobsters would enter banks to deposit duffel bags full of cash as the managers looked on.

Often, the planes that ferried cocaine would return loaded with enormous bags of cash, but when that was no longer possible, my father resorted to other methods of importing money into Colombia. For example, he started importing washing machines.

His men would remove the insides and fill the shells with wads of bills. They would also hide money in industrial machinery, new cars, motorcycles, televisions, stereos, and all sorts of appliances.

After a while, my father was banking not just money but also all sorts of weapons, as it became necessary to protect the shipments. It wasn't hard. At the time, Colombia's major airports had what was known as "magic mail," a sort of parallel customs system that made it possible to bring anything into the country without leaving a paper trail—in exchange for a fat bribe.

The demand for cocaine in the U.S. market was skyrocketing, so drug runners got creative in finding ways to move all their shipments. Every cartel had its own methods, but my father found the most profitable one of all. The authorities called the route "La Fania," but my father actually referred to it as "Fanny," named for a ship anchored at sea off the coast of Ecuador. The ship was loaded with fish meal, and concealed inside its enormous refrigerators was as much as four tons of cocaine that always, always made it into the Miami port without a hitch. People close to my father told me that this was the route that had made him rich.

There was so much money flowing in that my father soon began to indulge in all sorts of excesses. At one point, he was going out to clubs every night, usually Acuarius or Kevin's. He would get to a club and immediately be surrounded by beautiful women who chatted and drank while he sipped water and smoked a joint. At around two in the morning he'd pay the tab and invite them all back to his apartment: a luxurious penthouse in a building near the El Diamante baseball stadium, across from the headquarters of the army's Fourth Brigade in Medellín. My father would leave the club trailed by a procession of at least five cars full of women who were ready to continue partying all night.

He started spending money more and more lavishly. From the large house in Provenza—where my father flew in the Argentine group Los Chalchaleros to perform at my mother's seventeenth birthday party—we moved to a mansion in the Santa María de los Ángeles neighborhood, a block and a half from the Medellín country club.

At one point my father attempted to join the club, but the board of directors rejected him because, despite his great wealth, he lacked the pedigree required by Medellín's conservative elite. Used to getting his way, my father flew into a rage. He contacted some of the club's employees and paid them a fortune to start a strike complaining of low wages. For the first and perhaps the only time, the posh club was forced to shut down for several days.

Almost a week after the strike began, he met with the employees.

"Boss, can you tell us how much longer you want us to stay on strike?" they asked.

"Keep it going another fifteen days, and I'll pay everything you need. And do me a favor, take the dump truck, fill it with dirt, and drive around the golf course to tear it up. Then dump all the dirt from the truck into the swimming pool."

They followed his instructions.

IN OUR HOUSE IN SANTA MARÍA DE LOS ÁNGELES, AT ONLY FOUR years old, I received my first motorcycle, a small yellow Suzuki that my father had equipped with wheels on either side, like a bicycle's training wheels. That same day he taught me to ride it at lunchtime before going back to the office. He took off the side wheels and ran behind me, holding the motorcycle, before eventually letting go. I remember that as the day I fell in love with motorcycles and the indescribable feeling of freedom when riding.

The drug boom enabled my father to buy his first two aircraft: a white, red, and mustard-yellow Hughes 500 helicopter, registration number HK-2196, and a twin-engine Aero Commander plane. Once, when we were discussing those acquisitions, my father recalled that on his first trip in the chopper, he went to see someone very special to him: Don Fabio Ochoa Restrepo, whom he visited at Ochoa's La Clara estate in Angelópolis in southeastern Antioquia. Afterward, he took several of his neighborhood friends out for a ride over the Peñol dam, and an hour later, they landed to have coffee in a shop. The pilot was afraid that one of the dozens of curious onlookers who imprudently came near to see the helicopter as it landed might be killed.

As the market for cocaine grew rapidly, they continuously had to establish new smuggling routes. For example, they started running drugs through Mexico, sending shipments in airplanes that took off from secret airstrips in Urabá, La Guajira, Fredonia, Frontino, and La Danta. The Mexico route was known as "the onion route," as the cocaine was hidden in tractor trailers carrying bushels of onions that crossed the border near Laredo and then headed to Miami. Each truck transported between eight hundred and a thousand kilos. Leonidas Vargas was my father's Colombian partner on that route, and Amado Carrillo Fuentes was their Mexican connection for getting the cocaine into the United States.

Another method they used was "dropping bombs." From small airplanes flying at low altitudes, they'd dump the cargo into the sea near the Miami coast and send motorboats or sailboats out to pick it up. They also dropped these "bombs" in the Everglades swamps south of Miami. But at first a lot of the cocaine was lost because the packages weren't sealed properly and the contents would get wet.

My father rarely bragged about his achievements in the underworld, but there was one time he couldn't resist: when the news described a new trend in drug trafficking—blue jeans impregnated with cocaine. My father grinned for a while and then said he'd come up with the idea to soak jeans in liquid cocaine and legally export them to various cities in the United States. The buyers, he explained, would wash the garment with a special fluid, extract the cocaine in liquid form, and set it out to dry. Though they couldn't use the method for large shipments, my father said it had been a safe bet for several months because the authorities weren't expecting such a brazen move. He added that to prevent the drug-sniffing dogs from discovering them, they'd sprayed the jeans with a special fluid that kept the dogs away.

The cocaine-soaked-jeans route was shut down after a snitch in the United States reported it to the authorities. Yet only a few days later, my father, smiling again, said, "Boys, you remember how they shut down the jeans route?"

"Yes, boss."

"Well, I've kept on sending the jeans, and it's driving the DEA guys crazy because they keep washing them and washing them, and they're not finding anything. What we're doing now is impregnating the cardboard boxes the jeans are packed in and retrieving the drug when they throw the boxes in the trash."

Thanks to these successes, my father gained fame as a powerful capo. More and more people realized that you could make a lot of money in the business and started joining up, including much of Medellín's upper class. I used to visit my father at his office, where it wasn't unusual to see at least a hundred cars parked in the lot. Some of the employees later told me that on an average day as many as three hundred people would stop by with some sort of business proposition. Many of these visitors wanted my father to include ten or fifteen kilos of their own product in his shipments, as they knew they were guaranteed to turn a profit.

My father got visits from bootblacks, bikers, reporters, businessmen, politicians, police officers, soldiers of every rank, and even foreigners who wanted to become involved in trafficking. Almost all of them asked that some of their cocaine be included in the *Fanny* shipments. Visibly impatient, hundreds of people would wait their turn for two or three days in a row, without changing their clothes or bathing or even leaving their spot, hoping for "an appointment with Don Pablo." It was also common to see young

Carlos Castaño bringing messages from his brothers or other capos.

But not all of the propositions that my father fielded were illegal. One day, a prominent Medellín executive suggested that my father invest in a corporation to install the city's first residential natural gas infrastructure. In a serious voice, my father simply replied, "I'm very sorry, but I don't get involved in legal business dealings."

A couple of times I became worried when policemen arrived and entered my father's office. I thought it must be a raid, but they reappeared a few minutes later. They were there to collect money.

My father had proven that he had the safest drug-running routes. They were practically foolproof, and he even went so far as to offer insurance for the shipments, placing his personal fortune on the line to guarantee a full refund of expenses plus lost profits if a shipment didn't arrive. My father and Gustavo also did something unique: they would occasionally give a few lucky loyal acquaintances the equivalent of five or ten kilos of coke in cash without any investment or participation in the business on their part.

But just as he helped those he considered closest to him, my father was also capable of unimaginable violence. One day, I was told, two hundred million pesos that had been hidden in my father's office disappeared. The guard who had been on duty the previous day—a former soldier and friend my father had rescued years earlier from the prison island of Gorgona—immediately became suspect. The man's fate was sealed only a few hours after suspicions were raised, when my father's employees found the money at the soldier's house. They took the man down to the office, and my father called all of his employees to the pool. There, they tied the soldier up and threw him in the water.

"I'll kill anyone who steals a peso from me," my father announced to the speechless crowd once the soldier had drowned.

A few weeks later, my father decided to invest a small part of his money in Miami. In 1981, he bought a house in Miami Beach's exclusive Alton Road area. He paid seven hundred thousand dollars in cash, which he'd brought from Colombia and declared in U.S. customs. It was a massive two-story mansion with an imposing entrance, five bedrooms, a swimming pool with a view of Biscayne Bay, and one of the few private docks in that part of the city. Gustavo wasn't about to be left behind and purchased an enormous million-dollar apartment.

My father set about expanding his real estate holdings and soon acquired a two-hundred-condo complex in northern Miami. He paid in cash that he declared in customs and toted through Miami International Airport in two briefcases. Managing those properties ended up becoming a huge headache for my father. People frequently called to complain that crocodiles from the nearby lakes were wandering down the corridors of the complex.

Against my father's objections, Gustavo sold his apartment, sensing that things were about to take a complicated turn for the two of them in the United States. But my father was stubborn and thought he wouldn't have any trouble since he'd declared the money used to purchase the properties.

My father's increasingly frequent business trips to the United States took us to Washington, D.C., where he planned to test the security measures in place at the entrance to the FBI building. Heedless of the risk, he presented false papers at the reception desk while my mother handed over her passport and mine. Fortunately we had no problems. My father had scammed the U.S. government, and the three of us were given a tour of the building. From there, we headed to the White House, where my mother took the famous photo of my father and me at the gate.

At the end of 1981, as their business flourished, my father and Gustavo formed their own fleet of airplanes and helicopters. They bought three Aero Commanders, a Cheyenne, a Twin Otter, and a

Learjet along with two helicopters: a more modern Hughes 500 and a Bell Ranger. The intermediary for these purchases was the former race car driver Ricardo "Razor" Londoño, who brokered the sales through his import/export business in Miami. I once heard that Razor was an experienced airplane pilot who sneaked into the small private airports around Miami, stole planes, and sold them for good money in Medellín.

There's been a good deal of speculation about a possible relationship between my father and former Colombian president Álvaro Uribe Vélez. Over the years, Uribe's critics have repeatedly claimed that as head of the Colombian Civil Aviation Authority between January 1980 and August 1982, he provided illegal licenses and thus helped facilitate the growth of drug trafficking in Medellín. But this book has no hidden agenda or political loyalties, no wish to unjustly praise or smear anyone, so I did a thorough investigation to find out for sure what kind of relationship they had, if any.

I consulted my father's trusted friends and lieutenants, and their answers surprised me. As it turned out, my father had actually offered five hundred million pesos for Uribe's head. The reason? For much of his time at the head of the Civil Aviation Authority, Uribe had made life more difficult at Medellín's Olaya Herrera Airport, with more frequent searches and stricter entry and exit procedures for airplanes.

My father's efforts to get rid of Uribe didn't end with offering a reward for his death. His own men actually made at least three failed assassination attempts. The people I spoke with on the subject told me that my father's bribery of officials was ultimately more effective than the orders Uribe issued from Bogotá.

Much has also been written about my father's supposedly close relationship with his cousin José Obdulio Gaviria, currently a senator from Antioquia. But these claims are utterly groundless. I remember seeing my father condemn his cousin for believing he was better than my father. My father rarely mentioned him—he had no reason to, since José Obdulio never behaved like family—but on the rare occasion that his name was mentioned, my father referred to him as "that fucking cousin of mine." In the thousands of family photographs we have going back to the 1970s, José Obdulio doesn't appear in a single one.

In the early '80s, my father had no enemies or scores to settle with the law. But his growing economic power made it necessary to hire his first bodyguards: Rubén Darío Londoño, also known as "Cassava," a young delinquent from La Estrella, and Guillermo Zuluaga, known as "Catwalk."

Soon afterward, he realized that he also needed someone to accompany him on motorcycle at all times, riding alongside the driver's window. He searched and searched, interviewing and testing numerous candidates, but nobody could keep up with him until he met Luis Carlos Aguilar. Known as "Crud," Aguilar passed a difficult test in which my father went the wrong way down one-way streets, sped around traffic circles at high velocity, and drove up onto sidewalks. Crud started working with my father in 1981 and was immediately given a powerful Honda XR-200 motorcycle and a gun.

My father came home with his first three bodyguards and announced that they'd accompany us twenty-four hours a day. My father, my mother, and I—and, from the day she was born, my sister—were constantly under the protection of a delinquent army.

Because of the life we led, I shared a good portion of my childhood with some of the worst criminals in the country. My playmates while we were in hiding or who traveled with me were figures I knew only by their nicknames: "Toothpick," "Archivaldo," "Worrywart," "Stud," "Otto," "Crud," "Pinina," "Catwalk," "Skinny Skull," "Shooter," "Corn Liquor," "Squirt," "Séforo," "Chimp," "Smurf," "Ears," "Eyebrows," "the Jap," and "Mystery," among many others. I remember that my father's enemies used to say he had an army of assassins, but he would make sure to clarify, jocularly, that what he had was an army of cocksuckers.

Of the individuals who joined my father's group of delinquents, one is particularly worth describing: "Tabloid," a young man who stood out for his tough attitude, his swagger, his exquisite mastery of *lunfardo*—an underworld slang originating in Buenos Aires— and his taste for "narcobitches," as he used to call his many lovers, whom he had sculpted naked and in solid gold on pendants, necklaces, rings, bracelets, and watches. He always had his .38 caliber Smith & Wesson at his side and an AK-47 in his hands.

I didn't have any playmates my age in my father's hideouts, so I played soccer or Nintendo with his bodyguards. When there weren't enough of us, we'd just play keep-away. I always ended up being the one in the middle, and it frustrated me that they wouldn't give me the ball.

The real reason for my lack of friends my age was that a number of parents at the San José de la Salle School had forbidden their children—my classmates—from interacting with me. After all, being the son of Pablo Escobar Gaviria wasn't quite the same as being the son of Gabriel García Márquez. And that brought with it various kinds of discrimination.

I didn't grow up at the country club despite living so close to it. I wasn't friends with society's elite because that sort of people approached my father only to offer to sell him their properties or artwork or to make a business proposal, not to make friends. Instead, as my father was always surrounded by the world's toughest element, from the time I was a kid I saw them as a huge family. That was the world I grew up in, my only tangible reality.

The construction of the Nápoles estate would transform the lives of my whole family. The estate became a sort of staging area from which, night and day, planes loaded with cocaine took off for Mexico, Central America, the Caribbean, and the United States.

I remember one night during the first New Year's we spent at Nápoles, my father got into his Nissan Patrol SUV and drove to the airstrip because, as I heard him tell his men, a flight was coming in from Mexico. It was eleven o'clock on that clear night of December 31, 1981. He and his workers set up flaming rings of diesel fuel that burned for a long time, along with lanterns and torches, and the plane landed smoothly. It couldn't have taken more than ten minutes for them to load the cocaine, change the registration number and flag painted on the plane, and guide it as it took off again. Then they turned out the lights and headed back to the party.

My father tried to keep me from getting involved in his affairs, but at times it was futile: I could see everything from the estate's soccer field, where we used to set off the holiday fireworks.

Those I talked with for this book all noted my father's talent for deceiving the authorities. If they located and destroyed one airstrip, he'd quickly find another one. If they raided a lab, he'd have another one up and running within a few days. One of the tricks that almost everybody mentioned involved an airstrip located an hour from the estate, near an area called Lechería. The plain was perfectly flat and almost two-thirds of a mile long. My father had instructed that grass be planted in a curvy line so that when you reached the site, all you saw was a winding road and a country house at the center.

My father had designed the property to confuse the air force's reconnaissance planes and the police's antinarcotics helicopters, which saw only a pretty landscape when they passed overhead. But the house was actually mounted on a wheeled platform that could be hooked up to a truck and pulled a few yards to the side to allow airplanes to land. When a cocaine shipment was coming in, someone would move the trailer, and a thousand-yard dirt airstrip would appear. The grass created a bucolic illusion for anyone who wasn't in the know.

Because drug trafficking was in a constant state of flux, and every link in the chain had to be kept secret, my father and Gustavo continually sought out new and better routes to send cocaine to the United States. One of the routes they carved out was through the island of Cuba. Several of the men who worked for my father remarked that he had moved many shipments through there with the complicity of high-ranking officials in the Cuban government.

To manage this route, they sent Jorge Avendaño, known as "Crocodile," to Havana. He would meet the planes coming in from Colombia on an airstrip on the eastern coast of Cuba and then reship the cocaine on speedboats to Islamorada, a village in the Florida Keys located between Miami and Key West.

This complicated route worked seamlessly for two years before my father's Cuban military accomplices were discovered, charged with treason, and executed in 1989 after a long criminal trial. I never spoke with my father about these events, but it was clear from his men's interest in the Cuban scandal at the time that something very serious involving him had happened.

After years of wrangling with the various phases of the cocaine-trafficking business, my father decided to stop processing coca paste due to the constant problems in the labs, which the authorities had started raiding more often. He was also tired of the incompetent handling of chemical supplies, which frequently led to explosions that caused death and injury.

From then on, he stopped manufacturing cocaine and only transported it along his own routes, which remained safe—especially the Fanny and banana routes. Despite the high prices he charged narcos who wanted to send their product abroad, my father quickly became one of the biggest cocaine runners in the world.

6

Excess

This account depicts a period in my family's life that ended more than twenty years ago. Our opulent life at that time was a whirlwind of excess, lavish expense, and extravagance. I have no wish to brag, only to describe the world in which I happened to grow up.

- On my ninth birthday, in 1986, I received a unique gift whose significance I was too young to understand at the time: a small chest containing original love letters written by Manuelita Sáenz to the great Latin American liberator Simón Bolívar. I was also given several of Bolívar's medals.
- The chocolates and invitations for my first communion were brought from Switzerland in my father's private jet. My mother sent Gregorio Cabezas—our full-time chef at the Mónaco building, one of our properties in Medellín— to Switzerland to select the chocolates and the card design and paid for him to take the best chocolate-making course available. On its way back, the jet stopped in Paris to pick up twenty bottles of 1971 Petrus, one of the most expensive wines in the world. Nineteen of those bottles would end up in the garbage years later because no one drank them—and someone said to throw them out because they were old.

- In 1988, when I turned eleven, I already had a collection of nearly thirty high-speed motorcycles along with the best motocross bikes, three-wheeled motorcycles, ATVs, go-karts, and dune buggies money could buy. I also had thirty water scooters.

- When I was thirteen years old, to minimize security risks, I was given my own bachelor pad; it had two large bedrooms, mine with mirrors on the ceiling, a futuristic bar, a zebra skin in the living room, and a Venus chair.

- Some facts about the Nápoles estate: it had its own gas station and body shop for repairing and painting cars and motorcycles; twenty-seven artificial lakes; one hundred thousand fruit trees; Latin America's largest motocross track; a Jurassic Park with life-size dinosaurs; two heliports and a thousand-yard airstrip; 1,700 employees; and 7,500 acres with three zoos and ten residences.

- For the six or seven New Year's Eves we spent at Nápoles, my father imported numerous boxes of fireworks from China. He spent fifty thousand dollars on each box. He'd give half of them to his men, and the rest were for his family. In the first days of January, so many of the fireworks would remain unused that entire boxes hadn't even been opened yet.

- At Christmas, one of my father's helicopters was used to distribute custard, doughnuts, and even blood sausages to family members—certainly an exotic way to bring the family together.

- Family parties often featured raffles for paintings and sculptures by famous artists and rare antiques.

- The towels at each estate were embroidered with the estate's name: La Manuela, Nápoles, etc. The maids wore special outfits and took makeup classes, and my mother paid for their manicures.

- Flowers for our two-story, 16,000-square-foot penthouse in the Mónaco building were picked up twice a week in Bogotá in my father's plane and transported to Medellín. When my mother asked for permission for this, my father replied, "Darling, if Onassis sent for warm bread from Paris for Jacqueline, then I can send a plane to bring you flowers from Bogotá." Dinners at the Mónaco building were always accompanied by a violinist.

- My mother used to commission Venetian artisans to make linen tablecloths for the twenty-four-place dining table in the Mónaco building. Because of their enormous size and intricate embroidery, each tablecloth took the artisans between three and four years to make. The renowned Danish silversmith Georg Jensen designed and made a set of silver dishware with a monogram of the Escobar and Henao names intertwined. When my mother put in the order, they told her they hadn't received such a large order for centuries. The final cost: $400,000. The entire set would be stolen in Medellín in 1993.

- First prize for the Mónaco building's private tennis tournament was a brand-new car. Only family members and friends participated, and if the winner was rich, he or she would donate the car to a poor family.

- My parents wanted to build their dream house on one of the best lots in Medellín's El Poblado neighborhood. They hired famous California architects, who sent the plans and a model of the 50,000-square-foot project. My mother's decorator kicked up a fuss: "These architects are crazy— the foyer of this house is larger than the InterContinental Hotel's, and you could drive a car down these hallways!"

- My father's car collection included an army-green Mercedes-Benz limousine that had belonged to Carlos Lehder and, before that, to a high-ranking German official during the Second World War; an Italian Moto Guzzi motorcycle that had belonged to a general who was part of the dictator Benito Mussolini's inner circle; a black 1977 Mercedes-Benz convertible; an Old West stagecoach imported from the United States, with a leather interior, curtains, and wood trim; and a brown Porsche Carrera, his first race car.

- My mother loved themed parties—so much so that she'd send a tailor to the house of the invited families with instructions to custom-design costumes for each guest. All at our expense. We celebrated the five-hundredth anniversary of the discovery of the Americas with three built-to-scale caravel ships in the swimming pool and period outfits. There was also a Robin Hood–themed party with bows and arrows, swords, and horses. Every gathering my mother organized was also attended by our personal photographer, who later on would even be at my father's wake. The Halloween party was particularly special, and prizes were awarded for the best costume.

- A makeup artist and hairstylist made up my mother every day. While my mother was pregnant with Manuela, she traveled to Barranquilla, on the Caribbean coast, several times in my father's jet. A well-known fashion designer made her maternity clothing.

7

Nápoles: Dreams and Nightmares

When I die, all I want is for you to bury me here and plant a kapok tree on top of me. Oh, and I don't want you to ever come and visit me. The body is merely a tool given to us so that we can be on earth."

This was the third and final time my father told my mother and me what we should do with his remains after his death, which he understood was on the horizon. It was a peaceful Saturday afternoon, and we'd gone out for a drive around the Nápoles estate's zoo in his Nissan Patrol SUV when he stopped and pointed out the exact spot where he wanted to be buried.

But we haven't been able to fulfill his wishes, and to this day he is buried in a cemetery in Medellín.

WITHOUT QUESTION, NÁPOLES WAS THE PIECE OF PROPERTY that meant the most to my father. He first arrived in the balmy Magdalena Medio region in Antioquia in early 1978, after searching for more than a year for a place that had jungle, water, and mountains all at once. Using the first helicopter he'd bought when he started to get rich from cocaine trafficking, he traveled through Caucasia, Santa Fe de Antioquia, Bolombolo, and a significant portion of the rest of the Antioquia Department without finding a place that fulfilled those three requirements. One day, Alfredo Astado, my mother's relative, came to my father's office and told him that the *El Colombiano* newspaper had published a for-sale ad for a farm in Puerto Triunfo that was located near the highway being built between Medellín and Bogotá. Alfredo explained that the area, which was in the center of the country, was very pretty and was guaranteed to be prosperous, since construction of the new highway had already begun.

My father agreed, and Alfredo arranged a meeting with the real estate agent to see the land the following weekend. They ended up being delayed for three months because my father and Gustavo were always running into some sort of trouble.

Finally they were scheduled to meet at two o'clock one Saturday afternoon at the roadside restaurant Piedras Blancas, on the outskirts of the town of Guarne. Back then, my father and Gustavo were obsessed with motorcycles and were competing in a few races, so naturally they decided that it would be fun to make the trip by motorcycle.

The adventurers packed a small bag full of clothes for the weekend, but they hadn't thought of the heavy rains in the region at that time of year and didn't bring raincoats. As soon as they set out, a sudden downpour soaked them to the bone, but they decided to keep going so they wouldn't be on the road all night.

After numerous falls and scrapes, and several marijuana smoke breaks, they reached San Carlos close to midnight, still only halfway to their destination. There was hardly a light on in the town, and my father and Gustavo went from house to house waking people up to find the owners of the clothing store, restaurant, and hotel. In no time, the three businesses had opened their doors. At one in the morning, after showing off their new clothes and eating copious amounts of food, my father and Gustavo headed to bed.

On Sunday they crashed their motorcycles at least four times before they finally reached the Hezzen estate in Puerto Triunfo, where the real estate agent introduced them to the owner, Jorge Tulio Garcés, who turned out to be my father's old enemy, the same one he'd brawled with years earlier at a party in La Paz.

The two said hello without mentioning the matter and went out to survey the property on horseback. After the tour, my father offered to buy the land, but Jorge Tulio responded that it wasn't for sale because it had been passed down through his family.

The next day they scoped out more properties. Their search ended when my father saw a beautiful, two-thousand-acre estate known as Valledupar. Beside it was another, smaller property: Nápoles.

After a long wrangling process during which Jorge Tulio demanded exorbitant sums so he could avoid selling the land to Pablo, my father and Gustavo ended up with Valledupar for 35 million pesos—915,000 dollars at the time. But it didn't seem like enough land, so over the next four months he kept buying—first Nápoles, and then nine other estates—until the lot totaled 4,700 acres and 90 million pesos (2.35 million dollars). It was exactly what he wanted: an enormous property with rivers, jungle, mountains, and a pleasant climate.

I was one year old, and my father threw himself into building the project he'd envisioned, traveling to Puerto Triunfo by chopper every weekend. First he rebuilt and expanded the main house at the Valledupar estate, which he soon renamed Nápoles in homage to 1920s mobster Al Capone, whose father was born in Naples, Italy. My father admired Capone and read every book or newspaper article he could find on him. In one of the few interviews Pablo agreed to give, a Japanese journalist asked if he thought he was bigger than Al Capone. He replied, "I don't know how tall Al Capone was, but I think I've got an inch or two on him."

In record time, a hundred workers built the house for the freshly rechristened Nápoles estate. The two-story mansion, known as La Mayoría, was somewhat architecturally eccentric but full of luxurious amenities.

My father's bedroom didn't really fit in with the rest of the place. It was fifty-four square feet, quite small and out of proportion with the total square footage of the house.

On the first floor were eight bedrooms, all practically identical and each able to sleep eight people. In the rear of the house were three large garages; they were originally intended to house up to five vehicles each, but over time we had so many guests that my father filled them with bunkbeds and installed bathrooms.

Beside the pool, in a semi-enclosed area with a terra-cotta–tile roof, was a TV room that held thirty people. Next to that was a huge bar with ten four-person tables decorated with enormous whiskey bottles and full of the newest arcade games, including Pac-Man, Galaxian, Donkey Kong, and many others.

One day a worker brought a mamoncillo tree, and my father promptly had it planted next to the pool. When the tree grew, he would climb smugly to the top and throw mamoncillo fruits at anyone who happened to be taking a swim.

At some point my father decided to buy the largest crane available in Colombia at the time and use it to transplant large trees to Nápoles. He also planted thousands of fruit trees—mango, orange, guama, and lemon. His dream was to be able to pick fresh fruit without even having to get out of the car.

The pantries where we stored food looked like wine cellars, and eight people could have fit inside each of the three refrigerators in the kitchen. There were servants everywhere you went, always prepared to provide whatever was needed: bathing suits for people of all ages, diapers in case someone forgot to bring them, shoes, hats, shorts and T-shirts, even imported candy. If someone wanted a shot of *aguardiente,* they'd give him a whole bottle. Nápoles was supposed to be a place where other people would always take care of our needs and those of our guests.

My mother and her friends often played tennis on the courts and even organized tournaments. If someone didn't know how to play, they'd hire a private teacher and bring him in by helicopter from Medellín. I don't know where my father got the idea of building several life-size dinosaurs and a woolly mammoth, but they were constructed by a famous Magdalena Medio artist known as "the Devil" long before Steven Spielberg produced *Jurassic Park*. The massive, brightly colored cement animals are still there on the grounds. Years later, during a raid, the authorities would punch holes in them, believing they were stuffed with cash.

The Escobar and Henao families loved Nápoles and visited almost every weekend. During the estate's heyday, my mother would call up visitors and ask whether they wanted to travel by helicopter, private plane, SUV, or motorcycle and their preferred arrival and departure times. I've never been to Michael Jackson's Neverland Ranch in the United States, but I think Nápoles must have been just as impressive. It was pure adventure from the time you arrived to the time you left.

My father loved extreme sports, and his favorite place on the estate was a spot along the Claro River. To make things more exciting, he called his friend, the race car driver Ricardo "Razor" Londoño, in Miami and ordered a large number of airboats, a Rolligon, dune buggies, and ultralight planes. His weekend hobby was driving the noisy airboats. Sometimes he'd crash on the rocks as he hurtled up and down the river, and each damaged vehicle was immediately replaced with another. He and I went downriver swimming side by side or in inner tubes, and once I even came very close to drowning.

The constant recreational helicopter flights over the rivers around the estate—among them, the Doradal, one of the largest rivers at Nápoles—gave my father the idea of damming one to generate energy and create a lake for practicing water sports. Seven hundred workers showed up to work on the enormous construction project, but he canceled it after a year due to the astronomical cost and lack of technical expertise. The project was going so badly that a few experts had even warned my father that if it continued, he ran the risk of flooding the small village of Doradal and other nearby communities, which would cause unimaginable destruction. One day, my father returned from the Veracruz estate, owned by the Ochoa Vásquez brothers, intent on opening his own zoo. The Ochoa Vásquezes had built a beautiful place in the town of Repelón near the Caribbean coast; the estate featured a large number of exotic animals that had fascinated my father. He went to the Ochoa estate several times for guidance on how to set up a zoo and learned that the animals' survival depended on their habitat. To make sure he understood, he bought the National Geographic encyclopedia, studied the local climate, and selected the species of animals that would be able to adapt there.

The goal of having his own zoo began to become a reality in 1981, when my father traveled for the second or third time to the United States with my mother and me. Like good Antioquians, we were accompanied by a throng of family members: all of my father's siblings and their spouses and children, a couple of cousins, and my grandparents Abel and Hermilda.

According to my mother, the family spent shocking amounts of money in the United States, buying everything in sight and filling dozens of suitcases with clothing and all sorts of trinkets. Each family unit had a consultant who advised them on shopping and sightseeing as well as a driver, and they got whatever they wanted on that trip. They spent so much money that one day, when my relatives went to Mayor's Jewelers in Miami, the employees closed the store so they could give my family exclusive attention. Nobody was armed or had bodyguards—our family life hadn't yet become encumbered by such complications. That was the only period of pure pleasure and lavishness that my father enjoyed.

On our way back to Colombia, my father assigned Alfredo the task of finding a zoo in the United States where he could buy elephants, zebras, giraffes, camels, hippopotamuses, water buffalos, kangaroos, flamingoes, ostriches, and other species of exotic birds. He removed tigers and lions from the list because he wanted all the animals to roam freely.

A few weeks later, Alfredo informed him that he'd contacted the owners of a wildlife breeding center in Dallas, Texas, that captured animals in Africa and brought them to the United States. Excited, my father organized another trip with the whole family to carry out the negotiations. When we landed at the Dallas airport, we were surprised to find eight or ten limousines waiting for us on the runway. There were so many that I got to ride in one all by myself, watching Tom and Jerry cartoons on the television and drinking a huge glass of chocolate milk.

My father was delighted by the variety of animals available. He eagerly rode on an elephant's back for a few minutes before negotiating with the breeding center's owners and settling on a price of two million dollars in cash. He promised to send for his animals soon.

Back at the hotel, my father bought me a helium-filled balloon, and we went up to play with it in the room. He suddenly smiled and asked me, "Grégory, do you want to see your baby bottle fly through the sky?"

"Yes, Papi!" I replied with innocent enthusiasm.

"All right, well come help me, and we'll tie it on together so it won't come loose and fall off."

I was thrilled because my bottle was going to be flying soon. He tied the string, and together we threw the balloon out the window. We even took a photo with a Polaroid camera. But then I noticed that the bottle wasn't coming back, and I started pointing and demanding it.

"Son, I don't think your bottle is coming back down anytime soon—look how it's floating up into the sky. It's time for you to start drinking out of a glass, the way men do," he told me.

The first large group of animals for the Nápoles zoo arrived in a rented boat that docked in the port of Necoclí on the Caribbean coast, 250 miles from Medellín. Because boat travel was slower and exposed the animals to greater risk, my father decided to transport later shipments on clandestine flights. For the task, he appointed his friend Fernando Arbeláez, who rented several Hercules military transport planes that would land at Medellín's Olaya Herrera Airport after the day's operations were over. He was able to pull this off because security measures at the airport were rather ineffective, and my father owned two hangars next to the main runway.

Arbeláez carried out his duties with great precision, and the airplanes arrived a few minutes after six in the evening, when the control tower and the runway lights had already been shut down. The Hercules planes landed, not even turning off its engines, and trucks and cranes and numerous employees swarmed out of my father's hangar and unloaded the crates of animals with astonishing rapidity. Then the airplanes took off again. When the authorities showed up, alerted by the noise, they found only some empty wooden crates with feathers and fur littered around them. After that, Arbeláez was nicknamed "the Animal Man."

This strategy allowed my father to fill up Nápoles with animals very quickly, just as the Medellín–Bogotá highway was about to open. But they still didn't have a pair of rhinoceroses. To bring them from the United States, my father hired an old DC-3 plane whose pilot, an experienced aviator, agreed to attempt a landing at Nápoles itself, even though the plane required a 4,000-foot runway—the runway at Nápoles fell 1,000 feet short.

After measuring the distances and calculating the braking time, the plane descended from the skies above Nápoles and made a spectacular landing. Just as it touched down, the able pilot made it spin at least ten times on its rear wheel until it finally stopped just short of tumbling into the Doradal River. On the nose of the plane was painted an enormous fish with sharp teeth, a mischievous look in its eye, and a lit cigar in its mouth.

The zoo was almost ready, but my father wanted more and more animals. And he had expensive tastes. Like the pair of black parrots he bought in Miami, where he'd gone to collect on a seven-million-dollar debt from a cocaine distributor. Though he had an appointment with the distributor at two in the afternoon, he decided to go see the birds' owner instead, who had asked to meet at the same time on the other side of the city. At four hundred thousand dollars, the parrots were the most expensive animals in the zoo. Weeks later, furious, my father called to complain after a veterinarian found that they'd been neutered.

My father spent long hours admiring the enormous cages where the world's most exotic birds were on display. Parrots were his favorite, and he had them in every color. But not even that was enough. On a trip to Brazil in March 1982, he discovered a blue parrot with yellow eyes, the only one of its species and protected by Brazilian law. My father didn't care, and he arranged for his pilot to smuggle it out of the country. The parrot traveled alone in my father's private plane. The cost? One hundred thousand dollars.

The last animals to arrive at the zoo were a pair of pretty pink dolphins that my father bought in the Amazon. They lived in one of the lakes he'd had built at Honduras, an estate ten minutes from Nápoles, and in the afternoons I used to go play with them even though they gave off a foul odor.

At last my father deemed the zoo, which now housed nearly 1,200 exotic animals, ready to open to the public. But he realized something was missing: the entrance. So he ordered the construction of an enormous white gate with the word "Nápoles" on the main columns. And above that, also white and with a blue stripe painted along its side, they mounted a Piper PA-18 single-engine monoplane, registration number HK-671.

That airplane has been the subject of endless speculation. People have suggested, for example, that it was the one my father used to transport his first cocaine shipment. The reality is quite different. The small plane had belonged to one of my father's friends until he'd crash-landed next to the Olaya Herrera runway in Medellín. The aircraft sat there, abandoned, for several months until my father saw the wreckage and asked his friend for it. He had it brought to Nápoles, where they took it apart and restored it, but without the engine. The airplane's exterior was covered in cloth, which made it unique.

There are also lots of stories about the old car, riddled with bullet holes, that my father placed at the entrance to the first of the zoo's main areas. The most widely circulated version claims that it was the car in which the notorious American bank robbers Bonnie and Clyde were killed in May 1934. My father was a great admirer of that couple, and we watched every movie that Hollywood made about them together. But in truth, the car was actually assembled by Alfredo Astado out of parts from two different cars. The first was the chassis of a Toyota SUV, the only piece that was still usable after the violent traffic accident that had killed Fernando, my father's younger brother, when he'd taken a new car out for a drive with his girlfriend. The second was the body of an old 1936 Ford that Alfredo had received as a gift. Alfredo had used these pieces to construct a single car.

But Alfredo hadn't expected that one day, while he was running errands downtown, my father would discover the remodeled Ford at his house. Without even asking, my father had it taken to Nápoles and put on display. The next weekend, when he came to see how the vehicle looked, my father pulled out his submachine gun and ordered several of his men to grab their weapons, and they fired at the car to simulate the 167 bullets that had hit Bonnie and

Clyde's original car. The rain of bullets almost ended in tragedy, as they suddenly heard the cries for help of an employee who had fallen asleep inside the vehicle.

And so, with the plane at the estate entrance, the bullet-riddled car nearby, and hundreds of beautiful exotic animals, my father opened the estate to the public. It was an instant success, as not only was entrance free but also tourists could drive around the vast park in their own vehicles. One holiday weekend, nearly twenty-five thousand automobiles entered the property. Entire families from all over Colombia traveled to Nápoles.

My father was happy, and I asked why he didn't charge an entrance fee, since he could have made a lot of money.

"Son, this zoo belongs to the people," he explained to me. "As long as I'm alive, I'll never charge an entrance fee. I like that poor people can come see this marvel of nature."

The flood of tourists became so overwhelming that my father paid to build a new highway, as even he was having trouble getting there. The seven-minute trip from the estate entrance to the main house could take up to two hours.

The zoo opening went along with an intense social life. There were frequent parties with either our families or my father's friends, though parties with the former were more reserved. For our first New Year celebration at Nápoles, the festivities lasted a month— mid-December to mid-January. Performing were the Venezuelan singer Pastor López and his band, who would begin playing at nine at night and finish at nine the following morning. On some nights, as many as a thousand people, many of whom we didn't even know, would show up to party. The Nápoles airstrip looked more like an airport. One weekend I spotted a dozen planes parked there. Back then, my father had a lot of friends—nobody was after him—and many of his guests arrived with gifts and crates of liquor.

Everything was done with the utmost luxury. My uncle Mario Henao had a plane too, and he'd frequently leave Nápoles early in the morning, shouting: "I'm going to have breakfast in Bogotá; I'll be back for lunch. I'll bring Pablo some of that cheese stuffed with guayaba paste that they sell in the airport."

On another occasion, my cousin Nicolás—who weighed almost three hundred pounds at the time—was craving a hamburger that was only available at the Oviedo shopping center in Medellín. He had them start up the chopper, and a couple of hours later he was chowing down on his double hamburger with a huge serving of french fries.

The zoo was always my father's baby, and he took great care of every detail. One day as he was driving around the estate, he noticed that the flamingoes had lost their beautiful pink color, and their plumage was almost white. Convinced that the color change was the result of a poor diet, he consulted a veterinarian and, on the vet's incompetent advice, fed them shrimp for six months. It didn't work, of course. Another time, he noticed that the elephants seemed bored with their food. My father's men didn't really know what to feed them; they tried every variety of grass and even sugarcane, but the pachyderms continued to eat very little for a long time. Among many other attempts, one day my father ordered three tons of carrots to perk the elephants up. That didn't make a difference either.

Once when my father and I went out on our own around the zoo in a blue open-top Nissan SUV, he asked me to hold the submachine gun while he drove and examined the animals' condition. An hour after we'd set out, we found a deer lying beside the road with a broken leg. The little animal, with long, white legs and a brown coat with yellow spots, was writhing in pain; the bone was poking out through the skin. Seeing how seriously injured it was, my father said our only option was to kill it. He headed for the car to get his legendary black nine-millimeter Sig Sauer P226 pistol, which he loved because it was very accurate and was hard to fire accidentally. Also, it was the only one of the many he'd owned that didn't jam.

"Do you want to do it, Grégory?" he asked. Without giving me time to answer, he told me to aim at the deer's head and shoot.

He must have seen fear in my face because then he told me to wait in the car. But I insisted I could do it. Overwhelmed with panic, I took the gun and had to use both hands to press the trigger. Even though I was very close, less than three feet away, I missed the first time and fired into the earth. I missed the second shot too, but not the third.

There was only one species of animal that wouldn't adapt to the Nápoles habitat: the giraffes. The six animals that my father had bought in Texas—three males and three females—rejected their feed and never learned to use the feeders built for them in the treetops. In the end, they all died and were buried away from the estate.

Nápoles became so famous throughout Colombia that on May 31, 1983, my father loaned the property for the filming of a one-minute commercial for Naranja Postobón, the soft drink arm of the Ardila Lülle corporation. For the filming they used my father's Twin Otter plane, the amphibious vehicles and dune buggies, and of course the zebras, elephants, giraffes (which were still alive at the time), swans, kangaroos, elk, and ostriches. Naturally, I couldn't be left out, and you can see me in profile toward the end of the clip, filming my friend Juan Carlos Rendón—son of Luis Carlos Rendón, who collaborated with my father in his dirty dealings in the United States—who was dressed in yellow overalls and a green T-shirt.

A couple of days later, an enormous floral arrangement with fine chocolates, nuts, and a bottle of liquor arrived at our house in Medellín's Santa María de los Ángeles neighborhood. The gift had been sent by the soft drink company to my father.

The excess of money was not only apparent in the luxuries we enjoyed. As long as his wealth lasted, my father always made an effort to help people. I remember that on a couple of Christmases, there wasn't a single village nearby that didn't have presents for their children. I traveled with him to several communities to deliver the gifts, which were of high quality, and we spent entire afternoons in the back of a truck handing out two or three toys to every child.

He didn't restrict his gift-giving to the Antioquia Department either. He chose the country's poorest areas, and once even had four of his helicopters take off from Nápoles full of medicine and presents for the indigenous communities in the jungles of the Chocó region.

The community most grateful for my father was Puerto Triunfo, as Nápoles offered jobs and free entrance to the zoo. That gratitude was reflected at dawn one New Year's Day when my whole family went to the early mass at the church, which had been built with the help of my father and Gustavo.

When the service was almost over, the priest addressed my father and gave him a cardboard key, which he said referred to giving the keys of heaven to someone who helped others. But the touching moment was interrupted by a drunk.

"Father, don't you have a copy for me?"

The parishioners roared with laughter.

UP UNTIL NOW, MY PORTRAYAL OF THE NÁPOLES ESTATE HAS BEEN a positive one. My father was happy on the land he found and then molded to his liking. It's clear why he told us on three separate occasions that he wished to be buried there beneath a kapok tree. But this account would be incomplete if I didn't acknowledge that bad things happened at Nápoles too. Lots of them.

From the time he started building the estate, my father foresaw how it would be useful for protection against his enemies and of course for cocaine trafficking. He was already a powerful drug trafficker at the time, with a dangerous criminal apparatus at his command and a desire to engage in the country's political life.

My father wanted to distract me with all the toys at the estate, but the brutality of war was impossible to conceal. Nápoles was his center of operations, and I spent a good part of my childhood there.

The first thing he did when construction started on the main house was devise a hiding spot for emergencies. In the closet of his bedroom, he installed a medium-sized safe to store some money and a small .38 caliber revolver that he used to carry strapped to his ankle. To the left of that he built a hiding place, six feet tall, six feet wide, and ten feet deep, that was accessed through a small, secret door.

The first time I entered the hiding place, it contained at least one hundred Colt AR-15 and Steyr AUG rifles, pistols, and UZI and MP5 submachine guns. There was also a valuable Thompson submachine gun, a 1930 original, with a helical magazine that held three hundred rounds. That same day, my father took it out to show it to his men, who admired it.

Guns were often around at Nápoles, so I was used to them. In fact, my father had installed an antique antiaircraft battery next to the swimming pool; it had a seat, four large feet, and cannons with buffers. As the authorities attempted to come after him for the assassination of Rodrigo Lara Bonilla, the minister of justice, my father knew Nápoles would be raided for the first time, so he ordered that the antiaircraft battery be hidden in the jungle. It was never found again.

Along with having the hiding place built in the main house, my father also designed two other shelters in different places on the estate: Panadería and Marionetas. Panadería was a small, modern, one-story house with large wooden beams located in one of the most remote areas of the estate, about four miles from the main house, in the middle of the jungle. The place was full of snakes that appeared from every corner, so we had to fumigate and check under the pillows every time we spent the night there. Marionetas was an austere four-bedroom house reachable only by traveling several miles along a winding road full of turnoffs and dead ends to confuse anyone who dared enter.

Naturally, my father's henchmen came to the estate often. I met almost all of the members of my father's cartel there, from the lowest to the highest ranks. Most of them liked to show off to their girlfriends by inviting them to "the boss's estate."

The Mexican was at Nápoles several times, though my father preferred to take us to his estates, where we'd spend a few days together. The Mexican was a man of few words, shy, able, and intelligent, and he seemed to be silent and pensive most of the time.

Carlos Lehder, another major player in the Medellín Cartel, also visited fairly regularly, always in camouflage pants, an army-green T-shirt, and a hat. He carried a large knife that would have made Rambo proud, a compass, flares and matches that lit even when they were wet, a .45 Colt pistol, and a crossbow, his favorite weapon. He liked to carry a couple of grenades on his chest and a G-3 rifle in his hands as well. He looked like a character out of a video game, armed to the teeth, with an athletic build and even rather good-looking. I'll never forget how pale he was, though, the striking greenish cast of his skin, as if he'd contracted a rare tropical disease on his long trips through the jungle.

At the end of 1986, Lehder was involved in a serious scandal that pissed my father off and got Lehder kicked off the estate. Early one morning, he sneaked into a small room beside the pool and with a single gunshot killed "Rollo," a tall man who led one of my father's gangs of hitmen. The journalist Germán Castro Caycedo was there, having one of his late-night conversations with my father, when they heard a loud bang, and my father ordered everyone to hide under the cars until he could find out what was going on. Lehder appeared from behind him with his G-3 rifle in hand and said, "I killed that son-of-a-bitch." He'd been angry because Rollo had been having a fling with a woman Lehder was interested in. Afterward, my father lit into Lehder and forced him off the estate immediately. That would be the last time they saw each other.

Once, a very special guest came to visit, a seventy-year-old man whom my father always addressed with the utmost respect. It was unusual for my father to display such deference toward anyone. "Grégory, let me introduce you to Don Alberto Prieto, the only boss I ever had in my life," he said, gesturing for me to shake Prieto's hand. Prieto's sway over my father was such that my father asked the older man's permission to tell me about Prieto's past activities, back when he smuggled electronics, cigarettes, and liquor. My father's gratitude to the man was apparent in his face: Prieto had been the first person to give him an opportunity to thrive in the underworld.

That night, in a surprising gesture, for the first and only time in his life, my father gave up his room to Prieto and took us to sleep in a different one.

Nápoles was also used as a recreation spot for the army of hired guns who worked with my father throughout his criminal career. "They're all so tough here, real badasses, but they don't even know how to shoot or hold a weapon," my father said, complaining that his men were always getting injured or even killed as a result of their inadequate weapons skills. He constantly had to correct his bodyguards because they were bad shots and useless when it came to heavy or long-range weaponry.

One morning in 1988 in the Nápoles dining room, when the war against the Cali Cartel had just begun, my father announced, "These boys need training. There's a foreigner coming who's trained some of the Mexican's people, and he seems pretty good. 'Carlitos' Castaño brought him in, an Israeli he met during a course he took with some Colombian soldiers abroad. He's going to show them security and protection techniques and train them in shooting at moving targets. He'll teach them how to enter houses commando-style, so these guys don't end up killing one another when they're on patrol or under attack."

My father was enthusiastic about the training. "We had to get hold of some stolen cars to practice and a place with a semiaban-doned house to simulate a hostage situation, to rehearse entering and bringing someone out." He laughed nastily. "Incredible, right? Apparently we have to bring someone in from the other side of the globe to show my boys how to break into a house, when that's what they've been doing their whole lives!"

Three days later I heard that the foreigner had arrived early in the morning and been taken to a distant estate that was accessible by truck. One of my father's men heard the foreigner's name: Yair.

Obviously the name meant nothing to me, and my father didn't pay much attention to the trainer's origins at the time either. Later, he'd discover that Yair was actually an Israeli mercenary who had come to Colombia to train the Mexican's army, which later evolved into the Magdalena Medio paramilitary group.

Of the two dozen men who trained with Yair, the brothers Brances and Paul Muñoz Mosquera, known as "Tyson" and "Tilton," stood out from the rest. They were two of my father's deadliest hitmen and members of a large evangelical family.

During the first days of the exercises, my father and I stood to one side of the airstrip to watch the men fire at bottles and cans set up on buckets full of sand, but they always missed. Their aim was so bad that the bullets would hit the pavement. A few days later, when the training was finished, my father asked them what they'd learned. They said it had been very productive, as they'd been taught a difficult new maneuver: firing and reloading two pistols at the same time. The rest, they said, they had already known.

Operations for using car bombs in terrorist attacks were also based out of Nápoles. My father had employed the services of an explosives expert known as "Chucho," who had trained in Cali with a member of a Spanish terrorist group. We never really knew why, but Cali Cartel leader Gilberto Rodríguez Orejuela had brought the Spaniard to Colombia after meeting him in a Madrid prison. The Rodríguezes and my father had been friends, not rivals, at the time. The cocaine market in the United States was huge, and each cartel had its own territory to sell in.

Chucho became one of my father's most trusted men and was given maximum protection, as my father couldn't lose someone who offered a strategic advantage in the face of any kind of danger. He trusted Chucho so implicitly that on a couple of occasions my father allowed him to take cover in one of his secret hideouts.

Chucho had learned a number of methods for detonating dynamite-laden vehicles and knew how to direct the blast of the explosion toward a particular place. My father's men later remarked that they'd used the Nápoles airstrip for practice runs—with stolen cars, of course—that had to be executed very carefully due to the dangerous explosions. The location they selected was the far end of the airstrip because a ravine right next to it offered shelter to prevent injuries or worse. On one of their test runs, the explosion was so powerful that the vehicle flew up and landed in a tree near the top of the hill.

Soon my father would decide to take on the Colombian government, and being on the run would become a normal part of life. The authorities' first move would be to raid Nápoles for any evidence they could use to prosecute him for anything at all, but my father had informants in every security agency and paid them high salaries to warn him of operations. When the agents arrived, they never found a single bullet, though the authorities still portrayed the estate as a haven for weapons, explosives, and drugs. Everything you can imagine went on there on that property, but none of what they showed in the media actually had anything to do with my father. And that made him angrier.

Even while in hiding, my father refused to believe that the government would seize the zoo animals just because they'd been brought to the country illegally. He always argued that confiscating them didn't make sense if they were just going to move the animals to places that weren't suited to them. What's more, he was convinced the estate was the best place for those species and that any other zoo in the country was vastly inferior to Nápoles.

On one of the increasingly frequent raids, agents from INDERENA, the National Institute of Renewable Natural Resources and Environment, confiscated the zoo's twelve zebras. When my father found out, he immediately ordered his men to obtain an equal number of donkeys.

"Offer the guard a year's salary," he told one of his most trusted employees.

And so the guard at INDERENA allowed my father's men to make the exchange, and in the middle of the night they painted the donkeys black and white and returned the zebras to Nápoles.

He did something similar on another occasion, when the authorities seized a large number of exotic birds and took them to the Santa Fe Zoo in Medellín. When he learned what had happened, he ordered his men to buy ducks, geese, and chickens and to make the exchange in the middle of the night. And so his birds returned to Nápoles once more.

8

MAS Mayhem

In July 1981, a colonel from the army's Fourth Brigade in Medellín gave a friend of my father's a cassette tape containing several recordings in which militants from the M-19 guerrilla movement discussed kidnapping a Mafia don to collect a hefty ransom.

A copy made its way to my father, who at the time had already amassed an impressive military apparatus with young men recruited from the poorest areas of the city. These men, called *sicarios,* worked for him as hitmen, drug runners, and bodyguards—even as my bodyguards, though I was only four years old at the time.

After carefully listening to the recording, which left no doubt as to the guerrilla group's intentions, my father immediately investigated. He discovered that the M-19's Medellín cell had ordered the kidnapping, and he decided to weed out the culprits. Through his network of contacts in the underworld and in government intelligence agencies, my father and his men identified and located fourteen members of the group within a week, including Martha Elena Correa, Luis Gabriel Bernal, Elvencio Ruiz—whom "Pinina" (so nicknamed for his high-pitched voice, which resembled that of the little orphan girl in a popular Argentine television program) had found holed up in a seedy hotel in Bogotá—and Jorge Torres Victoria, known as "Pablo Catatumbo."

On several occasions my father told me that he admired the

M-19, partly because it had pulled off some impressive feats when it had occupied the Dominican embassy and stolen Simón Bolívar's sword and four thousand weapons from an armory—but especially because its earliest activities had included ambushing milk delivery trucks and distributing the cargo in Bogotá's poorest neighborhoods. But it was one thing for the M-19 to challenge the state and something else altogether for it to take on the Mafia.

Correa, Bernal, Ruiz, and Catatumbo were hauled off to the offices of *Antioquia Al Día* (*Antioquia Today*), a regional TV program with a newscast. My father had purchased it so he could get involved in mass media and journalism, which fascinated him, but that was a front. Working out of the rear of the building was one of my father's criminal enterprises.

The four members of the M-19 arrived right on time and emerged from their inconspicuous vehicle, visibly nervous. Elvencio Ruiz was holding a grenade with the safety pin removed, which meant it could be detonated at any moment. My father talked with the guerrilla members about their planned kidnapping and showed them that the drug trafficking Mafia was an imposing force and that he had a powerful military arm that couldn't be intimidated. Basically, he explained to them that he was the king of Medellín. For that meeting with the M-19, my father told me, he had gathered eighty of his men, armed them with new weapons, and instructed them to keep the weapons in plain sight. The goal had been to scare the guerrilla group, not kill them. Even so, he warned them to be alert in case of a confrontation.

Despite the guerillas' implied threat and the glowering faces of my father's men, the meeting was fairly cordial, and at the end the guerrilla group agreed not to interfere with the Mafia or their families.

"Things are simple with me, gentlemen," my father said. "You don't mess with me, and I don't mess with you. See, you haven't even done anything yet, and I already know all about your plans.

Don't even think about going behind my back because I could wipe you all out—tell me I'm wrong." He went on, "Make no mistake, all I need is one name or address or telephone number, and I can find you in a heartbeat." He stared at Elvencio Ruiz.

Then, to drive the point home, he pulled out a notebook and one by one read off the names of the fourteen guerrilla fighters who comprised the Medellín cell of the M-19, and then described their safe houses and recent movements. Finally, several of my father's men said, he gave the four militants somewhere between ten and fifteen thousand dollars.

My father maintained a close relationship with the M-19 for a while, even sending Pablo Catatumbo to run a gas station near Miami Beach. At the time, the United States was facing a severe gasoline shortage. The authorities had decided to ration gas and distribute it based on whether license plates ended with an odd or an even number. In buying the gas station, my father had solved a logistical problem for his organization, as there he could fill up the vehicles used to distribute cocaine around Miami. Catatumbo remained in the United States for five months and then returned to Colombia.

The alliance with the M-19 fell apart on Thursday, November 12, 1981, with the kidnapping of his ally Fabio Ochoa Restrepo's daughter, Martha Nieves Ochoa, an act that my father considered a betrayal and a personal affront.

As soon as Jorge Luis Ochoa called with the news that three armed men had kidnapped his sister, my father raced to Don Fabio's house in Medellín's Prado neighborhood and led the effort to figure out who was behind the abduction. As he was going through the photos of graduates in her high school yearbook, he recognized two people he'd met with just four months earlier: Martha Elena Correa and Luis Gabriel Bernal. The M-19 had Martha Nieves Ochoa.

My father considered the next steps carefully, knowing that the guerrilla group would probably demand twelve million dollars in exchange for Martha Nieves's release. The rebels clearly believed the narcos would provide them an easy, safe source of funding. My father had shut down one kidnapping attempt already, but a week later the M-19 would also abduct, in Medellín, a woman with the last name of Molina and, in the city of Armenia, Medellín Cartel member Carlos Lehder, who managed to escape but was shot during the struggle.

Over the next few days, my father arranged a narco summit at Nápoles that was attended by no fewer than two hundred drug kingpins from all over the country and several army officers. Everyone agreed that they wouldn't pay for Martha Nieves to be set free but would instead attack the kidnappers and rescue her.

The Mexican, Carlos Lehder, and Fidel Castaño, who years later would found the ACCU paramilitary group with his brother Carlos, joined in the search mission. Castaño's father had been abducted and murdered by the FARC guerrilla group, so he was in favor of the armed approach. My father was touched by his personal story, and they became very close after that.

My father was the leader of the rescue team, which they called *Muerte a Secuestradores* (Death to Kidnappers), commonly known as MAS. To aid the operation, Gerardo "Kiko" Moncada, another of my father's partners in the Medellín Cartel, loaned them a huge warehouse right beside the Perpetuo Socorro church near Avenida Palacé.

My father also worked to protect his own family, and our life became one of confinement and curfew. The house in Santa María de los Ángeles filled with bodyguards who watched over us twenty-four hours a day, and we were hardly allowed to leave the house because no one knew how the M-19 was going to react to the pressure from MAS. They started taking me to nursery school in an armed Toyota Land Cruiser, and there was always an armed guard stationed outside the Montessori school. My father even made my aunt Alba Marina step down from her teaching position at the University of Antioquia, since Martha Nieves had been abducted with the help of one of her female classmates there.

My father typically would go to bed around eight or nine in the morning after carrying out search operations and raids for most of the night. He, Pinina, Tabloid, Shooter, Cassava, and Otto would dress in army uniforms and travel in military trucks borrowed from the infantry battalion headquarters in Villa Hermosa, where the MAS inner circle often met.

My father's personal security team included anywhere from four to ten men, but my mother was still concerned for his safety.

"Pablo, they're going to kill you," she complained. "Where is your commitment to your son, if you're going to let your friends get you killed . . . as usual? We haven't seen you in a month—what about us? Are we going to get to spend Christmas with you?"

"No, darling, if I don't help now, how can I ask others for help down the line? We have to be together in this so it doesn't happen again," said my father, who had thrown himself into the rescue operation as if Martha Nieves were his own sister.

Fidel Castaño, Carlos Lehder, narcos from all over the country, and army and police officials interested in how the rescue was going would gather in Kiko Moncada's warehouse night and day. The entire Ochoa family was confined to their estate in Envigado, protected by a wall of armed men, where they received extortionate phone calls and recorded conversations with the abductors.

In the meantime, my father's most trusted bodyguards recruited dozens of young men from the Medellín slums to act as informants. Within a few days, at least a thousand people had joined the search effort for Martha Nieves.

As my father and his men hunted the kidnappers, the regional newspapers published large ads from MAS that announced the creation of the organization, described the Ochoa kidnapping, and declared that MAS refused to pay the M-19 a single peso for Martha Nieves's release.

Not long thereafter, Lehder bought space in several publications to explain why MAS had been formed and the reasons for its anti-kidnapping efforts. In addition, on the second Sunday in December 1981, the organization used one of my father's planes to drop thousands of leaflets over Medellín's Atanasio Girardot Stadium and Cali's Pascual Guerrero Stadium declaring that the M-19 wouldn't get a peso for the kidnapping.

MAS's military might became evident as the days passed thanks to the powerful alliance between my father, his men, the army, and the police. Dozens of raids took place across the city and in the Aburrá Valley, leading to the capture of several suspects, who were then taken to the MAS headquarters and brutally interrogated.

My father also ordered the purchase of more than one hundred fifty walkie-talkies and passed them out to the young men from the slums. Some were to hang out near the pay phones in certain locations around the city and wait to see if anyone used them to make a call related to the kidnapping. Other young men in vehicles nearby would wait for a signal to capture the suspect.

The strategy worked. Members of the M-19 called the Ochoa family several times to negotiate their abductee's release. The family's phone was tapped, so the police were able to trace the call and alert my father's men as to its location. Several guerrilla militants were arrested that way.

These arrests and interrogations led MAS to a house in Medellín's La América neighborhood, where my father's men and the army engaged in a shootout with three militants who died during the battle. They found Martha Nieves's identification card, but it turned out she'd already been moved to another location. A thorough investigation suggested that they'd brought her to the nearby village of San Antonio de Prado, southwest of Medellín, where the authorities had unwittingly impounded the van from which the

M-19 had been intercepting and hacking the national TV broad-cast signal and airing their own propaganda. From there, Martha Nieves had been taken to La Estrella and Montebello, south of Medellín.

But they still didn't find her. So, on the night of December 31, as a clear message that they were right at the kidnappers' doorstep, MAS left Martha Correa, whom they'd captured during their raids throughout Medellín, chained to the main entrance of the *El Colombiano* newspaper office with a sign identifying her as one of the kidnappers.

My father spent New Year's Day with the Ochoas and decided to counterattack in early January 1982. The family ran an ad in several newspapers with a succinct, straightforward message: "The Ochoa Vásquez family refuses to negotiate with the M-19 abduc-tors who are holding Martha Nieves Ochoa de Yepes captive. It will not pay money for her release and instead offers the sum of twenty-five million pesos to any citizen who supplies information regard-ing her whereabouts."

The announcement didn't produce any new information, and MAS's leads were drying up. The captured M-19 militants who were being held in the warehouse—some twenty-five of them—showed real signs of having no idea as to Martha Nieves's where-abouts. In addition, some of the M-19 leaders incarcerated in Bogotá's La Picota prison sent a message in which they denied knowledge of her location.

Having lost track of Martha Nieves, the Ochoa family swiftly mobilized and secured the cooperation of former Venezuelan president Carlos Andrés Pérez, who sought contact with the M-19 leaders who were hunkered down in Panama at the time.

These efforts bore fruit, and two weeks later, after tough nego-tiations, the M-19 agreed to accept $1.2 million for Martha Nieves's release. The deal included the release of twenty-five people being held by my father at MAS headquarters. Elvencio Ruiz, still alive, was left by the side of the road near the Guaymaral Airport, north of Bogotá, having been held at the Colombian army's cavalry academy.

Ninety-six days after she disappeared, Martha Nieves was found safe and sound in the town of Génova in the department of Quindío and was immediately taken home to Medellín. Contrary to what might be expected, my father and the M-19 did not go to war. Instead, over the next few months, they would forge an alliance that would inflict great harm on Colombia.

9

Politics: His Biggest Mistake

By late 1981, my father had become the world's top cocaine trafficker. But he wasn't willing to be just another drug trafficker. That became clear to Gustavo when he went to my father one day, smiling, to tell him that three cocaine-laden planes had made it safely to their destination.

"Pablo, the three shipments made it with no problem."

"Excellent, so we have economic power," my father said. "Now we're going to go after political power."

My father was about to enter the shifting sands of politics, which ultimately were to be his downfall.

MY GRANDMOTHER NORA; JOSEFINA, A GOOD FRIEND OF THE Henao family; and Jorge Mesa, mayor of Envigado, were talking animatedly at lunchtime one day when my father and Carlos Lehder walked in. They sat down at the table, and within a few minutes the conversation shifted to politics. It was February 1982, and elections to overhaul Congress and select the new president of the republic were approaching.

Mesa, who was from a prominent local political family, mentioned there were open seats and suggested that my father get into politics, insisting that a lot of people would support him.

My father listened attentively. Judging by his expression, I could tell the idea appealed to him. He wasn't a stranger to politics: in 1979 he'd gotten a seat on the Envigado town council after being chosen from a list presented by the supporters of Antioquian politician William Vélez. But he participated in just two council meetings before handing the seat off to the alternate who had been chosen to stand in for him in his absence.

Before the discussion of the mayor's proposal could go any further, my grandmother Nora stood up, noticeably upset, and said, "Pablo, have you forgotten who you are and what you do? If you get involved in politics, there won't be a sewer in the world where you can hide. You're going to put us all in danger; you'll hurt all of our lives. Think about your son, about your family."

At hearing her harsh point of view, my father also stood, paced around the dining room, and responded with his usual confidence: "Mother-in-law, don't worry: I do things right. I've already paid the F-2 [secret police] to make the police records that mention me disappear."

Lehder remained silent while Mesa and Josefina insisted that my father had a guaranteed voter base as a result of his good works. He had financed the construction of soccer fields, basketball and volleyball courts, cycle tracks and roller-skating rinks, and health clinics, and he had planted thousands of trees in poor areas of Medellín, Envigado, and other communities in the Aburrá Valley.

The goal had been to build forty sports arenas in a very short time. Overseeing it were Gustavo Upegui—who was called "Major" because he'd once been a police official—and Fernando Arbeláez, the Animal Man. At the time, they'd already opened a dozen soccer fields in the towns of La Estrella, Caldas, Itagüí, and Bello, and in the Medellín neighborhoods of Campo Valdés, Moravia, El Dorado, Manrique, and Castilla. My father wanted the boys in those communities to get involved in sports instead of, paradoxically, drugs or crime.

My mother and I would sometimes attend the soccer games organized to celebrate the openings of the new fields with my father. We'd be struck by how the stands were always packed with spectators who cheered my father for his social projects. Bodyguards had to protect us from the crowds—so many people wanted to try to speak to my father. I was very little and was sometimes frightened by the eager swarms.

It was around that time that my father had met Father Elías Lopera, chaplain of the Santa Teresita Church in Medellín. The priest appreciated my father's compassionate nature and accompanied him to villages all over Antioquia. For a long time, they'd be allies on philanthropic projects and in politics.

For my father, politics and philanthropy were intertwined. On June 26, 1981, for example, a tree-planting day was held in the neighborhood of Moravia at which my father gave a speech. Afterward, Father Elías thanked him for his generosity and prompted the audience to applaud. In that speech, for the first time, my father attacked Bogotá's *El Espectador* newspaper:

"We have seen beautiful civic and social campaigns in Medellín's *El Colombiano* newspaper, but not in media such as *El Espectador,* which represents the voice of the Colombian oligarchy. It takes as its banner and guiding principle dishonest and cynical personal attacks. Worst of all, that newspaper distorts the news, injecting it with deadly poison and attacking people. It has forgotten that people have values, it has forgotten that people have families, and it has forgotten that people sometimes have the support and backing of the community."

In addition to these community projects, for more than a year my father had been engaged in a public campaign against the extradition treaty with the United States, signed in March 1979 by Colombian President Julio César Turbay. My father thought it was humiliating for a country to hand over its citizens to another country's judicial system. He had studied the subject thoroughly—and this was before anyone had requested his extradition or was looking to bring him to justice.

So my father made extradition his pet cause and started organizing meetings at Kevin's nightclub and the country estate La Rinconada in the town of Copacabana. He dubbed the informal get-togethers the National Forum of Extraditables, which quickly became something other than your standard political meeting. My father summoned the big kahunas of the Colombian Mafia to a meeting at La Rinconada, and nearly fifty dons from Valle del Cauca, Bogotá, Antioquia, and the Atlantic coast, including the Cali narcos Miguel and Gilberto Rodríguez Orejuela and José "Chepe" Santacruz, attended. Failure to show up was frowned upon, as the meeting was an effort to seek consensus in the Mafia nationwide, with the exclusive objective of abolishing extradition. I should clarify that none of the attendees were yet recognized as drug traffickers, nor did they have criminal records or convictions. They were "successful businessmen," as they were called among society's elite, men with whom people did business but didn't get their photo taken.

My father sat at the main table with former Supreme Court of Justice magistrate Humberto Barrera Domínguez, who spoke at length on the serious consequences of the treaty Turbay had signed on the drug trade, as well as Virginia Vallejo, a TV host who'd dazzled him with her charisma. He'd invited her to add some celebrity to the event. She became a moderator at the meetings, and she and my father engaged in a torrid affair and later even did some business together.

I don't know the details and we never discussed the subject, but my father's relationship with Virginia Vallejo would end badly. I remember seeing her once at the gate to the Nápoles estate, where they refused to let her in because my father had learned that she was having more than her fair share of affairs. The TV host sobbed at the gate for hours, begging them to allow her to enter. But the order had been given. And that was the last time she was close to my father.

AT MY GRANDMOTHER NORA'S APARTMENT, THE DISCUSSION OF whether my father should enter politics went on for two hours. At last he gave in to temptation and agreed to be included as an alternate on the Liberal Renewal Movement's (MRL) list of delegates for the Chamber of Representatives. My father knew that the MRL was backing the presidential candidacy of Luis Carlos Galán from the New Liberals, and he didn't have a problem with that. He respected Galán's political career, his impressive oratory skills, and especially his populist ideals.

My father took his candidacy seriously, and three days later he held his first rally in the La Paz neighborhood, where he gave a speech standing on the hood of a Mercedes-Benz. He told the thousand people in attendance, including some old partners in crime, that he'd always have a special affection for the neighborhood, and he promised to work from Congress for the poor people of Envigado and Antioquia.

The campaign took off, and my father built more soccer fields and planted more trees in the Aburrá Valley. At one of the many rallies held over the course of his eight-week campaign, an apparently intoxicated man ranted about politicians who didn't keep their promises, pointing at my father, who became quite angry. According to my father's bodyguards, two policemen forcibly removed the heckler, drove to a spot near the La Aguacatala neighborhood, and handed him over to my father's men, who riddled him with bullets.

As the days passed, my father grew more confident on his soapbox, and at a demonstration in the town of Caldas's main square, he railed against extradition and demanded that the government repeal the agreement signed with the United States. His speech was nationalist in sentiment, expressed using simple language, and clearly focused on voters from poorer areas.

But the campaign's momentum was brought to a sudden halt one night when Galán led a rally in Berrío Park in downtown Medellín and rejected the inclusion of MRL in the New Liberals' campaign, kicking out my father and his fellow candidate Jairo Ortega Ramírez. A few hours later, Galán ordered that the MRL's campaign office in Envigado be closed and their publicity materials destroyed. Though outraged, my father immediately shut down his campaign headquarters.

Jairo Ortega received a handwritten message from Galán explaining his decision: "We cannot tolerate links to people whose activities go against our tenet of restoring Colombia's moral fiber and politics. If you do not accept these conditions, I cannot allow your candidate list to have any ties to my presidential campaign."

Despite this setback, two days later Ortega met with my father and introduced him to the politician Alberto Santofimio Botero, the leader of a small movement known as Liberal Alternative, which was also nominating a slate of candidates for Congress. After a short conversation, they agreed that Ortega and my father would join Liberal Alternative, cementing their new alliance at a public event in Medellín. Santofimio and Ortega climbed onstage dressed in suits and ties and with red carnations in their lapels. My father—who hated formality—was in short sleeves and also donned a carnation.

The next day, Liberal Alternative ran an ad in the regional papers welcoming my father to the group: "We support Pablo Escobar's candidacy for the Chamber of Representatives because his youth, his intelligence, and his love for the most vulnerable make him deserving of the envy of cocktail politicians. He has the support of all the liberals and conservatives in Magdalena Medio, as he has been the Savior of this region."

The campaign picked up steam, and my father continued to

travel throughout Medellín and the Aburrá Valley. Eventually he reached Moravia, a slum where they had just finished extinguishing a huge fire that had swept through dozens of cardboard huts built on a foul-smelling, unsanitary garbage dump. There, he walked along the path used by the garbage trucks and personally witnessed the damage and debris, distributing mattresses, blankets, and other necessities.

My father was so moved by the poverty in Moravia that he decided to move its residents out of the area and provide free housing. He formed Medellín Without Slums, affectionately known as Barrio Pablo Escobar, his most ambitious project, with the plan to start by building five hundred housing units—and to erect five thousand of those units within twenty-four months.

To finance construction, he organized a fundraising bullfight at Medellín's La Macarena bullring. Posters from the event show that my father went all out to fill the arena. He had the bulls flown in from Spain's Los Guateles ranch, hired the famed matadors Pepe Cáceres and César Rincón, and invited the mounted bullfighters Dayro Chica, Fabio Ochoa, Andrés Vélez, and Alberto Uribe. He even invited Miss Colombia 1982, Julie Pauline Sáenz, and her first runner-up, Rocío Luna, along with other contestants from the national beauty competition. The bullfighters and beauty queens didn't take any payment for their attendance because it was for a good cause.

In addition to charity events, the narcos were another source of funding. My father's enterprise, famed for being the largest in terms of cocaine shipments, had made many others wealthy as well, so he took advantage of that success to request donations. Every drug runner who came to his office for business purposes was greeted by my father's insistent question: "How many houses for the poor are you going to give me? How many can I put you down for? Go on, tell me!"

To gain points with my father, almost all of them agreed to

contribute money. After all, his smuggling routes guaranteed their economic future. Of course, fear also compelled their generosity. According to my father, the mafia gave him enough funds to build nearly three hundred homes.

Throughout his life, my father never forgot the names and faces of anyone who made a move against him, and Galán's decision to marginalize him in the congressional campaign was no exception. He had his men investigate the decision further and found out what happened in early March, a few days after the election. The intelligence his men gathered indicated that the doctor René Mesa, who had long been denouncing my father, was the person who had informed Galán that my father was actually a powerful cocaine trafficker.

My father was especially upset by this betrayal, as he'd known Mesa for several years and was close to his family. Mesa had even performed the autopsies for Fernando, my father's brother, and his girlfriend, Piedad, who'd died in a car accident early in the morning of December 25, 1977. My father couldn't forgive the affront and ordered Shooter, one of his deadliest *sicarios*, to kill Mesa at his office in Envigado.

At last, after an exhausting campaign, on March 14, 1982, the final results revealed that my father had been elected as a representative to Congress. He had spent the day with Ortega and Santofimio at the headquarters of the Liberal Renewal Movement. My mother had stayed for a while, but as the count began to drag on, she went home, and my father kept her updated by telephone.

That night when my father got home, ecstatic, he told my mother, "Get ready to be the first lady of the nation." He was euphoric and hopeful and talked all night about his public works projects, which included building universities and hospitals—free ones. As soon as his election had been confirmed, my mother had started planning her outfit for his inauguration. My father said that he didn't want to wear a suit and that he'd enter Congress in his shirtsleeves.

Once the National Electoral Council certified the results of the election, the minister of the interior at the time, Jorge Mario Eastman, issued the certificate recognizing my father as an alternate representative to the House. The document had an additional value: it gave him parliamentary immunity, meaning that he couldn't be prosecuted for crimes.

My father declared it was time to celebrate. And what better way than with a trip to Brazil, which was synonymous with women, partying, and beautiful landscapes?

On April 12, more than twenty of us traveled to Rio de Janeiro on a commercial jet. The group included my father, my mother, me, some of my aunts and uncles and their spouses and children, my grandmother Hermilda, Gustavo, Gustavo's wife and children, and his parents, Anita and Gustavo. There were so many of us that we had to hire a bus to get around. It was a hassle to get tables in restaurants and tickets to shows, so we weren't really able to enjoy ourselves. My mother especially hated traveling in such a large group.

We still joke about that trip in my family because almost all of the couples—including my own parents, of course—were fighting by the time we got home, as the men had gone out to see dancers and prostitutes at strip clubs every night.

Back in Colombia, as the cocaine trade prospered, my father threw himself into political affairs. Not surprisingly, he decided to try to influence the ongoing presidential campaign. Only forty-five days remained till the presidential election, and the slate of candidates included Liberal Alfonso López Michelsen; Conservative Belisario Betancur Cuartas; Luis Carlos Galán from the New Liberals; and Gerardo Molina from the leftist Democratic Front.

Continuing his old custom of making allies by providing supposedly disinterested aid, my father and the other drug kingpins decided to jump aboard both the López and the Betancur campaigns to maximize their influence. According to people close to my father, the Mexican painted his Cheyenne II plane blue and loaned it to the Conservative candidate Betancur for his travels around the country. And thanks to the prominent engineer Santiago Londoño White, coordinator of the Liberal campaign in Antioquia, my father, the Ochoa brothers, Carlos Lehder, and the Mexican met in a suite at Medellín's InterContinental Hotel with López, national campaign director Ernesto Samper Pizano, Londoño, and other Liberal leaders.

Londoño introduced the capos as wealthy businessmen who wanted to help and immediately offered them tickets for a fundraising raffle. López was only at the meeting for ten minutes before heading to another campaign event in Medellín, and he left Samper in charge. In the end, my father and his business partners bought tickets valuing around fifty million pesos.

Some time later, when news that the Liberal campaign had taken money from the Mafia got out, López and Samper provided different accounts of what transpired. But the truth is the story I just told you, as related to me by my father. Proof of the collaboration between my father and the Liberal campaign is an editorial my father wrote when he was starting up his own newspaper to compete with the major national papers out of Bogotá and the regional Antioquian press. It was called *Fuerza* (Strength), and the inaugural issue circulated among his friends. A political gossip column in that first issue mentions one of my father's remarks at a forum about extradition: "Ernesto Samper Pizano attacked [Liberal Alternative's] Santofimio for supposedly taking dirty money. But at the anti-extradition forum, Pablo Escobar told Samper Pizano to watch out because Pizano's own hands were dirty from the twenty-six million pesos he'd accepted in the InterContinental Hotel's Medellín suite to support his political campaign and his marijuana legalization efforts. Don't worry, Samper, buddy, marijuana's legal anyway."

But support was not offered only in the form of money or assets. My father and Gustavo hired a large number of buses to take

Liberal voters to the polls on election day—May 30, 1982. Back then the government used to shut down the roads in and out of the city to prevent people from voting more than once, and Pablo and Gustavo transported people to the polling places in Envigado and at the Oviedo shopping center in Medellín.

In the end, unity among the conservatives was crucial in getting Betancur elected president in a four-hundred-thousand-vote landslide victory over López, who lost the race because, among other things, New Liberals leader Luis Carlos Galán's campaign siphoned off a lot of his voters.

Two months later, on July 20, my parents arrived at the capitol building for his inauguration in the luxurious army-green Mercedes-Benz limousine, on loan from Carlos Lehder, that had once belonged to a German official. My mother was wearing a red-and-black velvet dress by Valentino, the famous Italian designer, but she looked worried. My father had been determined to disregard the strict protocols for entering Congress—one of which was wearing a tie. He thought he could do anything he wanted, but the stern, exacting doorman wouldn't let him enter. My father tried everything he could think of, and after half an hour of futile insistence, he had no choice but to put on the tie.

There is a striking image from his inauguration: whereas everybody else is raising their open palm to take an oath, my father is raising his right hand in the shape of a *V* for victory.

That night, Santofimio, Ortega, and journalist Virginia Vallejo joined us at a large family dinner.

A few weeks later, on August 7, 1982, my father attended Betancur's presidential inauguration. He and the Mafia as a whole breathed easier that day when the new head of state did not mention extradition in his long speech, despite the U.S. courts' demand for the extradition of several drug traffickers. Though he and the other major drug lords were not yet on the list, my father was nonetheless relieved.

With political power within reach and a president determined to focus on pardon and amnesty for the guerrilla groups—the M-19, the FARC, the EPL, and the ELN—my father arranged another trip to Brazil. This time, unlike with his previous trip in April, his plan was to invite his closest friends, without their wives. To organize the journey, Gustavo called on the surgeon Tomás Zapata, whom he'd previously sent to Rio de Janeiro for a course on hair transplants and plastic surgery, as Gustavo was obsessed with restoring his thinning hair.

And so in the second week of August, twelve men traveled alone in two Learjets, one of them belonging to my father and the other rented. A Cheyenne turboprop plane—also my father's—carried the luggage. The group consisted of Jorge Luis and Fabio Ochoa Vásquez, Pablo Correa, Diego Londoño White, Mario Henao, Shooter, Otto, Cassava, Álvaro Luján, Jaime Cardona, Gustavo Gaviria, and my father.

Once in Rio, they stayed in luxury suites on one floor of the best hotel in Copacabana. From the very first night, the suite occupied by Jaime Cardona, a mobster who'd gotten into the cocaine trade even before my father, became the gathering place for wild indulgence and entertainment. They hired beautiful women from the best brothels in the city, and according to the men who went on the trip, thirty to forty women cycled through that suite daily. The bellhops received a hundred-dollar bill every time they delivered something to the rooms, ultimately making it a competition of who could attend to the extravagant Colombian tourists quickest.

The group's goal was to return to Colombia without a dollar left of the hundred thousand that each of them had brought. They rented six Rolls Royces and drove the cars out onto the field of Maracaná Stadium through the tunnel used by the soccer players. That afternoon, the Fluminense and Flamengo teams were playing as part of a local tournament, and the following day, a local newspaper reported on the visit from a delegation of "politicians and prominent businessmen" from Colombia. It was on that trip that my father smuggled out the beautiful and insanely expensive blue parrot for the Nápoles estate.

Weeks after his return from Brazil, my father received an assignment from the Chamber of Representatives: to be part of the official committee sent to independently observe Spain's 1982 general election and assess the legitimacy of its results. My father was elated. He packed the same clothes as always, but he also included one new item: a pair of hidden-heel shoes from New York that made him appear a little taller. On October 25, he flew first class with Alberto Santofimio and Jairo Ortega on Avianca's Bogotá–San Juan–Madrid route. Three days later, Felipe González from Spain's Partido Socialista Obrero Español (PSOE, the Spanish Socialist Workers' Party) would win in a landslide; the party would remain in power for fourteen years, until 1996.

By late 1982, my father must have thought that he had secured himself a spot within Colombian politics. He mistakenly believed that he could traffic drugs while also holding a seat in Congress. The months to follow would prove that the state was ultimately more powerful than he was. And he would refuse to accept that.

10

Better a Grave in Colombia

Who is Don Pablo, the Antioquian Robin Hood who provokes such excitement among hundreds of poor people whose faces reflect a sudden hope, an improbable emotion in this sordid environment?

"Just saying his name produces a mix of reactions ranging from explosive joy to deep fear, from great admiration to cautious contempt. But no one is indifferent to the name Pablo Escobar."

This description of my father appeared on April 19, 1983, on the front page of the magazine *Semana,* which was on its way to becoming one of the most influential publications in Colombia. The article introduced Pablo Escobar, benefactor to the poor and owner of a vast fortune of unclear origins.

"Sweetheart, did you see the myths the media are spinning?" my father said in reaction to the article, which years later would become a touchstone in discussions of him. "I wish I were Robin Hood so I could do even more for the poor."

The next day, in an interview for a local news program, my father used it to his advantage: "It's a pretty interesting analogy. Those who are familiar with the story of Robin Hood know that he fought for and defended the lower classes."

The *Semana* article was published just as my father had reached his peak. He was a multimillionaire. He had made his dreams reality at the Nápoles estate. The cocaine trade was booming. He had no pending prosecutions to worry about, and the government had dropped its investigation that had begun in 1976. What's more, he was a congressman, rubbing elbows with the crème de la crème of the nation's political class.

To top it all off, a survey had just revealed that Pope John Paul II, U.S. President Ronald Reagan, and Pablo Escobar were the most recognized figures in the world. When he would sit down with us to watch the news, he always asked what they'd said about each man. Anxious to do a good job as a legislator, he started to read a primer on economics and devoured several biographies of the Nobel Prize–winning writer Gabriel García Márquez in case reporters questioned him on those topics. To stay on top of minute-by-minute developments, he hired someone to record all the radio and television news programs and summarize the most important stories.

Anyone else would have been satisfied with such a favorable set of circumstances. Not my father. On the very day that *Semana* was portraying him as a Robin Hood, he had already begun carrying out a nefarious plot to exact revenge on the New Liberals for sidelining him during the congressional campaign.

Luis Carlos Galán, who was back in Congress after his failed presidential bid, was known for his integrity. It wasn't going to be easy to trap him. His second-in-command, Rodrigo Lara Bonilla, a senator from the Huila Department, made an easier target. Evaristo Porras, an old ally of my father's who had spent some time in prison for drug trafficking, pretended to be a businessman interested in collaborating with Galán's movement and finagled a private meeting with Lara that he would secretly record.

Lara and Porras met in a room at the Bogotá Hilton, the same hotel where years earlier my father had stayed while competing in the Renault Cup. It was Tuesday, April 19, 1983. They spoke for more than half an hour, and in the end Porras wrote a check for a million pesos in Lara's name.

Afterward, Porras recounted his meeting with Lara to my father. They now had the check as evidence that Lara had accepted drug money. But when they tried to play the recording of the conversation, they discovered that Porras hadn't set up the recorder properly.

With this ace up his sleeve, my father continued to serve in the Chamber of Representatives, though it was already clear that Galán and Lara were going to be a thorn in his side and that sooner or later he would clash with them.

Over the next few weekends, my father stayed very active in Medellín, opening soccer fields and other sports venues that he'd funded with his own wallet. On May 15, he made the opening kick in front of twelve thousand spectators attending the first match in the neighborhood of Tejelo in northwestern Medellín. In June, he inaugurated the new field in Moravia with a match between the reserve players from the Club Atlético Nacional team and local players from the neighborhood.

In early August 1983, President Betancur named New Liberals' Rodrigo Lara Bonilla his justice minister. Lara's first public statements as minister offered frank condemnations of the drug cartels and specifically of my father and a few other traffickers. He also claimed that dirty drug trafficking money was being laundered through soccer clubs. But he failed to mention the traffickers' enormous economic power.

Hearing these accusations, my father decided to fight back. Through Jairo Ortega and his fellow congressman Ernesto Lucena Quevedo—one of Alberto Santofimio's political allies—they challenged Lara to a debate on dirty money. But their true objective was to reveal the existence of the million-peso check that Lara had received from Porras. A few minutes before the minister entered the chamber, they placed a copy of the check on each legislator's desk. Carlos Lehder arrived with a large group of men and occupied one of the sections reserved for journalists. My father sat to one side in the oval room. This maneuver put Lara under a lot of pressure. He looked out of sorts during the debate and finally had to admit that he'd accepted the check.

Back in Medellín after the debate, as the Betancur administration scrambled to do damage control, my father met with my grandmother Nora, who was, as usual, very stern with him.

"Son, if you have a tail made of straw, don't swish it next to a candle," she said.

"No, don't worry, nothing's going to happen," he assured her.

"You're hardheaded, and you're not considering what's best for your family."

My father remained angry with Lara and grew irate when Lara criticized him on the news, talking back to the television every time he spoke or simply appeared on the screen. On a couple of occasions, when my father got home and found my mother watching the news, distraught, he'd say, "Don't watch those things" and turn off the TV.

Despite the apparent success of the attempt to smear Lara, who was at risk of losing his position, on August 25, a week after the debate, *El Espectador* dealt my father a devastating blow. The newspaper published a front-page article reporting that in March 1976 my father and four others had been caught with nineteen pounds of coca paste.

Though my father had paid to make the case files disappear and to have the DAS agents who'd carried out the investigation assassinated, the Bogotá newspaper was able to expose Representative Escobar as a drug trafficker. He'd been convinced that the police files fingering him had disappeared, but he'd forgotten to destroy the newspaper's archive. His house of cards was falling down.

From that moment, my father started plotting to kill Guillermo

Cano, the newspaper's editor in chief. His first move, though, was to send his men to buy every single copy before they reached Medellín's newspaper stands. He managed to pull it off, but the damage had already been done: the other media outlets picked up *El Espectador*'s story, and my father's emphatic insistence that "my money has no ties to drug trafficking" fell on deaf ears. Contrary to what he'd expected, his effort to prevent the newspaper from circulating in the Aburrá Valley only heightened interest in the story among journalists around the country.

My father normally planned his crimes carefully and never lost his temper or cursed even in the worst moments. One of his most trusted men told me that my father's face twisted with fury when he saw his photo in the papers and that he was angry with himself because he'd let down so many people who'd believed in him. For the first time, my father found himself at a crossroads, and in an attempt to defend himself, he accused Lara of slander and demanded that he offer proof of the drug trafficking claim. He also met with journalists in Congress and showed them his valid entry visa for the United States.

At the beginning of September, while pundits were still debating the issue of dirty money, my mother shared the good news that she'd finally become pregnant after six years of failed attempts, three miscarriages, and an ectopic pregnancy. At the same time, a few tabloid papers published articles on my father's relationship with TV host Virginia Vallejo, even claiming that they were planning to get married soon. Enraged, my mother fought with my father and kicked him out of the house for three weeks. But he called her constantly.

"Sweetheart, I need you to know you're incredibly important to me. You're the only woman I love," he'd say. "The journalists and magazines and other people are jealous of us and want to hurt our marriage. I want to come back to you and be with you forever." Then he would send flowers with a card that read, "I'll never trade you for anybody or anything."

Each time he called, my mother would respond that there was no need for him to worry, she wasn't the only mother without a husband by her side. She suggested that they go their separate ways, but he remained persistent. One Sunday night he showed up unexpectedly with a dejected expression on his face, and my mother didn't have the heart to turn him away. She let him come back home again.

The cascade of bad news didn't stop, and the scandal around my father only heated up. The Tenth Superior Judge of Medellín, Gustavo Zuluaga, reopened the investigation into the deaths of the DAS agents who had arrested him in 1976, and the U.S. embassy canceled his visa. And as if that weren't enough, on October 26, the Chamber of Representatives revoked his parliamentary immunity.

Even as my father's life crumbled around him, he tried to hold things together within the family. He still wasn't under indictment, and we spent that New Year's at Nápoles.

With his reputation shattered and his immunity revoked, on January 20, 1984, my father finally exited public life for good, submitting a letter of resignation that offered searing criticism of Colombia's politicians: "I will continue to fight against oligarchies and injustices, and against backroom deal making, which continues to nurture a blatant disregard for the people's needs, and especially against demagogues and dirty politicians, who remain indolent in the face of the people's suffering but are always on the alert when it comes to divvying up official power."

One of Pablo's closest colleagues, a man who went by "Neruda" and helped him write his speeches and press statements, reviewed the final letter, but my father wrote it himself. My father was hit hard by being forced out of politics; he'd always believed he'd be able to use his seat to help the poor. Over the next few weeks we returned to Nápoles, and he turned his focus back to drug trafficking.

But he hadn't counted on the fact that the justice minister, now in collaboration with the police antinarcotics unit and the DEA, would keep working to bring down the Mafia network that threatened to hijack the country.

ON THE MORNING OF MONDAY, MARCH 12, 1984, MY FATHER heard on the radio that there had been a raid on a cocaine-processing complex known as Tranquilandia in the jungles of Yarí in the southern Caquetá Department. Minister Lara and police colonel Jaime Ramírez, who was heading the operation, reported that the Medellín Cartel had built several labs there for processing coca paste on a massive scale. The Mafia, they said, had managed to build facilities catering to every phase of the trafficking operation in a single location, and the raid had been a major setback for Colombian drug-trafficking operations.

Tranquilandia boasted a mile-long airstrip that operated twenty-four hours a day and a power plant that supplied enough electricity for the kitchens where coca paste was processed. Large planes would fly in ingredients and supplies while others took off loaded with packages of cocaine. Fifty people lived on the premises, twenty-seven of whom were arrested and taken to the city of Villavicencio. I never talked to my father about the topic, and for years I thought that he, Gustavo Gaviria, and the Mexican had built the complex. Even the 2009 documentary *Sins of My Father,* in which I participated, included photos of the Tranquilandia raid and referred to my father and the Mexican as the owners of the narco-fortress.

After conversations with various people who were involved with my father back then, I have become convinced that my father, Gustavo, and the Mexican had nothing to do with Tranquilandia.

Why? My father had been tired of the coca-processing kitchens because of their sky-high accident rates and the increasing costs of transporting the chemical supplies. It turns out that the traffickers who actually owned the complex had some business dealings with my father, and that must have been why the government linked Tranquilandia to the Medellín Cartel.

Tranquilandia vanished, but an incident in one of the Mexican's coca-processing labs in the Magdalena Medio region would lead to two long, brutal wars: the first between the Mexican and the Revolutionary Armed Forces of Colombia (FARC) guerrilla movement, and the second, its product, the conflict between the paramilitaries and the Patriotic Union (UP), the political group formed as a result of the peacemaking efforts between the Betancur administration and the FARC.

Tensions first erupted when a FARC unit stole thirty kilos of processed cocaine from the Mexican's lab and killed a guard who turned out to be the Mexican's cousin from his home in Pacho in northern Cundinamarca. My father once commented that wherever the Mexican had a kilo of cocaine, he also had someone from Pacho there to guard it.

The Mexican refused to forgive the episode and declared war on the FARC. All over the country, wherever the guerrilla group was operating, he organized small bands of armed men to go after them. He didn't care how much money it cost. And so paramilitarism financed by the drug trade—and later also by businessmen and ranchers fed up with extortion and kidnapping at the hands of the guerrillas or the cartels—was born.

My father tried several times to persuade the Mexican to drop the conflict with the FARC, arguing that it was better to negotiate. He was convinced that the narcos and the guerrilla groups could coexist in peace and respect each other's turf. But Rodríguez Gacha, like my father, didn't take advice from anybody. "Tell them that you're in charge in this area and they should stay out. They can do whatever they want over there," my father told the Mexican once, in vain. Paramilitary leader Carlos Castaño would later become the Mexican's perfect partner in crime, as both were determined to wipe out the Colombian guerrilla movements, whatever it took.

The Mexican had immense political power. Every time he came to Nápoles, the Mexican was accompanied by no fewer than two hundred armed guards. The logistics for his visits were enormously complicated, and my father thought they brought too much attention to the estate, so he preferred going to visit the Mexican on his land in Pacho. When he once asked the Mexican to meet but requested that he not bring so many bodyguards, the Mexican replied, "No can do, compadre—I always travel this way."

While the Mexican was busy starting a "war" with the FARC, my father decided that he needed to end his conflict with the justice minister, whose condemnations of my father were becoming increasingly harsh. According to what I was told, when my father realized that Lara wasn't going to stop attacking him, he ordered the minister's assassination. He called in Shooter, Cassava, Pinina, Otto, Honker, and Mug and explained that the attack had to be carried out from an ambulance—or at least what appeared to be one. So the men modified a van in an auto body shop, adding metal panels for bulletproofing and drilling four openings in each side. They then painted it with Red Cross markings.

"The whole world is going to come down on us, but let's do it. I'm not going to allow that guy to get away with it," my father stated to his men when the plot to kill Lara was ready to be executed.

Contrary to the claims of Lara's family—that my father threatened him many times with menacing phone calls and by having him followed—Pablo Escobar wasn't a big fan of giving warnings. As he saw it, intimidation tactics only made people strengthen their security measures. Plenty of other drug traffickers hated the minister of justice as well, and they had all issued threats against him without consulting my father first.

The *sicarios* headed to Bogotá, checked in to various seedy hotels downtown, and started tailing the minister. After a few days, they learned that Lara got around in an unarmored white Mercedes-Benz, escorted by two vans with four DAS agents. They also identified the routes the driver used between the Ministry of Justice and Lara's house in northern Bogotá.

In mid-April 1984, the logistics were in place, and my father's *sicarios* awaited the best opportunity to assassinate Lara from the "ambulance." They ended up trying and failing three times thanks to the "ambulance" driver's lack of skill. When he heard of these mishaps, my father concluded that the operation was at risk and had them turn the ambulance into a flower delivery van. But then he altered the plan further, opting to add two more *sicarios* on a motorcycle to the group.

Pinina, who had a reputation as one of my father's best men, took charge of recruiting two others to join them. He went to the northeastern Medellín neighborhood where he'd grown up, Lovaina, which was a breeding ground for *sicarios* and one of the city's most dangerous areas. There he hired Byron Velásquez Arenas and Iván Darío Guisao, but he didn't inform them that the assignment was to kill a minister, just an important person who traveled in a white car.

The operation was again underway. Once, when the *sicarios* parked very close to the ministry while waiting for Lara to exit, his bodyguards, completely oblivious, leaned back against the side of the van, unaware that *sicarios* armed with AR-15 rifles were hidden inside it.

Finally, on the night of April 30, 1984, the motorcycle with Velásquez and Guisao and the fake flower delivery vehicle containing four men, a driver, and an additional man literally riding shotgun went out after Lara, who left his office and headed to his home in northern Bogotá as usual. In the account I heard many years later, the plan was for the men in the van to pull up beside the minister's car and fire their weapons through the openings in the sides. The motorcycle would ride behind them to fend off the minister's escorts.

But the *sicarios* were forced to adjust their plan due to heavy traffic. Their vehicle was stuck in a traffic jam, and only the motorcycle was able to stay with the target. Without hesitating, Guisao, who was seated as gunman that night and armed with a Mini UZI .45 caliber semiautomatic, told Velásquez to keep going. The two of them could carry out my father's order to kill the man traveling in the white Mercedes-Benz.

At around Calle 127, the motorcycle managed to pull up on the right side of the car, and Guisao strafed it with gunfire. It was seven thirty-five in the evening.

My father's instructions were that none of the *sicarios* should communicate with one another once the job had been completed. They had agreed on a rendezvous point in Bogotá from which they would immediately travel back to Medellín.

That night, at my grandmother Nora's apartment in the Altos building, I heard my mother and grandmother crying. They were holding each other in front of the television and talking about something serious and sad that had just happened.

After the assassination, chaos reigned. For the first time, the government declared total war on drug trafficking. It would hunt down the Mafia leaders, confiscate their assets, and extradite them to the United States.

After seeing the news reports, my mother—who was eight months pregnant—and I went to hide with a distant relative and stayed there for two weeks until my father sent for us. In the meantime, my father and several of the men who'd participated in the Lara assassination—including Pinina and Otto—headed bright and early one morning to the village of La Tablaza in La Estrella, from which a helicopter took them to Panama. At the same time, another helicopter picked up Gustavo's family at a turnoff on the way to Caldas, but that helicopter's gas tank ruptured midflight and was forced to make an emergency landing in the jungle, far from the Panamanian border. The passengers wandered around lost for several days until they reached a village that offered them assistance.

A few days later, a messenger sent by my father arrived and said that he'd pick us up in a helicopter the next day in a pasture in La Estrella. My mother packed a small suitcase with a few items of clothing for the two of us. She also included baby clothes—she and my father thought they were going to have another boy. The following day at the meeting spot, we were introduced to a doctor who would travel with us in case my mother gave birth early.

After an uneventful, two-and-a-half-hour trip, the pilot landed in a clearing in the jungle, where a van awaited us. We had reached the Panamanian border. We put on beach clothing so as not to arouse suspicion and immediately headed to Panama City, where we slept on mats in the apartment of one of my father's friends for three nights.

There we learned that the assassination of Rodrigo Lara had caused Colombia's major drug kingpins to scatter. Besides my father and Gustavo, Carlos Lehder and the Ochoa brothers, also of the Medellín Cartel, and the Rodríguez Orejuela brothers of the Cali Cartel were all in Panama.

From the first apartment we moved to an old, damp, stifling house in the historic section of the city. It was awful. The shower was mildewed and didn't drain properly, so you had to shower in flip-flops. As a precaution, for the first week the only thing we ate was chicken from KFC, which my father had one of his men deliver to us.

One day a Panamanian gynecologist came to the house to

examine my mother. After performing some tests, the specialist surprised us with the news that she was going to have a girl. My mother remained unconvinced. The checkups in Medellín had always indicated she'd have a boy. My father was delighted.

With this news, we now had to come up with a name for my sister. I suggested Manuela in memory of my first girlfriend, one of my schoolmates at the Montessori school I'd attended before we'd gone into hiding in Panama and I'd been forced to drop out.

"We'll send your sister to you to complain if she doesn't like it when she grows up," my father said when they agreed to the name.

On May 22, we moved to another house, this one quite comfortable and luxurious, owned by Panama's strongman at the time, General Manuel Antonio Noriega. Though we saw very little of my father, the situation seemed to be improving. Noriega sent several police officers to guard us in shifts, and we were allowed a bit more freedom.

During that period, my father gave me a 50cc Honda motorcycle. Because there wasn't anybody to accompany me as I learned to ride, he ordered Stud—one of his men who'd stayed behind in Medellín—to come up to Panama City. Stud would dress in white and go out jogging every morning while I rode the motorcycle.

Years later, during a long conversation, I asked my father what kind of relationship he and his partners in the Medellín Cartel had actually had with Noriega. He told me it was a lengthy story that began in 1981, when he met Noriega and gave him five million dollars in cash in exchange for permission to build several coca-processing facilities on the Panamanian side of the Darién Gap, the remote area of swampland and jungle straddling the Colombia–Panama border, and to launder money through Panamanian banks. Noriega agreed to let them work without interference, but he was explicit in stating that he would not engage in cocaine trafficking.

General Noriega didn't keep his promise. Months after the

money had changed hands and several labs had been set up, he launched a military operation, destroying the kitchens, arresting almost thirty people, and seizing a Learjet and helicopter that belonged to my father.

Furious, my father threatened Noriega that if he didn't give back the money, he would have the general killed. The message must have frightened Noriega, as almost immediately he returned two million of the dollars.

Though the relationship with Noriega had soured, the general had attempted to make up for the damage by allowing my father and the other capos to remain in Panama after Lara's assassination. That's how we ended up living at one of Noriega's houses in the city, though my father didn't trust the general, so we couldn't stay there indefinitely.

The 1984 Panamanian election gave my father an opportunity to seek an accord with the Colombian government in the aftermath of Lara's assassination. Right around that time, the local media announced that former Colombian president Alfonso López Michelsen and former ministers Jaime Castro, Felio Andrade, and Gustavo Balcázar would be acting as observers for the upcoming presidential election to be held in May. My father phoned Medellín to speak with Santiago Londoño White, who had been treasurer for López's presidential campaign two years earlier, and asked him to try to set up a meeting while López was in Panama City. He suggested calling Felipe, López's son and the owner of *Semana* magazine, and asking him to convince his father. Londoño made the calls, and a few hours later, the former president agreed to meet with my father and Jorge Luis Ochoa at the Marriott Hotel in Panama.

My father vaguely mentioned the meeting to my mother hours before he left. "Tata," he said, "we're going to see if we can solve this problem. We're meeting with former president López."

At the meeting with López, my father and Jorge Luis Ochoa

proposed that the drug traffickers were willing to hand over their airstrips, labs, and fleets of aircraft; shut down their U.S. routes; and destroy their illegal crops—in short, end the cocaine trade—if in exchange the government suspended prison sentences for those who had been convicted of any criminal activity and, most important, did not extradite them. López promised to communicate the proposal to the current administration.

Back home, my father briefly informed my mother, "Former president López is going to talk to the administration. Let's hope there's a negotiation."

My father heard that López traveled from Panama to Miami and met with former communications minister Bernardo Ramírez, a personal friend of President Betancur. The proposal was considered, and the administration asked the inspector general, Carlos Jiménez Gómez, to meet with the capos in Panama City.

As the inspector general was working out the arrangements for the trip, my sister Manuela was born on May 25. While my father, Gustavo, and I were at Noriega's house, we received the call that my mother was in labor, and my father raced us to the hospital. Sitting in a waiting room, he looked nervous, and Gustavo tried to reassure him. The wait seemed to stretch on forever, until finally a doctor entered, congratulated my father on his beautiful baby girl, and gave us permission to see them. We headed to the elevator and, much to our surprise, found a nurse carrying a newborn baby with a bracelet that said "Manuela Escobar." My father's face lit up when he saw her.

Inspector General Carlos Jiménez Gómez arrived in Panama the next day, May 26, and met with my father and Jorge Luis Ochoa at the Marriott Hotel. They repeated the proposal they'd outlined to López, and at the end of their conversation, the official promised to discuss it with President Betancur. But the plan was derailed a few days later, when the newspaper El Tiempo reported on the meetings.

That was the last time—the only time—that Colombia had a real possibility of dismantling 95 percent of the drug trafficking industry. With the leak, there was now no turning back.

ANY OPPORTUNITY FOR RAPPROCHEMENT WITH THE GOVERNMENT now lost, my father came home upset one day in early June and told us we had to flee.

"We can't go on the run with a baby," he said. "Tata, we can't leave you here or send you to Colombia. Our only option is to send Manuela to Medellín. They'll take care of her there. We don't know whether we'll be sleeping in the jungle or by a lake, whether there will be food for the baby. We don't have a lot of options. We can't take a baby with us if we're going to have to keep running." It was excruciating for my mother to abandon her newborn daughter. Because I was older—I was seven now—they didn't consider sending me back to Colombia; my father thought I was safer by his side.

My mother wept as she handed her daughter over to Olga, the nurse, who would travel to Medellín with one of my father's most trusted men.

Why was my father suddenly eager to leave Panama—so eager that he was willing to send his fifteen-day-old daughter back to Colombia? I asked him once, and he told me that the leak about the meetings had revealed his whereabouts to the Colombian and United States governments, and he was afraid they'd try to arrest him. In addition, it was likely that Noriega would betray him again.

And so my father searched for a plan B, reaching out to old M-19 contacts from the Martha Nieves Ochoa kidnapping. My father knew that the guerrilla group and the new Sandinista regime in Nicaragua were politically and ideologically aligned, and so he asked the M-19 to inquire about the possibility of moving to Nicaragua. Within days he received a message from the M-19: some members of the Nicaraguan junta were willing to offer refuge to him and the other capos and their families in exchange for economic aid, which they needed due to a U.S. economic embargo. The agreement included permission to use Nicaraguan territory as a platform for continuing the cocaine trade. I remember my father commented that Daniel Ortega, then a candidate for president of Nicaragua for the Sandinista National Liberation Front (FSLN), had dispatched a number of officials to help settle the narcos in Managua, the capital.

My father saw Nicaragua as a real opportunity to change his place of work and residence. So, after ascertaining that Manuela was doing fine in Medellín, my mother, father, and I flew to Nicaragua. We were met at the airport by high-ranking Sandinista officials who transported us in a government Mercedes-Benz to a huge old house, where we found the Mexican, his wife, Gladys, and four of their bodyguards. Not long afterward, my grandmother Hermilda and aunt Alba Marina arrived. Almost immediately, my father had Pinina, Tabloid, and another dozen of his men brought in to protect us.

From the very beginning, we hated the house. It was gloomy. It was surrounded by ten-foot brick walls, and every corner had watchtowers with heavily armed guards. We even found a book on the history of the place that claimed several massacres had occurred there in the past.

Everyday life became intolerable. Managua was unlivable, racked by civil war, and there was frequent gunfire. The United States was sending contras across the Costa Rican and Honduran borders to fight the Sandinistas, who had overthrown Anastasio Somoza's military dictatorship a few years before, in 1979. The city was under siege, and the effects of the conflict were visible in the crumbling buildings and shuttered businesses. We had plenty of food, but we didn't know where it was coming from, though it was clear that someone in the government was responsible for stocking the refrigerators. There were no supermarkets or drug stores. My father had millions and millions of dollars in the country, but there was nothing to spend it on.

I remember that I stayed quiet most of the time and cried a lot. I begged my parents for us to return at least to Panama. There weren't even any toys in the house, and in our haste to flee Panama, I'd had to leave my motorcycle and other belongings behind.

My only distractions were going with my mother and the Mexican's wife to a spa near the house, sitting with Pinina and listening to Colombian soccer games over the radiotelephone from Medellín, and betting on who could kill the most flies in five minutes in a room that was always swarming with them.

"For three months, the only way I could see my daughter was in the one photo I had," my mother mourned as we reflected on this time in our lives. Even though my uncle Mario took photos of Manuela every day, he was never able to send them in fear that it might tip off the authorities as to our location.

While we were living that perilous existence, my father, the Mexican, two Nicaraguan soldiers, and an American pilot named Barry Seal traveled around Nicaragua to explore new cocaine trafficking routes. For several days they surveyed the country's numerous lakes and chains of volcanoes by helicopter, trying to identify the best places to construct labs and airstrips.

They knew it might take a while to set up the infrastructure, so they decided to use the small Los Brasiles airport, not far from Managua, to send the first shipments of cocaine on direct flights to southern Florida. The first shipment of six hundred kilos of cocaine packed in large duffel bags was scheduled for the night of Monday, June 25, 1984, in a plane that would be piloted by Seal himself. But my father and the Mexican didn't realize that they'd actually fallen into a trap. While they and Federico Vaughan, an official from the Nicaraguan Ministry of the Interior, were waiting for the soldiers to load up the plane, Seal was snapping photos.

The aircraft took off without a hitch, and while Seal flew to deliver the shipment, my father and the Mexican continued their activities, unaware that disaster was imminent.

Meanwhile, I had finally convinced my father to let me and my mother leave Managua. I had been complaining of boredom for a while, but he'd always insisted we'd be killed if we went back. Now, he reluctantly had agreed. My mother promised him she wouldn't go out on the street in Medellín, though it seems my father had a different plan for her all together.

"No, Tata. We'll tell him you're going to be traveling with him. If we don't, he's going to be even more upset. But when we get to the airport, we'll tell him he has to go by himself. And that my man Tibú will be going with him," my father told her in secret.

And that's what they did. When they revealed to me at the airport that my mother wasn't joining me, I felt immense anguish. I felt abandoned. I clung to them and refused to let go.

"I don't want to go if Mamá isn't going too," I sobbed, but my father wouldn't budge, promising she'd meet me in a few days. My mother says she cried day and night. Her two children were gone, she was surrounded by armed men, and she had been left to her fate in tumultuous Nicaragua.

In despair, one day she approached my father on the subject: "Let me go meet with one of my sisters and her husband in Panama so they can bring me photos of our children and I can see how they're doing."

"All right, but you have to promise me, sweetheart, that you'll come back here after you talk to them."

Despite her promise, my mother had already planned to head from Panama to Medellín.

While my mother was in Panama, my father called repeatedly to ask after Manuela and me. On the fourth day she summoned up her courage and stated that she wouldn't be returning to Nicaragua. She was going back to Colombia to take care of her children.

"No, what are you thinking? You can't do that!" my father said. "You know they're going to kill you—there's no way out of it."

"I promise I'll stay in my mother's house and never go out, but I have a baby who needs me. She's been without her mother for more than three months."

Finally, terrified, my mother reached the Olaya Herrera Airport and went straight to the Altos building, where she found my grandmother Nora, who had lost almost seventy pounds and was sunken into a deep depression.

My mother's reunion with me and my little sister was very emotional. She and I couldn't stop hugging each other, but Manuela barely recognized her and would start to cry whenever my mother held her, as she was only used to the nurse and my grandmother.

Things were complicated enough for us in Medellín, but back in Managua, my father suffered another major setback. In mid-July, several U.S. newspapers published a series of photographs of my father and the Mexican sending the cocaine shipment from Nicaragua. The visual evidence was incontrovertible. It was the first time—and the last—that they caught my father red-handed. Barry Seal, who turned out to be a DEA informant, had betrayed my father, and he wouldn't forget it.

The release of the photos to the media did damage in two ways: it exposed my father and it implicated the leftist Sandinista regime for collaborating with the Colombian Mafia. The ensuing scandal was so great that my father could no longer stay in Nicaragua. Two weeks later, he and the Mexican and all of their henchmen returned to Colombia.

As soon as he reached Medellín, my father went into hiding and lived that way for a long time. We continued to stay with my grandmother Nora, and my father sometimes sent for us so we could spend weekends together.

On July 19, only three weeks after the photos had been taken,

Herbert Shapiro, a judge in Florida, issued an arrest warrant for my father for conspiracy to import cocaine to the United States.

Though the infrastructure that had been set up to send cocaine to the United States was still in place, and my father was still the biggest name in the business, he knew that, legally speaking, his situation was deteriorating by the minute. He was being driven to a point of no return in which sooner or later they'd come after him or force him to defend himself. He was haunted by the possibility of extradition.

For a couple of months after, we experienced a relative calm, but that was soon shattered on September 20, 1984, when my grandmother Hermilda called to say that several armed men had abducted my grandfather Abel from one of his farms on the outskirts of La Ceja in eastern Antioquia. My father made use of his experience with the Martha Nieves Ochoa kidnapping and organized a massive search operation, though it turned out to be somewhat less wide-ranging this time, as he quickly discovered that my grandfather had been taken by four petty criminals who'd heard of my father's financial station.

Two days later, my father placed an ad in the Medellín papers offering a reward to anyone who provided information as to my grandfather's whereabouts. It described the vehicles that had taken him: two Toyota SUVs, one red with wooden trim, license plate KD9964, and the other beige, with an official plate, 0318. The idea was to let the kidnappers know that he had them in his sights.

Just as he had with the Ochoa case, my father sent hundreds of men to keep an eye on Medellín's pay phones and installed call-recording equipment at my grandmother Hermilda's house. The strategy worked. Ten days later, he'd learned the kidnappers' identities and the place where my grandfather was being held, tied to a bed in the town of Liborina in western Antioquia, sixty miles from Medellín.

But instead of moving in on the abductors, my father decided to wait until they asked for a ransom and then pay up to avoid putting my grandfather in danger. In the first phone call, they demanded ten million dollars. My father's reply was stern: "You kidnapped the wrong person. I'm the one with money. My father is a poor farmer who doesn't have a penny. This negotiation isn't going to be what you expected. Come up with a realistic number and call me, and we'll talk," he shouted, and then he hung up to show them that even though they had his father, he had control of the situation.

After a couple of days, they asked for forty million pesos, and eventually came down to thirty. Through John Lada, Manuela's godfather, my father delivered that sum in cash, and my grandfather arrived home safe and sound. The kidnapping had lasted sixteen days, and the four criminals were tracked down a few days later on my father's orders.

In the meantime, my father's legal troubles were growing. Ten of the *sicarios* who had participated in planning and carrying out the Lara assassination were arrested; six more, Pinina among them, managed to escape and were in hiding with my father. In that case, the First Superior Judge of Bogotá, Tulio Manuel Castro Gil, brought charges against my father.

As a result of legal proceedings, the first major search operation for my father began in late December 1984. At the time we were at a country estate in Guarne, Antioquia. I was seven years old when I awoke to the barrel of a gun thrust against my stomach. The gun belonged to an agent from the F-2, the secret police. I remember I had been wearing an experimental elastic device that covered my head and chin. My doctors had prescribed it to correct a deviation of the jaw, and it made me look bizarre.

Just as I asked where my father was, a police officer walked in holding his white poncho.

"Look what he dropped as he ran," the agent said.

My father had easily eluded the first raid, but over the next few days the hunt would intensify.

Saturday, January 5, 1985, was a bad day for my father. At dawn he received a phone call informing him that a Hercules plane from the Colombian Air Force had taken four people to Miami that morning, their extradition orders authorized by President Betancur and Minister of Justice Enrique Parejo, who had replaced Rodrigo Lara.

The four detainees were Hernán Botero Moreno—president of the Atlético Nacional soccer club—the brothers Nayib and Said Pabón Jatter, and Marco Fidel Cadavid.

My father exploded. He thought the extradition of Botero was especially unfair because he had been accused not of drug trafficking but of money laundering.

He considered it worse than an injustice: President Betancur's decision to act on the extradition treaty with the United States was a betrayal. Though Betancur hadn't promised to do away with extradition, my father thought the politician shouldn't forget that they'd helped fund his campaign.

My father's actions had become more radical of late, and he called up Juan Carlos Ospina, who went by "Socket," and a criminal known as "the Bird" and instructed them to blow up Betancur's car. Several of my father's men told me that the head of state avoided being killed at least four times. His security detail changed routes frequently, and on some occasions it hadn't passed by the places where they'd set up the explosives; on other occasions, the convoy did pass by the bomb, but the remote control to activate it failed.

By early February 1985, my father had become obsessed with eliminating the threat of extradition. All those public forums and secret meetings with other narcos to warn about the humiliation of being tried in another country had been useless. Though he was convinced that he could resolve his legal problems in Colombia his way, the United States was a different story.

At that time, my father was close to a number of M-19 leaders, including their highest commander, Iván Marino Ospina. The two of them saw each other regularly and talked about everything under the sun. They got along so well that the guerrilla fighter even gave my father a brand-new AK-47 that he'd just received in an arms shipment from Russia. That rifle became Tabloid's trusty sidekick.

After many hours of conversation, my father and Ospina came to agree on a lot, especially their opposition to extradition. That shared vision must have influenced the M-19's decision to depose Ospina at their ninth conference in late February at the Los Robles estate in Corinto, Cauca Department. There, he was criticized for his militaristic tendencies and political shortsightedness, especially in lieu of the M-19's ongoing negotiations with the Betancur administration, which put their August 1984 treaty with the government at risk. Ospina's deposal was also related to his statement during a trip to Mexico that Colombian drug lords should retaliate against US citizens if the government extradited Colombians to the United States.

My father understood that, with the ouster of Ospina, the M-19 leaders wished to send a public message against drug trafficking, even if relations between the guerrilla movement and the cartel were unshaken in private. At the end of the Los Robles meeting, the M-19 agreed to allow Ospina to return as the group's second-in-command and appointed Álvaro Fayad in his place. Fayad continued dialogue with the Betancur administration until Thursday, May 23, when Antonio Navarro Wolff, a member of the insurgent group's upper leadership, was badly wounded in an assassination attempt.

Much has been said about that attack, which took place in a restaurant in the El Peñón neighborhood of Cali. Navarro, Alonso Lucio, and a pregnant M-19 member had been discussing whether the group should maintain its ceasefire with the Colombian government when a man threw a grenade at their table. It was said that the attack had been retaliation for a grenade thrown at an army bus that morning that seriously injured several soldiers. In the initial chaos, it had been thought that the culprits for the bus attack were members of the M-19, though it was later established that another armed group, the Workers' Self-Defense Movement (ADO), was responsible. Navarro once said that he knew the names of the military officials who'd given the order to assassinate him and even the identity of the person who'd thrown the grenade.

I heard a different version. My father told me that the person who'd carried out the attack was Héctor Roldán, a drug trafficker who owned the Roldanautos car dealership in Cali, the same man he'd met during the Renault Cup in Bogotá in 1979 and who was nearly named Manuela's godfather. Roldán was very close with high-ranking military officers in Valle del Cauca and had attacked Navarro not only as revenge for the injured soldiers but also as a display of the discontent among prominent business and military leaders over the government's talks with the M-19.

The story of my father and Roldán wouldn't end there. On June 19, 1985, three weeks after the assault, Carlos Pizarro, one of the M-19's leaders and a delegate to the government negotiations, announced the end of the ceasefire and the return to armed conflict.

A few days later, Iván Marino Ospina told my father that Álvaro Fayad had suggested to the M-19's inner circle that they peacefully occupy a public building and stage a trial in which they'd bring President Betancur to justice for, according to the group, failing to comply with the treaty he'd signed with them. They first contemplated the National Capitol, but they scrapped that option because the building was too large to control militarily without including additional personnel. Ultimately, they decided on the Palace of Justice, as it had a less open architecture and only two entrances, the main one and a basement entrance through the garage.

When he learned of the plot, my father saw an opportunity and offered to finance a significant part of the operation. He knew that the nine magistrates from the Constitutional Chamber of the Supreme Court of Justice were currently assessing various suits brought by cartel lawyers working to repeal the extradition treaty with the United States. The narcos were all pressuring the magistrates with death threats to force them to strike down the 1979 accord, and this would be another weapon in that fight.

While the plan was moving forward, I later found out, my father sought revenge on the judge Tulio Manuel Castro, who a few months earlier had issued a warrant for his arrest and then called him to trial for Minister Lara's assassination. His men shot the judge in downtown Bogotá right as he was preparing to move offices, having just been named magistrate for the superior court in Santa Rosa de Viterbo, Boyacá.

Once more, my father had followed through on his terrible rule of unleashing violence on anyone who dared to oppose him.

In the meantime, Elvencio Ruiz was appointed to head the M-19 operation and started training the group that would occupy the courthouse. My father met several times with Iván Marino Ospina and other M-19 leaders in a hideout near the Nápoles estate, where they worked out the details of the military and economic aid he'd give them. The occupation was tentatively scheduled for October 17, 1985.

My father had already decided he'd go all in to ensure the operation's success. After all, he would also benefit if the guerrilla fighters destroyed the files related to the extradition of narcos—including himself—that were being examined and held at the Supreme Court of Justice. He didn't hesitate to provide a million dollars in cash and offered an additional bonus if they made the files disappear. According to several men who accompanied my father to those meetings with the M-19, he also made several suggestions: that the guerrilla fighters bring in the weapons they needed from Nicaragua; that they enter the Palace of Justice through the basement, head to the cafeteria, and then occupy the building floor by floor; that they have radios inside and outside the building to keep tabs on what was happening; and that, to facilitate their escape, they wear the uniforms of Colombia's Civil Defense, the agency charged with disaster response.

On August 28, 1985, just as their plan was coming together, the M-19 suffered a crushing setback when the army killed Iván Marino Ospina during a confrontation at his house in Cali's Cristales neighborhood. My father mourned the death of a man he considered a warrior and feared that the occupation of the Palace of Justice might have to be called off. But the M-19 forged ahead, more determined than ever to hold a public trial for President Betancur.

A mistake on my father's part almost unraveled the complicated plot. In the first week of October, he told Héctor Roldán all about the planned occupation. Roldán, who was friends with a number of important generals, tipped them off. The M-19 had to cancel the operation, and all of its members went into hiding for several days. The army stepped up its patrols around the main square in Bogotá, and the police began developing security plans for the building and the magistrates. But as the days passed and nothing seemed amiss in the city center, those security measures were phased out. The occupation of the Palace of Justice was rescheduled for Wednesday, November 6.

The eventual assault led to that regrettable outcome that we Colombians know all too well: dozens of hostages killed or missing, eleven Supreme Court justices assassinated, and the records for thousands of criminal cases destroyed. During the two-day occupation, my father was in a hideout known as Las Mercedes in the

Magdalena Medio region. Pinina told me that when my father saw that the building had been set on fire, he was delighted. He knew the extradition files wouldn't make it.

IN THE SECOND WEEK OF JANUARY 1986, WHILE ON VACATION AT the Nápoles estate, I was walking by the pool at the main house when my father called me over. He was sitting behind a cage of several exotic birds.

"Grégory, come here. I'm going to show you something. Come on, son." He pointed to a sword he was holding between his thighs.

"What have you got, Papi?"

"The sword of our liberator, Simón Bolívar."

"What are you going to do with it? Hang it in the bar with the other swords?" I asked, not giving it much thought.

"I'm going to give it to you so you can put it in your room. Take good care of it; that sword's got a lot of history. Go on, but be careful. Don't start fooling around with it."

It was a month before my ninth birthday, and I have to admit my father's gift didn't interest me much. At that age, I preferred motorcycles and other toys. But I plastered on a smile and tried it out on the shrubbery.

The famous sword of the liberator Simón Bolívar turned out to be heavy and dull. It didn't slice through the bushes like I wanted it to, so I put the sword in my room at the Nápoles estate. I have only vague memories of it, as I was always surrounded by dozens of toys.

Bolívar's sword met a fate that is inevitable when a child receives such a gift. It ended up stashed away somewhere at some farm or apartment my father owned. I lost track of it because I didn't care about it.

Five years later, in mid-January 1991, Otto and Stud would

arrive with a message from my father telling me to return the sword. I refused at first and said that gifts couldn't be taken back. Patiently, they asked me to call my father about it.

"Son, return the sword," he said. "I have to deliver it to the friends who gave it to me. They need it so they can return it as a gesture of goodwill. Where is it?"

"I don't remember where it ended up," I said, "but I know it's around somewhere. I'll look for it and let you know if I find it in the next couple of days."

"All right, but make it quick. It's urgent. They already promised to return it, and I can't make them look bad."

I immediately started searching and sent my bodyguards to check the farms, houses, and apartments where we lived.

The next day, the men returned with the sword. Otto came to collect it right away, but before giving the sword back, I asked them to take a few quick photos of me wielding it. Looking back, I regret my attitude at the time and my lack of respect for such an important symbol of history.

Much later, I'd understand the significance of that moment. Having demobilized in exchange for pardons after the Palace of Justice attack, the M-19 had already relinquished all its weapons and gone back to civilian life. As an act of goodwill, they had promised to give back the stolen sword. On January 31, 1991, after more than fifteen years, Antonio Navarro Wolff and other members of the M-19 would return the sword in a special ceremony attended by then-president César Gaviria. But my father's war was just beginning.

EVEN AFTER BELISARIO BETANCUR'S EMBATTLED ADMINISTRATION came to an end in August 1986, my father wouldn't abandon his plan to exact revenge on him. Quite the opposite.

The idea was to kidnap Betancur and hold him captive in the

jungle. My father ordered a man known as "Godoy" to travel by helicopter deep into the jungle between Chocó and Urabá, make a clearing in the vegetation, and build a small, windowless cabin. Godoy found a spot and worked there for weeks with two other men. Supplies were dropped down to them by helicopter. Godoy had finished the project and was heading back to tell my father that the cabin was ready when a group of indigenous people unexpectedly passed through, startled to see white people in their territory. When he found out, my father said they had to go even deeper into the jungle to make sure nobody would ever see it. The new cabin was finished two months later. Nonetheless, despite numerous attempts, my father told me that Socket and the Bird were never able to kidnap Betancur. His cruel plan fortunately would never come to fruition.

11

Barbarity

Can you imagine some guy with a typewriter saying, 'Pablo Escobar Gaviria is being extradited to the United States'? I'm not about to let them extradite me. Me, young and rich, in a gringo jail? They don't know what they've got coming to them."

My mother didn't really know what my father meant with that statement, but she didn't ask; she was used to his secretive and cryptic manner.

Those first weeks of January 1986 were peaceful ones for us, the product of my father's repeated strategy of eliminating any obstacle that appeared in his path. With the occupation of the Palace of Justice two months earlier, his worries had evaporated.

In addition, Colombia was too busy caring for the thousands of families affected by the eruption of the Nevado del Ruiz volcano and rebuilding the high courts to worry about the Mafia. The government and police were so distracted that they didn't notice that my father loaned two of his helicopters to the relief effort, ordering the pilots to suspend all cocaine transport and help with whatever the aid organizations needed. We even saw the two aircraft on the news several times. Nevertheless, my father made it violently clear that he had no problem giving with one hand and taking away with the other.

And he continued to send that message on February 19, 1986,

when his men assassinated the pilot Barry Seal. My father had assigned Razor, a dangerous criminal from La Estrella, to organize the attack at any cost. "That guy's going to pay for it. . . . He's not getting out of this alive," my father assured him. Razor settled in Miami for a long time, trying to scrounge up information on Seal.

It wasn't such an easy task. The American pilot was a protected DEA witness. They had quite possibly given him a new identity, and he could be living anywhere in the country. Finally, my father's narco contacts in Miami informed Razor that Seal had refused to abide by U.S. authorities' security protocols and had instead gone on living as usual. They also told him exactly where: Baton Rouge, Louisiana.

Razor dispatched three *sicarios*, who shot Seal as he was getting into his white Cadillac in the parking lot of a Salvation Army community clinic. Two days later, Razor informed my father that the *sicarios* had been arrested on their way to the Miami airport. A long prison sentence awaited them. My father had known that there might be hell to pay because of this assassination, but his desire to avenge Seal's betrayal had been too powerful to resist.

From the day my father turned criminal, we never knew when he gave the order to commit a particular crime or have someone killed. He was adept at keeping his business dealings and criminal activity separate from his family life, and that was the case till the end of his days. We hadn't known that he'd sentenced Barry Seal to death, much less that his men were the culprits. He was always able to maintain his composure.

Five days after Seal's murder, on my ninth birthday, my father wrote me a two-page letter with advice that revealed much about who he was:

> *You're turning nine years old today. You're a man now, and that means a lot of responsibilities. On this day, I want to tell you that life has beautiful moments, but it has tough, difficult*

moments too. Those tough moments are the ones that make
us men. I know with absolute certainty that you have always
faced the difficult moments in your life with great dignity and
courage ...

That was my father. A man who could write beautiful letters and
who would go to any lengths for his family, but who could also
wreak terrible havoc. In his own way, he always had us in his heart,
even as he used terror to intimidate his enemies. He didn't hold
back in either area of his life.

Lurking in the background of his senseless violence was always the threat of extradition, which would take a big fight to get
erased from the national constitution. My father made full use of
the army of criminals he had at his command. And nothing could
stop him.

In northern Bogotá, a week before Belisario Betancur handed
off the presidential sash to Virgilio Barco, my father's men murdered a magistrate from the Criminal Bench of the Supreme Court
of Justice, which had ruled in favor of a number of extraditions. In
Medellín, they also shot a magistrate from the Superior Court of
Antioquia, which had ordered that my father be investigated for
the death of two DAS detectives.

With these two carefully targeted murders, my father sent the
signal that he would be merciless with any judge who followed
through on applying the extradition agreement or initiated judicial
proceedings against him.

To send yet another message, on November 6, 1986, a year after
the attack on the Palace of Justice, my father announced the for-
mation of the Extraditables, a secret group whose mission was to
fight extradition. The truth is that *he* was the Extraditables. There
was never a larger organization behind it. He came up with its slo-
gan, "Better a grave in Colombia than a cell in the United States."
From the Extraditables' very first press release, my father consulted

a dictionary to choose just the right words for the group's statements. He was also careful to use proper spelling and grammar.

My father assumed leadership of the Extraditables. He didn't consult with anyone about the contents of his communiqués or his military decisions, but he did charge the narcos monthly fees to finance the war. Some of them, such as the Mexican and Fidel Castaño, made substantial contributions. On November 17, the Mexican executed his plot to get revenge on the police colonel Jaime Ramírez, who had headed up the operation to destroy the Mexican's labs around the country. Other narcos were stingy, and my father would call them up in a menacing tone to remind them of their debt.

Extradition came to loom so large in my father's life that once he even dreamed that he'd been captured during a raid and was being extradited almost immediately. So he devised a plan to deal with that possibility in the event that it happened: He would hijack a school bus in Washington, D.C., and threaten to blow it up. And he'd go through with it, if necessary.

Soon, the murders, the intimidations, and the creation of the Extraditables led to the Mafia's first victory over extradition. On December 12, 1986, the twenty-four magistrates of the Supreme Court of Justice held that the law upholding the 1979 treaty with the United States was illegal because it had been signed not by President Julio César Turbay but by Germán Zea Hernández, the government minister who had been carrying out presidential duties at the time.

My father and the other narcos celebrated the decision, as it automatically invalidated the warrants out for their arrest, but they hadn't foreseen that President Barco would now turn to an old treaty with the United States: one that allowed the administration to extradite individuals without judicial approval.

An editorial in Bogotá's *El Espectador* touting the president's decision to restore extradition as a victory in the fight against the cartels infuriated my father, and he revived his old plan to seek payback for the newspaper's negative coverage. *El Espectador* gave the following account of my father's retaliation: "The crime took place at 7:15 P.M., when [*El Espectador* editor in chief] Don Guill-ermo Cano, behind the wheel of his vehicle, slowed down to turn north at the intersection of Carrera 68 and Calle 22. He was caught off guard by a man waiting for him at the end of the median in the crowded thoroughfare, who fired repeatedly into the driver's-side window."

When the sculptor Rodrigo Arenas Betancourt later donated a memorial bust of Cano to the Medellín city government, which placed it in Bolívar Park, my father considered that homage an insult. "We can't let them erect a statue of Guillermo Cano in Antioquia," he said once while smoking his nightly dose of mari-juana. He was sitting with Shooter, who offered to blow up the sculpture for free. And when the family rebuilt the bust and rein-stalled it in the park, Shooter again volunteered to destroy it, this time using a larger quantity of explosives. The sculpture was re-moved for good.

El Espectador was such a thorn in my father's side that he ordered his men to set fire to the newspaper delivery vehicles in Medellín and threaten the newspaper sellers in the streets. *El Espectador* soon disappeared from the city.

Retaliation against Cano and *El Espectador* would continue for years to come. When my father learned that the justice department had obtained several pieces of evidence identifying him as the mastermind of Cano's murder, he arranged the assassination of the lawyer representing the Cano family in the investigation. Two gunmen riddled his car with bullets in Bogotá on the morning of March 29, 1989. And at six thirty in the morning on Saturday, Sep-tember 2, Don Germán, a sixty-year-old man who belonged to Pinina's squad, blew up a truck loaded with almost seven hundred pounds of dynamite in a gas station across from the main entrance of the *El Espectador* offices in Bogotá. A few hours later, the Cano family's vacation home in the Rosario Islands was also destroyed.

After the murder of Guillermo Cano, we hid for several weeks at La Isla, by the El Peñol reservoir. I remember one morning I saw my father sitting at a table with Carlos Lehder, Fidel Castaño, and Gerardo "Kiko" Moncada, all poring over a book and taking notes. Though I didn't know what was going on and didn't dare to ask, I did catch a glimpse of the title: *The Man Who Made It Snow*. Years later I would realize that the four men had been less interested in reading than they were worried about the contents of the book, in which the author, an American man named Max Mermelstein who is now deceased, recounted his experiences working for my father and other capos from the Medellín Cartel.

According to the book, over the course of six years, Mermelstein brought fifty-six tons of cocaine—nearly thirty million dollars' worth—into Miami and southern Florida for my father and his partners. But when the Miami Police arrested him in 1985, things changed dramatically. While waiting for the cartel to pay Mermelstein's bail, one of my father's Florida associates grew nervous and threatened Mermelstein's family, whereupon Mermelstein switched sides and began to cooperate with the American authorities.

In early 1987, my father's band of assassins would demonstrate that they knew no limits, though they weren't always successful. For example, there was the failed assassination attempt against Enrique Parejo, the Colombian ambassador to Hungary. My father wanted him dead, according to what I've heard, because as minister of justice during Virgilio Barco's administration, Parejo had signed extradition orders for thirteen people. The plan was difficult to pull off, as Hungary severely restricted tourist visas and made it almost impossible to smuggle in illegal weapons. The ambassador was so well protected that my father's men concluded that the murder couldn't be organized from Colombia.

I don't know the details of the plot, nor did I ever ask about what transpired, but on the morning of January 13, 1987, an assassin shot at the ambassador five times, seriously wounding him. By that point, we'd learned that all of my father's violent acts had direct consequences for us, so we always opposed them.

A few days later, we were coming back from spending the weekend at the Nápoles estate, which, though it had supposedly been confiscated by the authorities, my father was able to enjoy freely. (For much of the 1980s, "confiscation" meant that government forces would swarm in and take photos of themselves occupying the estate to give the appearance of taking on my father, and then abandon it a few days later.) My father was driving a Toyota SUV with my mother and Manuela beside him; Carlos Lehder and I were in the backseat.

My father had sent two cars ahead of us that stayed no more than a mile apart so they didn't lose the radiotelephone signal in the mountainous terrain. It was lunchtime and the day was clear, with few clouds. My father generally only drove that route after two in the morning, but this time, eager to get the family back to Medellín, he was driving during the day. He was confident that his men would inform him of any law enforcement presence when he was still 2.5 miles away, giving him more than enough time to escape. Over the radiotelephone, we occasionally heard the voice of Luigi, a young man from Envigado who'd just started working for my father. He had gone ahead in an inconspicuous car, accompanied by Dolly, whose job was to conceal the radio.

In an even voice, Luigi said they'd just passed through the tollbooth in Cocorná, halfway between Nápoles and Medellín, and had seen a standard police checkpoint with four or five uniformed agents. "There are only a few cops," Luigi said reassuringly. My father kept driving, and I wondered why he wasn't stopping, but I didn't say a word.

"Pablo, aren't we getting awfully close to the checkpoint? How do you plan to get through it? I don't think it's a good idea to go in the same car as your family, do you?" Lehder spoke up.

"Yes, I know, Carlos. Hang on. Before we get there, there's a curve in the road on the hill right above the tollbooth, and we can scope it out."

We reached the curve. On the left-hand side of the road was a restaurant whose parking lot offered us a view of the checkpoint without having to leave the car.

Over the radio my father instructed Otto—who was behind us in a Renault 18 with Crud and Tabloid—to pull in beside us so he and Carlos could switch vehicles. He wanted my mother, Manuela, and me to travel on to Medellín by ourselves in the SUV. Otto helped move my father's gym bag, Lehder's backpack, and the food my mother had packed into his car. The plan was that we would go to Medellín, and he would hide at one of the farms outside the city.

Lehder exited the SUV with his rifle and stashed his crossbow in the trunk of the Renault. My father had his Sig Sauer pistol at his waist and a Heckler submachine gun hanging over his shoulder. I remember that gun well: my father carried it everywhere. At night he left it beside his shoes, tied to the laces, in case he had to take off running.

My mother drove toward the tollbooth as my father climbed into the backseat of the Renault 18 between Tabloid and Lehder. They hadn't realized that two plainclothes DAS agents having lunch in the roadside restaurant had witnessed all of their movements. The detectives started running toward the tollbooth, waving their handkerchiefs and shouting that there were armed men coming. We were already in line behind two other vehicles, waiting to pay the toll.

When I looked back, I saw the Renault 18 racing toward us in the wrong lane. It reached the tollbooth seconds before the DAS agents. Lehder stuck his head out the window, holding my father's submachine gun, and shouted, "We're F-2 agents! Don't shoot!"

Naturally, the agents didn't buy it, and a huge gunfight broke out. We hadn't gotten through the tollbooth yet, and we were caught in the crossfire.

A police officer took out his revolver and fired at the Renault's back windshield; the bullet hit right where my father's head had been. From the passenger-side window, Otto shot at a policeman, who managed to leap into a sewer pipe. And Tabloid fired into the air with his AK-47. Frightened we might be hit by stray bullets, I threw myself on top of Manuela to protect her. Finally, I heard the sound of squealing tires and the unmistakable roar of the Renault 18's engine growing distant.

It was utter chaos. We could hear the screams of the people at the tollbooth and the police officer's cries for help because he couldn't get out of the sewer pipe, which was more than ten feet deep. A police officer instructed my mother to drive on without paying the toll, but one of the DAS agents intervened. He'd seen the men responsible for the gunfight exit our SUV.

They made us get out of the vehicle, their guns trained on us, and searched all our belongings. They rounded up the two dozen other people who'd been passing through the tollbooth at the time and put us in a small administration hut where there was only enough room for us to stand. Manuela cried inconsolably.

Minutes and hours passed, and we heard only the shouts and threats of the police. "You'll see what we're going to do to you, narco bastards," they said through the windows. "You're not getting out of this, you murderers." My mother asked several times for her diaper bag so she could feed and change Manuela, but they ignored her.

We were there for nearly five hours when a police officer appeared and said he'd take us to the Antioquia police headquarters in Medellín. He drove my mother, sister, and me in the SUV that my father had been driving only hours earlier. The policeman spent a good bit of the journey lecturing my mother for having had children with a criminal.

Colonel Valdemar Franklin Quintero was waiting for us at the police headquarters. We got out of the SUV, my sleeping sister wrapped in her blanket. My mother went to pick up the diaper bag, but the officer snatched it and grabbed Manuela's blanket, waking her with a yank that almost threw her to the ground.

"Take this goddamn woman and that bastard's children and put them in a cell," the colonel shouted, and his men hastened to obey.

"Please, at least leave me the baby's blanket and the diaper bag so I can feed her," my mother pleaded. "She hasn't eaten for hours, and they didn't even give us a glass of water at the toll station. Are we going to be treated that way here too?" My mother sobbed but the colonel just walked off. His visceral hatred for my father was undeniable.

Once the place had quieted down, a policewoman gave my mother a baby bottle. It was almost one thirty in the morning.

"Here, ma'am, take this bottle for your little girl. This is all I can do," she said.

Suddenly we heard loud footsteps and angry shouts. We didn't know what was happening, but it was clear it had something to do with us. A man appeared, dressed in a suit and tie. It was the lawyer José Aristizábal, sent by my father.

"Ma'am, I've come on behalf of your husband. He's fine. Don't worry, I'll get you out of here tomorrow. The most important thing right now is that I'm going to take your children home."

"Thank you so much. Take them to their grandmother Nora's house," my mother said as she handed him Manuela, and he tried to figure out how to carry her without letting go of his briefcase.

I followed him out. I remember that he was walking quickly and saying, "Don't worry, son, it's over now. Let's get out of here before they change their minds. We're going to your father. He's anxious to see you."

We arrived at a house on the avenue known as Transversal Superior, where my father's main office had been located for years.

He was there with Lehder, Otto, Crud, and Tabloid. My father came over, kissed the sleeping Manuela on her forehead, and instructed the men to take her to Nora's house.

"Grégory, stay here with me and have something to eat. Are you hungry? Or would you rather go to your grandmother's house?" he said. "Don't worry, tomorrow I'm going to get your mother out of there. That asshole who refused to give your sister her bottle is going to pay. Come have something to eat in the kitchen, and after that I'll take you to your grandmother."

After the incident, Aristizábal told me about the conversation he'd had with my father before leaving to fetch us at the police station. "I'll never forget the expression on your father's face. That's the only time I ever saw him cry. He said to me, 'Who's more of a criminal? Me, who chose to be one? Or the men who hide behind the authority of their police uniforms to abuse my innocent wife and children? Tell me, who's more of a criminal?'"

A few days later, Carlos Lehder was captured in the town of El Retiro in eastern Antioquia after neighbors filed a noise complaint against the house where he was staying. The police offered to release him in exchange for five hundred million pesos. My father was willing to pay, but Lehder refused. The government took advantage of that unexpected reaction, and within just nine hours they sent Lehder off to the United States without any domestic judicial proceedings.

The threat of extradition on the table once more, my father and the other capos focused their efforts on striking down the administration's interpretation of the treaty that permitted extradition. And they succeeded on June 25, 1987, when the Supreme Court nullified the rule that allowed extradition without judicial process.

The new minister of justice, José Manuel Arias, had no choice but to lift all arrest warrants issued for extradition purposes. My father once more ended up free of any charges.

With this reprieve, we spent the second half of 1987 together as a family, as we hadn't been able to do for some time. And in the best place you can imagine: the Mónaco building, where my father spent nearly three months straight with us.

For several weeks, my father moved freely through Medellín in ten Toyota Land Cruisers, each carrying four or five men armed with AR-15 rifles. Once, four police officers on motorcycles stopped the convoy to examine their identity papers and letters of transit. The occupants of the SUVs got out and started to turn over their weapons, but when it was my uncle Mario Henao's turn, he aimed his submachine gun at the uniformed officers instead.

"Pablo, these fucking homos are the ones protecting you?" he yelled. "Four cops show up, and fifty bodyguards hand over their weapons. These are the kind of lions you have protecting you? You're fucked. Do me a favor, officers, and return those weapons right now, or you'll have an even bigger problem."

Terrified, the officers allowed the convoy to continue on its way.

But that untroubled period didn't last long. In late October 1987, some of the Mexican's hatchetmen killed Jaime Pardo Leal, former presidential candidate and head of the Patriotic Union, near Bogotá. The murder of the well-known leftist leader triggered a new hunt for the narcos, and my father went back into hiding, holing up in La Isla and managing his business dealings from there.

At around that time he received an unexpected visit from Jorge "Blackie" Pabón, who'd just returned to Colombia after spending a couple of years in a New York prison for drug trafficking. They'd known each other since my father was arrested in 1976 and Pabón had told the other prisoners to leave my father, Gustavo, and Mario alone. Pabón started visiting my father fairly regularly, and they'd smoke pot and talk for hours. My father really liked him, and they developed such a trust that he told Pabón that while he was looking for a place to live, he could stay in an apartment on the third floor of the Mónaco building. Pabón was grateful, and a few weeks later he moved into the apartment, which my mother decorated with Italian furniture gathered from other areas of the building.

Pabón came and went as he pleased and almost always visited my father in his hideouts. During one of their chats, Pabón complained about a minor disagreement, and my father's attempt to resolve the situation would instead escalate it into a war. Neither of them knew it at the time, but a bloody confrontation with the Cali Cartel was about to unfurl.

THE EVENTS THAT I AM ABOUT TO DESCRIBE WERE RELATED TO me by my father. I'd confirm them with Cali kingpin Miguel Rodríguez years later during our peace talks, when I demonstrated my ignorance of why the war had begun. Over the years, people have spun a lot of theories about the root causes of the split between my father and the Cali Cartel. The story goes like this.

During one of his visits, Pabón said he was upset because while he was in prison in New York, his girlfriend had had a fling with a man known as "Pineapple," who worked for Hélmer "Pacho" Herrera of Cali. When he finished his tale of woe, Pabón told my father he wanted revenge for the betrayal.

My father, who was always looking for a fight, even if it wasn't his, supported Pabón and promised to ask the Cali Cartel to hand over Pineapple.

So he got in touch with Gilberto Rodríguez Orejuela.

"This cannot stand. Send him to me," my father demanded, making it clear that continued good relations between the cartels depended on it.

Hours later, he got a no from Rodríguez. Pacho Herrera refused to hand over Pineapple, who was one of his most trusted men. The conversation turned into an argument that ended with one of my father's favorite mottos: "Anyone who's not with me is against me."

My father surreptitiously reinforced his security measures and ours. In this tense atmosphere, at the end of 1987, I celebrated my first communion in the Mónaco building with a party that my mother had spent a year planning. My father was in attendance with Fidel Castaño and Gerardo "Kiko" Moncada, but they stayed only for an hour before heading to El Paraíso, a hideout in the hills of San Lucas in Medellín.

The new year began chaotically. On January 5, 1988, the new justice minister, Enrique Low Murtra, reinstated the warrants for extradition for my father, the Mexican, and the Ochoa brothers. With the law breathing down his neck again, my father visited the Mónaco building unannounced at dawn one morning. I remember that we saw him only briefly. My mother had invited him to see her most recent acquisition: a huge oil painting by the Chilean artist Claudio Bravo. The funny thing about that sale was that Bogotá's Quintana Gallery had offered to sell the painting to her for a significantly larger sum than she'd paid, but when the gallery found out my mother had already purchased the painting, it called to offer to buy the painting from her for the sale price it had originally proposed to her because it had already negotiated to sell it to a narco for an even higher price.

"No, sweetheart, you keep it. Don't sell that painting, it's beautiful. Don't sell it," my father said when she recounted the story of the transaction.

In hiding once more, my father moved on to a new phase in his fight with the government. Now he would turn to kidnapping political leaders and journalists to put pressure on the government.

He spent long hours watching television in the hideouts and concluded that Andrés Pastrana Arango would be a good target. He fit the bill in a number of ways: he was a journalist, a landholder, the former director of the news program *TV Hoy*, a mayoral candidate for Bogotá, and the son of former Conservative president Misael Pastrana Borrero. My father sent Pinina to Bogotá to abduct him. The men Pinina brought with him included Giovanni,

Popeye, and others from Lovaina, Campo Valdés, and Manrique. My father remained behind to wait for the operation to unfold.

But at dawn on Wednesday, January 13, 1988, we were caught off guard by the explosion of a car bomb at our building. At the time, my father was hiding at El Bizcocho, a farm up on the La Loma de los Balsos Road, from which our eight-story building was visible. When the explosion occurred, he, my uncles Roberto and Mario, and Crud felt the earth shake and saw an enormous mushroom-shaped cloud rise up in the distance.

In the apartment, we didn't hear a sound. My mother and I were sleeping in the guestroom that night because the master bedroom was being remodeled. The concrete slab of the roof collapsed and pinned us to the bed, but luckily one of the corners caught on a small sculpture by the great Fernando Botero that was sitting on the nightstand.

I woke up because I was struggling to breathe. I couldn't move. My mother responded to my cries and told me to be patient while she tried to free herself from the rubble. A few minutes later, she managed to escape and went to fetch a flashlight. My mother heard Manuela crying and asked me to wait a moment longer while she went to get the baby. She found her safe and sound in the nanny's arms and immediately returned to help me. I tried to turn my face toward the window. I was still trapped between the concrete and the bed and could hardly breathe.

Eventually, my mother was able to locate one of the corners and, with a superhuman effort, lifted the heavy slab. Shouting and sobbing, I wriggled free. When I managed to stand on top of the debris from the roof, I was startled by the star-filled sky overhead. It was a surreal sight.

"Mamá, what would have happened if there had been an earthquake?" I asked.

"I don't know, darling."

Once we were reunited with Manuela and the nanny, my mother

lit up the hallway to locate the stairs, but a pile of rubble blocked our path. We cried out for help, and after a few minutes several bodyguards arrived and cleared a small opening in the wreckage.

Just then, the telephone rang. It was my father. My mother talked to him, distraught.

"They've ended us, they've ended us."

"Don't worry, I'm sending for you."

A maid handed my mother some shoes, but we couldn't find any for me, so I had to go down seven flights of stairs barefoot, stepping on splinters, shrapnel, pieces of glass, nails, bits of metal, broken bricks, and all kinds of sharp materials.

When we reached the ground floor, we climbed into an SUV that one of my father's men had parked in the building's visitors' lot and tore out of there. We had planned to go to my grandmother Nora's apartment, but we opted to stop by my father's hideout first because we knew he must be worried. When we got there, he pulled us into a long hug.

Once the panic had died down, my father continued discussing the situation with my uncles Mario and Roberto, but his cell phone soon interrupted. After talking for five minutes, my father thanked the person for the call and hung up.

"Those bastards called to find out whether I survived. I thanked them for the so-called support they offered. I know it was them who set off the bomb," he said, referring to the possible culprits. He didn't specify whom he meant, but we later learned that the car bomb was a declaration of war from the Cali Cartel.

From El Bizcocho we went to the small apartment of one of my maternal aunts, who put us up temporarily. The attack had been so traumatic that for more than six months we were unable to sleep with the lights off.

Much later, one of my father's men who'd participated in the search for the culprits told me that Pacho Herrera had hired two men for the job. One of them was Germán Espinosa, also known as "the Indian," who lived in Cali. It wasn't easy to go after them on their own turf, so my father offered three million dollars as a reward for information as to their whereabouts. For weeks after the attack, criminals of all stripes would visit my father's office or the Nápoles estate to request information about the suspects. One day, two friendly-seeming young men came for the information on the Indian, and my father advised them to be careful because he was a very dangerous criminal.

A month later, when they'd return with several photos of the Indian's corpse, my father would be surprised by the young men's efficiency. They would explain that the Indian had been a real estate agent and was selling a house. They'd pretended to be a gay couple interested in buying. The Indian had fallen into their trap, and at their second meeting to negotiate the property, they'd killed him.

"We didn't believe in those boys, but it's a good thing they killed the Indian. That guy would have done us a lot of damage," my father would comment.

A few weeks later, I'd hear that Pinina had captured the Indian's partner, who'd driven the explosives-laden car. The partner revealed that the car had been loaded with 1,500 pounds of dynamite in Cali. With that quantity of dynamite, it was no wonder the explosion had caused such damage to the building and neighborhood. What's really incredible is that the Indian had the car bomb stored at Montecasino—the Castaños's mansion—for four days before the explosion. I should make it clear that Fidel and Carlos Castaño had been deceived by the Indian and had nothing to do with the attack.

Despite the authorities' manhunt, my father remained at El Bizcocho for several days rather than continuing his rotation of hideouts. At night he would gaze at the ruins of his building through the telescope and contemplate how to get revenge on the Cali capos. He determined that the first step was to drive them out of

Medellín by attacking their chain of drug stores, La Rebaja, and a number of radio stations that belonged to the Rodríguez Orejuela brothers. Then he would go after them at their properties in Cali and the rest of Valle del Cauca.

As my father prepared for the incipient war, Pinina called to say he'd caught the journalist Andrés Pastrana and would take him to the Horizontes farm in El Retiro in Kiko Moncada's helicopter the next day. My father and my uncle Mario Henao traveled there to talk with Pastrana, whom they planned to hold for a long time. The idea was to hide their identity, so they put on hoods before entering the room where he was tied to a bed. But my uncle messed up and called my father "Pablo," so Pastrana immediately realized who had him—not the M-19, as Popeye had led him to believe when he'd grabbed Pastrana from his campaign headquarters on Pinina's orders.

Given Pastrana's importance in the social and political sphere, my father thought that if he could kidnap other prominent people as well, the state would have no choice but to halt extradition.

Kidnapping served a dual purpose: it offered my father a means of intimidation to pressure politicians to repeal the extradition treaty, and it also provided him the money to finance his war against the government and the Cali Cartel, which was consuming more and more resources. According to what his men later told me, my father organized two groups to kidnap, in Miami, Chábeli Iglesias—the daughter of the Spanish singer Julio Iglesias—and, in New York, a son of the industrial magnate Julio Mario Santo Domingo. The plan was to bring the abductees to Colombia from Miami on a private plane. But it was never fulfilled.

While Pastrana was being held on a farm in El Retiro, my father set in motion yet another scheme to put pressure on the government: this time, by kidnapping the inspector general, Carlos Mauro Hoyos, who visited his mother in Medellín almost every weekend. Hoyos had taken office in September 1987, and my father had been waiting for him to make a public statement opposing extradition, as he'd promised during a private meeting. But he'd clearly reneged, and once more, my father assigned the abduction to Pinina, who recruited six of his best *sicarios*.

They struck on the morning of Monday, January 25, as the inspector general arrived at José María Córdova Airport in Rionegro on his way back to Bogotá from his mother's. But it all went wrong. The two DAS agents protecting the official fired back when the *sicarios* cut them off at the roundabout leading to the airport terminal. One of Pinina's men, Smurf, was seriously injured in the shootout; he wasn't wearing a bulletproof vest because that morning he'd had to return the one he'd borrowed from Shooter for another assignment. During the exchange of gunfire, Smurf hit the inspector general in the left ankle. A few minutes later, the two agents were killed, and Pinina gained control. Because of his injury, the inspector general couldn't walk, and the sound of gunfire had alerted airport authorities, complicating the situation. Still, they managed to take Hoyos to the San Gerardo ranch in El Retiro, only six miles from where Andrés Pastrana was being held.

As the hours passed, a massive search operation closed in around my father's men. When he was informed by radiotelephone, my father said, "Our only option here is to kill the inspector general. He's within the military's perimeter, near Andrés Pastrana, and we can't give the government a dual victory right now. Let them rescue both Andrés Pastrana and the inspector general? No. No, we can't come off looking like a bunch of pussies. We're going to bring the government down a peg or two."

The original plot to acquire a more valuable hostage as leverage couldn't have gone worse. Pastrana actually ended up being freed when the police arrived to search the farm and my father's men ran for it. Pinina shot the inspector general eleven times, killing him.

That afternoon, on my father's instructions, Popeye called into the Todelar radio station in Medellín and made an announcement on behalf of the Extraditables: "We have convicted the inspector general, Carlos Mauro Hoyos, as a traitor who was willing to sell out the nation. You can be sure this war isn't over."

Though his strategy had failed, my father devised new and more violent ways to fight extradition. At the same time, though, these events also served to give new energy to the forces hunting him. As his son, I felt powerless in the face of my father's brutal methods. He no longer listened to anyone's advice or pleas. There was no way to persuade him to stop.

IN THE MEANTIME, THE CAPOS OF THE CALI CARTEL MUST HAVE concluded that my father's forces were spread thin across too many battlefronts. They decided to go after his weakest flank: me.

After the attack on the Mónaco building a month earlier, my father had ordered that his new enemies' economic interests be destroyed, but they weren't going down without a fight. That may be the only explanation for an incident that took place on February 21, 1988, when I was set to compete in a motorcycle race through the streets of the failed urban housing project Bello Niquía, north of Medellín.

I was raring to go when ten pickup trucks full of armed men suddenly appeared and blocked the race course. My father climbed out of one of the vehicles and ruffled my hair in front of hundreds of spectators. "Don't worry, son. Some people were planning to kidnap you during the race by making you crash and grabbing you, since it would be the only time you'd be alone without any bodyguards around. I'm going to leave Pinina and a few other men here to take care of you. Go ahead and race." He kissed my cheek, patted me on the head, and wished me luck, telling me to drive well and strap my helmet on tight.

A few weeks later, a high-ranking military official was added to my father's long list of adversaries. General Jaime Ruiz Barrera's first act as commander of the Fourth Brigade was to direct a massive operation to nab my father. At around five in the morning on Tuesday, March 22, two thousand soldiers, three helicopter gunships, and several tanks took over El Bizcocho.

My father and ten of his men were sleeping at the time. A peasant couple acting as lookouts warned them about the soldiers over the radio. So did two guards hiding in the hills above the Vía Las Palmas, who saw the soldiers descending the mountain toward the hideout.

My father managed to escape along with Otto, Albeiro "the Champion" Areiza, and seven other bodyguards, but they had two major scares on their way to another hideout. The first came as they were creeping across the mountain and suddenly encountered a soldier in the brush, who stabbed his rifle barrel against my father's chest and ordered the men to raise their hands and not to move.

My father, unfazed, stood up to talk to the soldier. "Relax, man, relax, we're all going to turn ourselves in. See, I've got one, two, three men with me," he said, and as three of his men moved forward to distract the soldiers, my father made his escape with Otto and the Champion. The soldier saw through the ruse, however, and got off several shots that came very close to hitting my father. He once told me that he could feel death at that moment, that the bullets were so close they kicked up dirt that hit him in the face.

They were able to get away unscathed. A quarter mile down the road, when the group reached the Las Palmas highway, another soldier tried to intercept them. My father pointed his gun and yelled, "F-2! We're F-2! Let me do my work, man, I've got some prisoners here! Get out of my way!"

The soldier, caught off guard, obeyed and moved aside, as if he were taking orders from a general. Then my father, Otto, the Champion, and two other guards walked single-file down the mountain, my father in front leading the fully armed men. That moment was captured by a photographer from the *El Colombiano* newspaper, who'd been alerted by the military deployment and came to see what was happening.

My father had gotten away, but General Ruiz Barrera had plans for his family. That morning, the army raided the Torres del Castillo building at the intersection of Transversal Inferior and La Loma de los Balsos, where they arrested my mother. One of my aunts was afraid for her and asked to be arrested too. They were taken to the Fourth Brigade's headquarters and were held there for a day without being allowed to speak to anyone.

Almost simultaneously, though I was only eleven at the time, soldiers headed to the San José de la Salle School for me. But when they arrived, one of the school security guards notified my bodyguard, and we ran to take refuge in the headmaster's office. From my hiding spot under the headmaster's desk, I could hear the sound of boots as the soldiers entered, asked for me, and then left.

Carlos, my maternal grandfather, who was seventy-six years old, was approached by soldiers when he was driving his Volvo down a street in Medellín. They seized his vehicle and drove him to a military base in Envigado.

I remember Popeye, the jokester in the group, laughing about my grandfather's car being impounded. "Thank God they took Don Carlos's car away. There haven't been any traffic jams in Medellín since."

After the failed military operation at the El Bizcocho hideout, my father issued the order to assassinate General Ruiz. Pinina and seven of his men rented an apartment near the Fourth Brigade so they could keep an eye on the general's movements. They loaded a car with powerful explosives and planned to detonate it as his caravan passed by. That was among the first car bomb plots in Colombia, but they weren't able to pull it off. They stalked General Ruiz all around Medellín, just waiting for him to drive past the car bomb so they could set it off by remote control. The officer was very clever in his movements, so their opportunities were limited. Whenever they did have the chance, at least five times in total, the remote control would fail.

At one point, one of the general's secretaries, who handled sensitive information, became ensnared in my father's quest for revenge. After following her for several days, Pinina told my father that when she left in the afternoon, she always took a taxi at the entrance to the brigade headquarters. They put several of my father's taxis into service at that hour of day, until she finally climbed into one and was kidnapped.

A few weeks later, the army offered its first reward for my father, asking citizens to send any tips to a post office box. In response, he flooded the military with information to hamper their search. He sent one of his men to the La Paz neighborhood and paid numerous families to write letters providing wide-ranging and contradictory clues as to his supposed whereabouts. Each message had to tell a different story, with different handwriting and paper, and be written from a different area. To make them believable, my father paid to have the letters mailed from far-flung places. The purpose was that even if the army did receive accurate information, it would be buried amid the barrage of useless reports.

And the strategy must have worked, because for several months my father hid in relative tranquility.

Then 1989 arrived, and it would turn out to be a tumultuous year for Colombia and for our whole family, as my father's war against the government escalated.

According to what Shooter told me, in February, on the instructions of my father—and after a consultation with the Mexican—Carlos Castaño had attempted to assassinate the head of the DAS, General Miguel Maza Márquez, in northern Bogotá.

Shooter explained to me that Castaño was the right person for the job because he had informants inside the DAS. Castaño himself was even known to be a DAS informant. For several months he had provided vital information that had helped take down major players in the criminal underworld, and that role gave him access to Maza, with whom he had met many times. Castaño was able to obtain privileged information from both sides and use it to his advantage.

From what I heard afterward, my father and the Mexican had reasons to go after Maza. My father knew that the DAS director had a suspect relationship with Miguel and Gilberto Rodríguez from the Cali Cartel. And the Mexican resented Maza's condemnation of the paramilitary movement that he was building in Magdalena Medio.

The operation against Maza failed when Castaño's men activated the car bomb too early, causing the explosion to hit one of the vehicles carrying Maza's bodyguards instead, but my father ordered Castaño to keep his group active and make another attempt. A new opportunity came several weeks later, when Maza fell ill and needed medical attention. My father's men offered Maza's nurse a lot of money to poison him, but for some reason the plan never came together.

An attempted helicopter attack on the Nápoles estate by the Cali Cartel failed when the Rodríguezes' aircraft crashed. In response, my father told me, he dispatched Otto to the United States to learn to pilot Bell Ranger choppers, with the aim of ultimately bombing the Cali Cartel in retaliation. The course cost $272,000 and was taught near the port of Miami by a former Nicaraguan guerrilla fighter.

In mid-June, my father was at the Marionetas hideout on the Nápoles estate when the seven o'clock news announced that at the New Liberalism convention that day in Cartagena, Luis Carlos Galán had decided to rejoin the Liberal Party on the condition that the party call a convention to nominate its candidate for the May 1990 presidential election. In the same speech, Galán mentioned extradition once more and claimed it was the only effective tool to fight drug trafficking.

Though he remained composed, those who were with my father at the time heard him utter what sounded like a death sentence: "As long as I'm alive, you will never be president. A dead man can't be president."

He immediately contacted the Mexican and arranged to meet a few days later on one of the Mexican's farms in the Magdalena Medio region. After a long conversation in which they considered the legal and political repercussions, they agreed that my father would head up an operation to assassinate Galán when the politician made a campaign stop in Medellín. My father instructed Ricardo Prisco Lopera to go to Armenia, buy a vehicle, and have it registered to Hélmer "Pacho" Herrera, the Cali capo, so the authorities would trace the attack back to him instead.

Meanwhile, in early July my father's *sicarios* made a deadly mistake when they carbombed the caravan of Antioquian governor Antonio Roldán Betancur—not, as they believed, of Antioquian police chief Colonel Valdemar Franklin Quintero.

When he heard that the car bomb had killed Roldán instead of the colonel, my father was furious. I later heard that Tabloid had mistaken Roldán's car—a blue Mercedes-Benz—and bodyguards for the colonel's security detail, and his signal to his partner, "Sucker," led to a powerful explosion that killed the governor and five others.

My father's campaign to intimidate the judges expanded in the months that followed, when his men killed a judge from the Public Order Bench and a magistrate from the Supreme Court in Bogotá. As my father stopped weighing the consequences of his actions, the list of Colombians who'd died in this terrible war had grown longer and longer.

On August 1, my father heard on the news that Luis Carlos Galán would be giving a lecture at the University of Medellín. This was their chance. He ordered Prisco and his men to plan the assassination, which would involve launching two rockets at the podium where the candidate would be standing.

On the morning of August 3, everything was ready to go. Prisco instructed his men to park the vehicle purchased in Armenia—a Mazda station wagon—in a semiabandoned lot two blocks from the university. They would launch the rockets from there. But the plan failed when a woman spotted suspicious activity from the second floor of her house and alerted the police, who sent several uniformed officers to investigate. Having been discovered, the men abandoned the car and projectiles and fled.

My father called the Mexican, and the two of them arranged to meet up again. I later learned that during the conversation, they determined that a new attempt would be made in Bogotá, this time under the Mexican's command. The name Carlos Castaño resurfaced, since his plan to attack General Maza Márquez was still in place.

In charge of this plot as well, Castaño turned to his DAS contacts and obtained detailed information on Galán's security protocols and personal schedule. In mid-August, Castaño told my father that all was ready except for one detail: he hadn't been able to find a MAC-11 subcompact machine pistol, whose size and versatility made it ideal for the task. Two days later, my father sent a MAC-11 to Pinina, who passed it on to one of Castaño's men.

Through his informants at the DAS, Castaño found out two days ahead of time that Galán would be holding a rally in the main square in Soacha, south of Bogotá, on the evening of Friday, August 18, 1989. With that general information in hand, my father and the Mexican gave the assassination plot the go-ahead. The plan was to have several men infiltrate Galán's security team once Galán had reached the rally location. Castaño swore he wouldn't fail.

My father knew that there would be major blowback from the assassination of Galán. The government would come down hard on the narcos, especially him and the Mexican, who were known to be Galán's primary enemies. He ordered his men to bulk up the security measures at his hideout known as La Rojita, a red house along the highway between Medellín and the town of La Ceja in eastern Antioquia, where he was staying at the time. We had still been living in the Altos building, but we moved to 00, a penthouse in the Ceiba de Castilla building.

As usual, my father slept until around noon that fateful Friday. When he woke up, we called to inform him that early that morning, at around seven, a squad of six men under the direction of Jhon Jairo Posada, who went by "Tití," had mowed down Colonel Valdemar Franklin Quintero when his vehicle stopped at a traffic light in Medellín.

The crime had gone down in true Sicilian mob fashion: the *sicarios* had placed themselves in front of the colonel's car and fired until they'd emptied their rifles. According to my father, the officer was hit about one hundred fifty times. In those days, my father was always going on about Salvatore "Totò" Riina, one of the most famous members of the Sicilian Mafia, from whom he'd adopted the terrorist methods of car bombs and targeted assassinations.

That afternoon, President Barco announced new and more drastic measures to combat the Medellín Cartel's terror tactics. But the upheaval in Colombia only increased later that night, with the news that presidential candidate Luis Carlos Galán had died after sustaining serious injuries. Carlos Castaño's plot had been successful.

At dawn on Saturday, August 19, Fidel and Carlos Castaño arrived at La Rojita to speak with my father. We weren't there at the time, but I was later told that they talked about the efficiency of the men who'd participated in the assault and predicted that the cartel would now face a series of massive raids and manhunts. My father promised the Castaños that he would cover the cost of the operation that had taken out Galán, an estimated 250 million pesos, which he would give them in cash the following week.

But Fidel refused to accept: "Don't worry about it, Pablo, you don't owe us a thing. I'll pay for it as my contribution to the war."*
Careful not to stay too long in one place as the number of agents searching for him swelled, my father left La Rojita and went to El Oro, a farm a few miles from the port of Cocorná in Magdalena Medio. That's where he was with my uncle Mario Henao and Jorge Luis Ochoa when, at six in the morning on November 23, they were warned that several helicopters and men from the national police's Elite Antiterrorist Unit had just left the Palanquero military base and were heading their way.

As usual, my father didn't believe the operation had anything to do with him, so he remained unfazed. But minutes later, a helicopter gunship appeared and pursued them. My father had had his men place dozens of long poles tied together with steel cables on the ground, so the aircraft was unable to land. As they attempted to escape, the agents started firing from the air. In the turmoil, my father and Jorge Luis Ochoa managed to get away, but my uncle Mario hadn't been able to take cover.

That operation killed my father's closest friend, the only person he ever listened to and even feared. "I will be your most loyal

---

* As I finish this book, the politician Alberto Santofimio of Tolima is still serving a long sentence for his supposed participation in Galán's murder. He was convicted for allegedly advising my father to kill the presidential candidate. As I have already said elsewhere in this book, I do not wish to condemn, absolve, or antagonize anybody. From what I have heard, my father didn't participate in other people's plans, and it's extremely unlikely that he would follow the advice of someone who had previously been his adversary through his alliance with the Cali Cartel. Galán had garnered a lot of enemies among Colombia's politicians and drug traffickers because honest men like him, who refused to become involved in corruption and organized crime, were a threat to their interests. Pointing to a single person as being responsible for Galán's death raises serious doubts about whether Colombia is getting the administration of justice that it deserves—justice should offer a model of truth and healing, not the opposite. My father made his decisions without asking anybody about them. I remember that his closest friends had a joke that summed up my father perfectly: "Pablo was a very democratic man; in his democracy, what he said went."

brother," says one of the postscripts of a letter he wrote to his best buddy after his death.

With all of the government security agencies engaged in the manhunt, my father, holed up in another hideout, received a visit from one of his lawyers, who begged him to call off his terroristic campaign. But my father refused: "The United States brought Japan to its knees in the Second World War by bombing it. I am going to do the same with this country."

And he did.

Over the next few weeks, my father sowed chaos throughout the country. His men, who were becoming much more efficient at detonating car bombs and other explosive devices, inflicted serious damage at several political headquarters in Bogotá, at the Hilton Hotel in Cartagena, and at the offices of the *Vanguardia Liberal* newspaper in Bucaramanga, among others.

Convinced that the government would be willing to negotiate a settlement like the one attempted in 1984 after the assassination of Justice Minister Rodrigo Lara, my father asked the lawyer Guido Parra* to try to arrange a meeting with his godfather, former minister Joaquín Vallejo Arbeláez.

As bombs went off all over the country, my father, Vallejo, and Parra secretly met and developed a peace proposal: the Extraditables would turn themselves in in exchange for substantial judicial protections, including safeguards against extradition. Vallejo quickly went to Bogotá to discuss my father's offer with the general secretary of the presidency, Germán Montoya Vélez.

But just as it had five years earlier, news of these communications was leaked—this time by the *La Prensa* newspaper, owned by the Pastrana family. The year before, journalist Andrés Pastrana had been kidnapped by my father and then escaped during the res-

---

* On April 16, 1993, Los Pepes would kill Parra and his son as part of their retaliatory campaign against my father and anyone associated with him.

cue raid. With this disclosure, the government had no choice but to state publicly that it had received the Mafia's proposal but rejected it outright.

With the possibility of negotiation destroyed once more and the Barco government with the upper hand, Shooter explained to me, my father and the Mexican set their sights on the favored presidential candidate: César Gaviria. Not surprisingly, the Liberal candidate had continued Galán's support for extradition. My father and the Mexican once again had Carlos Castaño start organizing a new plot, but Castaño quickly realized that Gaviria's heavy security would make it difficult to attack him using the standard methods.

Castaño decided that the only way to get Gaviria was to take out the plane he'd be traveling on. According to Shooter, afterward, my father and the Mexican gave the operation the nod and Stud— as the prosecution noted when he was put on trial some time later—built a bomb with a powerful explosive inside a briefcase. At the same time, Castaño persuaded a young man from a poor family who had serious health problems, basically a terminal illness, to carry the bomb aboard and detonate it once the airplane had taken off. In exchange, he offered a substantial sum of money for the man's family. In the Antioquian drug-trafficking world, the young man was known as a *suizo,* a clumsy abbreviation for the word *suicidio.*

Shooter told me that Castaño secretly altered the bomb to go off not by remote control but automatically once the airplane reached an altitude of 32,000 feet. Though he was unable to learn the details of Gaviria's schedule from his campaign or security team, Castaño managed to confirm with the Civil Aviation Authority that the candidate would be flying that Monday, November 27, on Avianca flight 1803, which would leave Bogotá for Cali at 7:13 A.M. The airplane blew up as it was flying over Soacha, the same town that Galán had been assassinated in.

But Castaño's information proved to be incorrect. Gaviria hadn't been on board.

More than one hundred innocent lives were taken, and I never forgot that atrocious act. Over the years I've had the opportunity to meet many family members of my father's victims and ask for their forgiveness on behalf of my father.

MY FATHER'S ABILITY TO CREATE TURMOIL SEEMED LIMITLESS, and the government appeared incapable of neutralizing the army of assassins he deployed all over the country.

On December 6, 1989, Carlos Castaño had a *suizo* drive a bus loaded with dynamite into the DAS headquarters in central Bogotá to kill General Maza. Shooter later told me that my father had instructed Castaño to turn the DAS building to rubble, so Castaño had had the bus's suspension reinforced to support the weight of eleven tons of dynamite, which he calculated to be the necessary amount to bring down the building. Castaño's men started loading the massive quantity of dynamite along the floor of the bus up to the level of the windows so as not to arouse suspicion. But my father later noted that because of the way they arranged the dynamite, they could fit in only seven of the tons and had to leave the remaining four in the warehouse. The bus blew up right next to the building's main entrance, injuring a hundred people and causing enormous material damage. But they still didn't manage to get General Maza.

That night, as the TV news and official sources reported that the bus had been loaded with 1,500 pounds of explosives, my father remarked, "Those assholes don't know anything! They always claim it's ten percent of the actual amount of dynamite I send them."

The violent conflict took a radical turn on Friday, December 15, when my father heard on the news that the Mexican had been taken down in a police operation in the Caribbean seaport of Coveñas. My father deeply mourned the loss of the Mexican. He considered his ally a warrior who'd been there for him in good times and bad. My father was even the godfather of one of the Mexican's children.

Despite his affable appearance, Rodríguez Gacha had some eccentric habits. He had people disinfect all bathrooms with alcohol before he entered them, got manicures several times a week, and had toilet paper shipped in from Italy.

My father once told us that the Mexican had expressed concern for his life. They were bunkered down in La Isla, and the Mexican revealed that he'd heard that the police and the Cali Cartel had him in their sights because someone in his organization was ratting him out. He was so paranoid that he left La Isla and went by truck to a farm in the town of Barbosa, Antioquia, fleeing there two weeks later, sure that his enemies were catching up with him. My father suggested that he come back to La Isla, but the Mexican said he'd rather go toward the coast.

"My friend," my father advised the Mexican, "you should stay with me—the coast is way too dangerous. There's no jungle there to hide you, and the gringos can easily sniff you out. It's much worse at the seaside."

With the Mexican now dead and with no apparent prospect of negotiating with the government in sight, my father once more resorted to violence and kidnapping to confront the state.

Five days after the operation to take down the Mexican, with the country still celebrating the blow to the Medellín Cartel, the media reported that in Bogotá, my father's men had kidnapped Álvaro Diego Montoya, son of the general secretary of the presidency, Germán Montoya; and that in Medellín, they'd abducted Patricia Echavarría Olano de Velásquez and her daughter Dina, daughter and granddaughter, respectively, of the industrialist Elkin Echavarría, who was the father-in-law of President Barco's daughter.

After these kidnappings, the government secretly offered my

father a new opportunity to turn himself in. The Montoya family sought the assistance of the tycoons J. Mario Aristizábal and Santiago Londoño, who in turn asked the lawyer Guido Parra to try to persuade my father to free his captives.

Through Aristizábal and Londoño, my father got the impression that he might be able to garner special consideration in his prosecution. And so in mid-January 1990, he freed three of his hostages and issued a communiqué in the name of the Extraditables that acknowledged the government's victory and announced a unilateral truce. In a demonstration of good faith—just as then-President of the United States George H. W. Bush was on an official visit in Cartagena—my father relinquished a cocaine-processing complex in Urabá, a school bus loaded with a ton of dynamite, and a helicopter.

My father drew up a document outlining the conditions of his surrender, and the government began subtly delaying the processing of several extraditions. President Barco even noted at the time, "If the drug traffickers give up and turn themselves in, we could negotiate an agreement."

I often asked my father to find a peaceful solution to his problems and urged him to end the violence completely and focus instead on his family. Yet another assassination would stymie the possibility of a negotiated settlement for my father on March 22, 1990, when leftist leader and Patriotic Union presidential candidate Bernardo Jaramillo Ossa was murdered and Minister of Government Carlos Lemos Simmonds—who had accused Jaramillo of belonging to the FARC guerilla group—subsequently resigned.

Almost immediately, the authorities named my father as the culprit in Jaramillo's death. In a letter, he denied the accusation and wrote that he'd actually liked Jaramillo, as the politician had opposed extradition and was open to negotiating with the cartels. At the end of the missive, my father quoted an interview with Jaramillo published in *Cromos* magazine in which he'd even said,

"Everything gets blamed on Pablo Escobar now. He will be the scapegoat for all the evil perpetrated in the country over the next few years. But there are prominent government figures with ties to the paramilitary groups, and they will have to answer to the country for the crimes they've committed."

After his death, my father claimed that Jaramillo had begged him to intercede and ask the Castaños not to kill him. "Fidel and Carlitos are the ones responsible," he insisted, "but they're my friends, so I can't come forward and say anything."*

Minister Lemos Simmond's resignation revealed to the Colombian people that the Barco administration had secretly opened the door to negotiations with my father after the abduction of Álvaro Diego Montoya the previous December. The officials who had participated in that process—Germán Montoya among them—came forward to claim publicly that protection from extradition had never been on the table and that the narcos' only option was unconditional surrender.

Convinced that he'd been deceived by the administration, on March 30, 1990, my father announced through the Extraditables that the war against the government would resume. Over the following weeks, his criminal apparatus unleashed a terrible new wave of terrorism that was utterly unprecedented in Colombia. Some of his men said they'd set off bombs in Bogotá's Quirigua and Niza neighborhoods, in downtown Cali, and at Medellín's InterContinental Hotel. My father also ordered a direct attack on the police's Elite Antiterrorist Unit, a special group created specifically

---

* Fidel and Carlos Castaño were also responsible for the assassination of Carlos Pizarro Leongómez, presidential candidate for the M-19 Democratic Alliance, on April 26, 1990, as he was traveling on an Avianca flight from Bogotá to Barranquilla. This murder, too, was blamed on my father, but he told me that he was Pizarro's friend, that he'd liked the man and had no reason to go after him. Again, he explained, he couldn't deny the accusations at the time because it would have escalated into war with the Castaños.

to hunt him down. Two car bombs detonated as trucks carrying those agents passed by.

At the same time, my father kept detailed records of the violent acts perpetrated by city authorities in trying to track him down. There were often massacres in the lower-class neighborhoods of Medellín, committed by gunmen hoping to decimate my father's private army. One news program even reported that a military patrol had thwarted a massacre and arrested several DIJIN agents.*

In retaliation, my father decided to combat the Medellín police using two extremely brutal methods: The first, Pinina later told me, was targeted dynamite attacks using suicide bombers—the so-called *suizos*. These were people who started out selling small quantities of cocaine and were paid regularly to earn their trust. Later, they would unknowingly carry not cocaine but dynamite, packed the same way as the white powder, and as they went through checkpoints or passed police stations, men who were strategically positioned would activate the explosive by remote control. My father said the remote controls initially purchased on the advice of Chucho, the Spanish terrorist he'd hired to train his men, didn't work well, so he had his men buy the kind used for model airplanes.

The second method was known as the "pistol plan." This involved retrieving dozens of weapons that had been stored in hidden caches around the city and distributing them to gangs in the Medellín slums so they could defend themselves and also kill any police officer they saw on the streets. More than three hundred policemen were killed in a short period all over the city. The gunmen would receive a reward based on the rank of the dead officer, and it was said that all the assassin had to do to collect was go to one of

---

* In 1998 the Colombian government acknowledged before the Organization of American States' Inter-American Commission on Human Rights that it was responsible for the massacre in Villatina, a poverty-stricken area on the eastern slopes of Medellín, carried out by armed men later identified as being with the police. Seven young men between the ages of fifteen and twenty-two had been killed.

my father's offices with the newspaper clipping reporting the officer's death. "The only way they're going to call us to negotiate is if we create total chaos," my father told the lawyer Aristizábal.

Medellín felt like a war zone, and squads of armed men from both sides prowled the city. It was like being in a civil war.

At the beginning of June 1990, my father moved me out of the country under the pretext of watching the Colombian team play in the World Cup in Italy. He sent me with a family member, Alfredo Astado, and Pita and Juan came along as bodyguards. Afraid his enemies would track me down abroad, my father had new papers drawn up for me. He bragged that those documents would make it through any immigration or police checkpoint in the world.

And he was right. On June 9, we attended the opening match between Italy and Austria in Rome's Stadio Olimpico, and over the next few days, I cheered on the Colombian team during its matches with Yugoslavia and Germany in Bologna and Milan. I went to every arena with my face painted yellow, blue, and red; I covered my head with a flag; and I wore dark sunglasses that made me unrecognizable.

While in Europe, I couldn't help poring over newspapers and magazines, which arrived after an eight-day lag, for information on the turmoil in Colombia and my father. That's how I found out that on June 14, the police killed Pinina, the true military leader of my father's organization.*

The Italian hotels were full, so we traveled by train to Lausanne, Switzerland, and checked into the Hôtel de la Paix. I didn't go out sightseeing but instead stayed in and played cards with Pita and Juan. The hotel's concierge must have become suspicious of the

---

* The police announced Pinina's death with great fanfare. According to the official account, Pinina had engaged in a shootout with the Elite Antiterrorism Unit. But my father received an anonymous package containing several photos of Pinina being removed from a nearby building. They show him, his leg broken from jumping out of a window in his apartment, being led toward a gray Mazda by armed men dressed in civilian clothing.

foreign guests who never left their room, and he alerted the local authorities. At midday when we went out to get some air and have lunch at a Chinese restaurant, ten police officers appeared, searched us, and took us away in handcuffs. Outside the restaurant were additional police and no fewer than ten patrol cars with their sirens blaring; the block was cordoned off with yellow tape.

They separated the three of us and took me to a house belonging to the secret police. It had a cell with red doors and bulletproof glass. There, they had me undress and searched me a second time. Five hours later, a man and woman led me to a vehicle and drove me to another house, where they interrogated me for two hours.

They said they didn't understand why a thirteen-year-old boy would be wearing a ten-thousand-dollar Cartier watch. I explained that my father was a rancher in Colombia and that he'd bought me the watch by selling a few head of cattle of his more than three thousand five hundred animals. In the end, they found no reason to detain me, and I was soon reunited with Alfredo and my bodyguards, who had also been released. The police, embarrassed, asked where they could drop us off. We told them just to take us back to the Chinese restaurant.

THE WAR RAGED ON BETWEEN MY FATHER, THE GOVERNMENT, AND the Cali Cartel. On the night of Saturday, June 23, 1990, the same day that Colombia was knocked out of the World Cup by Cameroon, a band of men barged into the Oporto nightclub located on a rural estate in El Poblado and known for its popularity among Medellín's upper class. Around twenty men, dressed in black and armed with submachine guns, arrived in two black vans with tinted windows, intimidated the attendees, and forced them to walk down to the parking lot in single file. There, the men shot them indiscriminately, killing nineteen young people between the ages of twenty and twenty-four and wounding fifty.

Again, the authorities quickly fingered my father, arguing that he despised the Medellín elite. Later, while we were stuck in a hideout, I'd ask him about that massacre, and he'd tell me he'd had nothing to do with it.

"Grégory, if I'd done it, I'd tell you. I've done so many things, why wouldn't I admit to one more? There's an Elite Antiterrorism Unit checkpoint very near there, and the killers got through without a hitch. I think agents from that unit targeted that club because several of Otto's men used to hang around there. But only one of my men died there. The rest were innocent people."

Despite the luxuries we enjoyed in Europe, I was anxious to know what was happening with my father and what the future held, so I wrote him several letters. He responded with a lengthy note dated June 30, and I received it a week later.

Dear Son:
I am sending you a big hug and a heartfelt greeting.

I miss you and love you very much, but at the same time I am happy to know that you are enjoying your safety and freedom. I have decided to send your mother and your little sister to be with you because in the letter you sent you said you wanted everyone to be here when you got back, and you know the situation here has been getting a little difficult.

You must never forget what I've always told you: you must believe in the destiny of human beings. They are marked, whether for joy or for suffering.

In the paper I recently read the letter to President Carlos Menem of Argentina from his son, who condemned his father for having driven his family out of the presidential palace and accused him of lacking courage and being corrupted by power.

I was startled and unnerved by it, so I reread your previous letter several times and felt proud and reassured. All I want is for you to enjoy peace and happiness. And understand that sometimes families have to be apart for a little while because that's the way life is.

I want you to approach everything with confidence and imagine that we are apart not because of an unpleasant situation but because, even though we're such a tightknit family, I as a father have made a great effort to allow you to go study for a while so that the future will be brighter.

Let's imagine I've had to sacrifice a lot of things. Let's imagine we've had to sell our house to allow you to stay there abroad and study for a few months. How sad it would be for all of us if something like what happened with the president of Argentina and his son happened to us!

What greater sacrifice could I make than to endure your absence?

If you appear calm with your mother and little sister, they will be calm, and if you laugh, they and I will also laugh. Enjoy all of it. When I was thirteen like you, I didn't have anything, but nobody was happier than I was.

Don't fail to take advantage of this opportunity to study languages so you can learn things and be exposed to other cultures.

But be careful: remember that you're not in your country and so you mustn't do anything that isn't legal. Don't let anybody give you bad advice. Just do what your conscience tells you.

Remember that I have always wanted to be not just your father but your best friend.

Brave men are not those who drink a shot of liquor in front of their friends but those who don't drink it.

Please excuse all this philosophizing and such a long letter, but since it's Saturday I wanted to devote some time to you, just as if you'd come to pay me a visit. For my part, I'm doing very well. Lots of work, lots of organizing, but everything's going well.

We are making progress. Your mother must have told you, and I'm really happy because the torturers are being exposed. The most important ones have been stripped of their uniforms, and that's very positive.

I want you to send me more photos and tell me what you're doing and how you spend your time. Don't waste a minute. Enjoy life and walk around or play a sport.

If you play a sport, you'll be able to find the place where happiness hides. I'll write again soon, and I'll be waiting to hear from you.

I love you so so so much. June 30, 1990

When the World Cup was over, we traveled to Frankfurt, Germany, where we met up with my mother, Manuela, and other relatives. After visiting several cities, we returned to Lausanne, and my mother and I enrolled in a language school to study English till the end of the year.

We had attended the first few classes when we received a new letter from my father, dated July 17, in which, for the first time in a long time, he sounded truly optimistic about his personal situation and that of the country: "I've decided to change strategy and end the war when the new government takes power. The president-elect has said that he's not committed to extradition and that whether it's used depends on what the public-order situation is like, so the public-order situation will be good then. The members of the National Constituent Assembly will be chosen very soon now that the people have voted, and I'm positive that the first constitutional article it will write will be the one prohibiting the extradition of Colombians. And the best news of all is that when this change is made, all the danger will be over, and you'll be able to come home."

But despite the good tidings in my father's letter, on August 12, 1990, only five days after César Gaviria was sworn in as president, the police in Medellín killed Gustavo Gaviria, my father's cousin, accomplice in crime since they were kids, and loyal business partner.

According to Gustavo's widow, six police officers raided the Gavirias' house with the intention of taking Gustavo into custody. But when he hung on to the door jamb so tightly that they couldn't pull him out, they shot him instead. His widow also said that Gustavo had been unarmed and had even called Medellín's emergency services number to ask for help because he knew they were going to kill him.

Far away in Switzerland, in early September, we heard that my father had returned to his old method of kidnapping prominent people, this time to put pressure on the new and less experienced administration. We learned that a group headed by Comanche, one of my father's *sicarios,* had apparently kidnapped the journalists Diana Turbay, editor in chief of *Hoy por Hoy* magazine and daughter of former president Julio César Turbay; Azucena Liévano; Juan Vitta; Hero Buss; and the cameramen for the TV news program *Criptón,* Richard Becerra and Orlando Acevedo.

The order had also included instructions to abduct Juan Gómez Martínez, the editor of the newspaper *El Colombiano,* but my father's men failed when he barricaded himself in a corner of the house with a revolver and they couldn't get him out.

Diana Turbay and the others were held on a farm in the town of Copacabana, and as soon as she learned that my father was the one holding her, the two began to exchange letters. Comanche acted as their go-between, and according to my father, Pablo promised Diana several times that he would respect her life no matter what.

The strategy of extorting the upper crust worked, and on September 6, President Gaviria announced a dramatic change in the fight against drug trafficking. He issued Decree 2047, which offered reduced sentences and the promise of no extradition to anyone who turned himself in and confessed. My father examined the decree and told his three lawyers, including Santiago and Roberto Uribe, to talk to the government, as the benefit didn't appear to extend to him and the content should therefore be modified.

Continuing the intimidation, two weeks later, on September 19, my father's men abducted Marina Montoya, owner of a trendy Bogotá restaurant and sister of Germán Montoya, the general secretary of the presidency, as well as Francisco Santos Calderón, editor in chief of the newspaper *El Tiempo*.

Having amassed enough hostages to negotiate with the government, my father turned his attention to another front in his war. The Cali Cartel had recently made several failed attacks against him and, in the past, even two attempts to kidnap me. That was one of the reasons my father had sent us out of the country.

So on Tuesday, September 25, twenty gunmen led by Tyson and Shooter attacked and occupied the farm Villa de Legua in southern Valle del Cauca Department, as they knew that that night the Cali capos would be playing a soccer game there. In a fierce gun battle, my father's men killed nineteen people, including fourteen players, but Pacho Herrera, who owned the property, and the other cartel bosses managed to escape through the neighboring cane fields.

Back in Medellín, Shooter showed my father Pacho Herrera's personal appointment book, which he'd left behind at the soccer field. My father flipped through it and burst out laughing—the notes revealed that his enemy was quite stingy. He had written down his employees' miserably low salaries and kept track of even the smallest expenses. In the nearly three years since the war between the cartels had begun, my father's men had destroyed fifty branches of the La Rebaja drug store in Medellín, Pereira, Manizales, Cali, and other smaller communities, which had been sources of income for Cali.

My father also hired three men to analyze the thousands of phone calls between Medellín, Cali, and the Cauca Valley. The massive lists were supplied by workers at the local phone company. My father's employees would go through them armed with a ruler, a magnifying glass, and a highlighter, cross-checking incoming calls against a list of the phone numbers of the Cali capos. If the two lists coincided, they would give them to my father, who'd send his men to carry out raids and abductions. The same fate befell any cars driving around Medellín with license plates from Cali or other parts of southwestern Colombia.

In November, we received a new message from my father that reminded us that the war in Colombia was far from over.

"When you all left, I was really optimistic because Gaviria was asking me to call and promising me heaven and earth. I sent a delegate, who had an audience with the man himself for two or three hours. Gaviria's wife even wrote to me. But afterward they started coming out with a bunch of nonsense, and I couldn't accept that after what they did to my partner [Gustavo]. What happened to my partner was really destructive. They thought it would finish me off, but now they're running scared, and I know that everything's going to turn out OK."

We were forced to leave Europe in early December, when we discovered that two men were tailing us everywhere. I became aware of our shadow when we had to go to a number of supermarkets to find plantains. I immediately informed my father, who arranged for us to return to Colombia at once, suspicious that they had been sent by Cali.

We reached my father's current hideout, a large apartment on the seventh floor of a building on Medellín's Avenida Oriental, kitty-corner to the Soma Clinic. Also there were Fatty and his wife, Popeye, and "the Indian Woman," a sensual woman Shooter had recruited to help him with jobs and certain other things. Our stay in that apartment was extremely tedious. We couldn't even look out the windows because the curtains were always drawn. There was no cable TV, so we played board games or read books. We'd moved from confinement in Switzerland to an even worse one.

While we were there, my father shared some details on how he was persuading the government to grant him a reduced sentence and reject extradition requests. Of course, he had a powerful method at his disposal: kidnapping. His hostages now included Diana Turbay, Francisco Santos, Marina Montoya, and the journalists and cameramen from the TV news program *Criptón,* as well as Beatriz Villamizar and Maruja Pachón de Villamizar—sister-in-law of Luis Carlos Galán—who had been kidnapped a few weeks before by an armed group led by Socket.

My father had secured a commitment from the administration to modify Decree 2047. He and his lawyers had argued that extradition should be denied with the mere appearance of an implicated party before a judge, and they had relayed some suggested wording to the Ministry of Justice.

It is clear that the recommendations reached the Casa de Nariño, the presidential palace, as President Gaviria made reference to the topic on a visit to Medellín in that first week of December 1990: "We are willing to modify that decree—number 2047—because we are interested in bringing peace to the country. We are interested in having those Colombians who have committed crimes submit to our justice system. For that reason, over the course of this week, we are going to shed as much light as possible on the decree and eventually incorporate a few modifications."

Over the next few days, my father would sit for long periods watching the news programs at noon, seven and nine in the evening, and midnight, and he drove us crazy switching from one channel to another to find out what each was reporting. When we started complaining, he bought a split-screen television. That way, he could watch multiple channels and turn on the sound for whichever program he wanted.

Though my father was very interested in the terms of surrender offered in the government's decree, on December 9 it became evident that, as always, he had a plan B. He was paying close attention to the results of the election to choose the seventy constituents who would amend the national constitution that had been in place since 1886. When the National Electoral Council announced the winners who would begin their terms in February, a sardonic smile formed on my father's face.

"This decree business doesn't give me a lot of confidence. Even if they announce the changes I want, they can go back tomorrow and change them again once I'm in custody," he said. "But if the changes are in the constitution, they can't screw me over."

Then my father explained that in October—when we'd been in Europe—as the election campaign was ramping up, he'd received a message from the Cali Cartel asking him to join with them in promoting candidates who would promise to eliminate extradition from the new constitution.

"I told them to do what they had to do, to bribe whomever they had to bribe, and I would do the same," he said, adding that he'd already secured a large number of votes.

On December 15, my father arose at noon as usual and saw in the newspaper that the government had issued a new decree, number 3030. The newspapers published the text in full. After his brunch—as always, ripe plantain diced and fried and then scrambled with egg, rice, and ground beef—he stayed in the dining room and carefully read the new decree under which the government hoped he would turn himself in.

"Let's see if they've given me what I asked for," he said, and then lapsed into deep silence for hours. By the end, he'd marked up almost the entire text with a ballpoint pen and filled several sheets of paper with notes.

Sometime after five in the evening, worn out, he told us he had objections to several aspects of the decree and was going to send his suggestions to the government so that a new one could be issued. That same night, he sat down to write a long letter with instructions for his lawyers to take a message to the Casa de Nariño. It also contained instructions for what Pablo's advisers should say to the media in the name of the Extraditables.

Just as he requested, the media reported that the Extraditables had informed the government that they considered Decree 3030 a declaration of war and would not consent to it. Through his lawyers, my father insisted that the requirement that the narcos confess in order to receive reduced sentences and other benefits must be eliminated. He found the clause unacceptable.

Three days later, my father was surprised to learn that Fabio Ochoa, the youngest of the Ochoa brothers, had turned himself in and was already being held in the high-security prison in Itagüí. Three weeks later, Jorge Luis and Juan David Ochoa followed suit. My father didn't understand why his friends had accepted the conditions of the government decrees. Though he thought they had surrendered too hastily, he decided to wait and see what happened.

In early 1991, we were once more confined in the depressing hideout on Avenida Oriental in Medellín after spending New Year's Eve with my uncle Roberto. My father considered it safer to keep us with him. He was now prepared to go to any length in his war against the government because he knew that this year would be decisive.

The government still hadn't responded to my father's proposed modifications to Decree 3030, so, as Shooter told us afterward, my father chose to assassinate Marina Montoya, whom he was still holding hostage. We were shocked. And though the government had publicly sworn not to try to liberate the abductees by force, pressure from their families now led them to renege and provoked a major crisis at the end of January. In a failed rescue attempt at a farm in Copacabana, Diana Turbay died from several gunshot wounds as she was fleeing with the cameraman Richard Becerra. Though the Gaviria administration and the police claimed that the kidnappers had shot the hostages when the police arrived, my father always said he'd been very clear in telling his men to keep the hostages alive, just as he'd promised Diana Turbay.

A couple of weeks later, when the uproar had died down and my father was still publicly expressing his willingness to turn himself in, he received a message informing him that a large group of agents from DIJIN—a secret police unit—was parked in a truck under the Avenida San Juan bridge, 150 feet from the La Macarena bullring. Later, I heard Giovanni say that my father had sent him in a white Renault 9 loaded with three hundred pounds of dynamite. The car blew up, and eighteen people died: three noncommissioned officers, six DIJIN agents, and nine civilians.

My father was sure that the DIJIN agents also belonged to a secret organization out of Bogotá known as Los Rojos (the Reds), which carried out targeted assassinations against the Medellín Cartel. Despite my father's rationale, my mother and I thought he'd gone too far. And so, after the incident at the La Macarena bullring, which left dozens of people wounded in addition to the eighteen deaths—I asked him to stop.

"What's wrong, son?" he said.

"I'm tired of all this violence, Papá. Very tired and very sad about the deaths of all those innocent people. Our friends and relatives go to those bullfights all the time, and any one of them could be killed by one of those bombs going off indiscriminately, even grandmother Hermilda. That's not the way to solve your problems. It'll make everybody's problems bigger instead."

I remember the three of us were alone in the dining room. My mother hugged me as she said, "What in God's name are you doing, Pablo? Listen to the pleas of your son, of all of us, please, and put an end to these tragedies."

"Look, my love. And look, son. A few innocent people may have died, but I also killed a lot of people who have been responsible for targeted assassinations in this city. War is war, and some people are going to die. A person's fate is already written, whether for joy or for suffering."

But my father seemed to hear our point of view, and over the next few weeks he made an effort to remain in contact with the government and up-to-date on the deliberations of the Constituent Assembly in Bogotá. He knew that the extradition issue would be up for discussion in early June and that the assembly would wrap up its session and present the new constitution at the end of July. It seemed like a simple enough task, using the votes of the assemblymen that he and the other drug cartels had gotten elected to abolish extradition by constitutional mandate. The rumor at the time was that the Cali Cartel had spent fifteen million dollars, and my father five million, in their efforts to make sure that extradition would be struck.

A few days later, on April 16, I went to El Vivero, next to Montecasino, Fidel Castaño's estate, to celebrate the birthday of my mother's youngest sister. It was the first time I'd seen so many people gathered together for a social event since I'd come back from Switzerland. The guest of honor and I had practically grown up together as brother and sister. She'd invited some of her friends from high school, including Andrea, a beautiful seventeen-year-old girl. I was too shy to ask her to dance, but I asked my aunt to introduce us. From that moment, we started talking and didn't stop.

As fate would have it, my family had a series of first communions, birthdays, and other events during that mini-vacation. My aunt invited Andrea to each, and I kept flirting with her. After a month and a half of phone calls, flowers, and letters with poems, I took the leap and kissed her at a hideout on Avenida Las Palmas that offered a spectacular view of Medellín. Ever since, we have been united in a beautiful, passionate relationship that has lasted twenty-three years and counting.

Right around the time my relationship with Andrea began, the priest Rafael García Herreros paid my father a visit. It had occurred to Don Fabio Ochoa Restrepo that his old acquaintance might somehow sway my father to put an end to his violence, free the hostages, and turn himself in with full guarantees that he would be safe and would not be extradited. Host of the evening TV program *The Minute of God*, Father García Herreros was a man who transcended good and evil.

Don Fabio had told my father about his plan to introduce them, and Pablo immediately accepted. The priest agreed to become involved and even sent an initial hidden message to my father one night through *The Minute of God:* "They've told me you want to turn yourself in. They've told me you want to talk to me. Oh, sea at Coveñas, at five in the afternoon, when the sun is setting, what should I do?" The phrase "Oh, sea at Coveñas" became famous, but it was actually a sort of code between my father and the priest. In Spanish, the phrase is *"Oh, mar de Coveñas,"* and *Omar* was the secret identity of "the Doctor," a man in hiding with my father at the time who would pick up the priest at Don Fabio Ochoa's farm to take him to the hideout in the event that they met in person.

My father and the priest had exchanged letters expressing their interest in meeting, and for weeks *The Minute of God* became a medium of communication between them. "I want to serve as your guarantor to make sure they respect all of your rights and those of your family and friends. I want you to help me so I can know what steps I should take," the priest told my father in one of his messages.

While the country tuned in to the voice of Father García Herreros, we heard on the news that my father had once more demonstrated that he wouldn't forget those who had defied him in the past. Former minister of justice Enrique Low Murtra was killed as he was leaving a class he taught at La Salle University in Bogotá.

My father and García Herreros had finally agreed to meet on May 18 somewhere in Medellín. According to what my father told me afterward, the priest must have been afraid to attend the meeting, as he came up with several excuses to cancel, including claiming that he had lost his glasses and couldn't see anything. In response, my father's men immediately took him to the optometrist. Every excuse he gave was resolved in a matter of minutes.

And so the Doctor picked up the priest at Don Fabio Ochoa's farm. They were able to travel under the cover of a windstorm that was raging through the area, which scared off the police officers who were supposed to be manning several checkpoints along the way.

My father and García Herreros met at last in an apartment in the city after my father's men switched the priest from car to car several times in case they were being followed.

Things moved at a dizzying pace afterward. On May 20, my father freed Maruja Pachón and Francisco Santos, the last of the hostages he was still holding. Two days later, the government issued Decree 1303, which included all of his demands. The administration also agreed to allow him to be confined in a prison that he himself had built. My father had everything under control.

On June 18, 1991, after having spent several days in Las Vegas, Los Angeles, and San Francisco, we arrived in Miami, Florida. My father had thought it best for Manuela and me to travel to the United States because, although he was confident in his own power, he was afraid the government might use us to pressure him during this potential turning point.

Once we were checked in to a hotel, we asked our bodyguards to call our father from a pay phone. He was hiding near Medellín, and it wasn't hard to locate him through a UHF frequency. After we'd described the places we'd visited so far, my father told me that extradition was going to be abolished in the new constitution. The next day, June 19, he was going to turn himself in.

My parents met in the La Paz neighborhood of Envigado. He was eleven years older than she, and they had an intense, turbulent relationship that ended only with my father's death.

In 1976, my father was transferred to the prison in Pasto from Yarumito Prison in Antioquia, where he was incarcerated for drug trafficking for the first and only time. The guards let him leave the prison to meet my mother, pregnant with me at the time, and grandmother Hermilda at the Morasurco Hotel.

A few months after my birth in February 1977, my family began to reap the financial rewards of drug trafficking. My parents left the La Paz neighborhood and went to live in the best areas of Medellín.

To compete in the Renault Cup, my father bought ten Renault 4 cars and a mechanic's truck full of replacement parts, and rented an entire floor at the Hilton Hotel in Bogotá.

My father and his cousin Gustavo Gaviria bought these two expensive Porsches. They were shown in various exhibitions at the Renault Cup in 1979.

Over the course of the year-long Renault Cup, my father placed in races several times but never won.

My father and me at the Renault Cup.

My father and Gustavo Gaviria posed for these photos during a trip to Las Vegas.

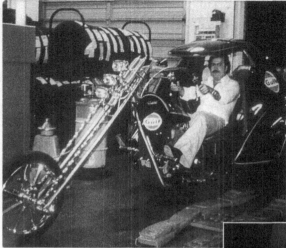

In Miami, 1980, my father bought this motorized tricycle for his motorcycle collection at Nápoles.

This dinner service with twenty-four place settings cost $400,000.

Wealth was on display everywhere: stacks of bills were included among the surprises in piñatas.

This previously unpublished photograph shows my father riding an elephant in the Dallas, Texas, wildlife breeding center. On that trip, accompanied by a large part of the family, he bought dozens of animals that were later transported to the Nápoles estate.

Although Nápoles was occupied by the authorities on numerous occasions, my father always arranged it so he could remain there and live as usual. Here he is riding a Jet Ski on one of the estate's lakes.

This original stagecoach from the American West was imported by my father and joined the long list of eccentric items at the Nápoles estate.

Nápoles was the start of my father's empire. It was a paradise where he made all of his dreams a reality. But he also used the estate as the headquarters for his activities as a drug trafficker.

For several years the estate was the preferred recreation spot for the Escobar and Henao families. We went there almost every weekend.

This photo, taken at Nápoles, shows perhaps the only time my father was drunk, after he consumed several cocktails known as a Rasputin.

My father and me in front of the White House in 1981.

My father and I always had a very close relationship. Not even his time in hiding drove us apart. He always made an effort to be there for the most important family events.

My maternal uncle Mario Henao was the only person my father was afraid of. They maintained a close friendship up until my uncle's death.

My father first became involved in politics in 1982. He thought he would be able to effect major changes in Congress. That was his big mistake.

Alberto Santofimio's political movement welcomed my father after Luis Carlos Galán sidelined him within the New Liberals.

In a lightning campaign, my father was elected as an alternate representative to the legislature in 1982.

During his political campaign, my father created Medellín Without Slums to build housing for three thousand poor families. As a fundraising event, he organized a large bullfight at Macarena bullring. Here is a poster for the event.

APUNTES BIOGRAFICOS
DE CUATRO REJONEADORES ANTIOQUEÑOS
DEBUTANTES

The bullfight at Macarena, which benefited Medellín Without Slums. To the left of my father are Santofimio and Jairo Ortega, and to the right are me, my mother, and my grandfather Abel.

My father was in Congress for more than a year but was forced to retire from politics because of accusations of drug trafficking. Here he is being sworn in.

President Belisario Betancur met my mother at a charity event in Bogotá. Afterward they had a long conversation.

My sister Manuela was born in May 1984. We were in hiding in Panama because Justice Minister Rodrigo Lara Bonilla had been assassinated a few days earlier, and my father was a suspect.

In April 1985, despite my father's legal problems, American Express issued him this credit card, good for two years.

My father had a close relationship with the M-19, so close that in 1986 one of the guerrilla leaders gave him the sword of Latin American liberator Simón Bolívar. We kept it until 1991, when my father returned it. Before giving it back, I posed for this photo.

The bombing of the Mónaco building, where we were living, set off the war between the Medellín and Cali cartels in 1988. Manuela, my mother, and I miraculously survived.

This is the room where my mother and I were sleeping at dawn on January 13, 1988, when a car bomb went off. The ceiling caved in on us. It was a harrowing and intense experience.

This photo was taken at Nápoles a few days before the extradition of Carlos Lehder. The journalist Germán Castro came to speak with my father.

Father Rafael García Herreros played a crucial role in my father's turning himself in to face justice.

During the year that my father was incarcerated in La Catedral, we spent almost every weekend with him.

We were able to reestablish our family life while my father was in La Catedral. In these photos, my father is wearing the hat I sent him from New York.

My father's cell in La Catedral.

It was difficult to be in prison with my mother. But we did have moments of joy, such as on her birthday.

I founded a business called Escobar Henao to sell clothing inspired by unpublished documents from my father's life with unambiguous messages of peace.

Meeting the sons of Luis Carlos Galán and Rodrigo Lara Bonilla was a historic moment. I asked their forgiveness for the harm my father had caused them, and they told me they considered me also a victim of the violence in Colombia. (Photo courtesy of Iván Entel)

To celebrate the International Day of Peace in 2010, the UN screened the documentary *Sins of My Father*.

The screening of *Sins of My Father* took me to more than a dozen countries. The documentary won seven prizes.

My father.

12

Tales from La Catedral

Don't worry, son, I'm doing well. Things are great. I need you to do me a favor and buy twenty-five or thirty warm coats and have them sent down here on a direct flight. We need them urgently. Everything is fine here. The men who are taking care of me are the same ones who have always taken care of me."

It was hearing the calm in my father's voice, three days after he'd entered the La Catedral prison in June 1991, that convinced me that turning himself in was going to be good for my father, for us, and for the country as a whole.

In that third week of June, we'd just arrived in New York, forty-five days into our prolonged family trip to the United States. My girlfriend Andrea had already asked for permission to extend her stay with me for the third time, which had caused problems with her family and at her high school, where she was in the process of completing her final year. I had promised to put her on a direct flight back to Medellín after we'd spent a few days together in the Big Apple.

My father's men had reserved rooms at the St. Regis, one of the best hotels in the city, an architectural gem from 1904. But I wasn't so sure about staying the night there. When they gave me a tour, the place didn't feel the least bit luxurious or elegant. Quite the contrary, I found it old and ugly and depressing. I must have been one of the only customers in the history of the St. Regis to take one look at the hotel and then leave with all his luggage. Of course, they refused to refund the money we'd paid for our five rooms.

"I want a modern place, boys, a hotel up in a skyscraper with a good view of the city. I'd rather be in a Holiday Inn than this old dump," I said, back in the car.

So we went to the Hyatt, which turned out to be just what I'd been looking for—a modern place and a room on a floor so high up that you had to change elevators to get there. The view was incredible.

It was a hot summer, and I quickly realized that I didn't like New York at all. It felt as if the sun had a hard time reaching the earth with all those massive shadows cast by the buildings, which seemed to be piled one on top of the other.

Endless and aimless wandering around the city made the trip tedious and boring, but I perked up when I discovered a huge electronics store right beside the hotel. I went in with my uncle Fernando and went nuts buying gifts for family members and friends back in Medellín: thirty of the latest model of Sony Discman, water-resistant, plus five photographic cameras and five video cameras.

That night my uncle came to my room and told me that the store owners had invited us to stop by early the next morning, as they wanted to show us "in private" some electronic items that we might be interested in. I was curious, so at nine we headed back to the store. As soon as they saw us, the owners lowered the blinds to keep other customers from entering. They must have recognized that we had money to spare.

They ushered us to a back corner of the store and set a black leather briefcase on the counter. Inside it were small boxes containing various kinds of microphones. There were pens, calculators, keyrings, and tiepins, all with tiny microphones implanted in them. There was also a very small camera for photographing documents, with a special miniature roll of film.

I was fascinated and felt as if I were James Bond being shown Mr. Q's latest technological advances.

I thought these devices would be the perfect gift for my father now that he was in prison. It was never easy to surprise him with gifts. He didn't like fancy watches or jewelry, didn't wear rings or chains. So I bought four wireless FM microphones whose batteries would last for a month of continuous use, a dozen microphone pens and keychains, two calculators, and the micro-camera.

When I asked if they had anything better than what they'd shown me, they said to come back the next day so they could check their warehouse.

The next morning they had new microphones with a range of 650 feet and a voice-activated recorder. I added four to the order. They opened a briefcase that held a receiver for all microphones within a one-mile range. I added one of those and told the body-guard to pay the bill.

My father's surprise was ready. It was just then that he had called to request the coats. Buying winter clothing in summer proved a challenge and took us all over the city, but we eventually found what we were looking for. Andrea helped me choose what to buy. We filled four suitcases and sent them with one of my father's men on a direct flight from New York to Medellín.

Two days later I received another call from my father thanking me for the coats but requesting more, and much thicker this time, because the cold in La Catedral was awful, almost unbearable. So we headed back to the same store, and after searching and searching I discovered the famous black, Russian-style fur hat that later appeared in a photo of my father inside the prison. This time I bought the best cold-weather wear they had, including hats and gloves normally used for mountaineering. Again, another employee departed for Colombia with five suitcases. When he received the shipment, my father called and told me he loved the Russian hat and wore it all the time.

I had traveled to the United States while Colombia was at war, but I returned home a month and a half after my father's surrender to a country at peace, at least in terms of the conflict between the government and Pablo Escobar. It was a strange sensation.

"The Nose," "Sausage," and ten other bodyguards picked us up at the airport, and as we neared Medellín, I noticed they had changed our route. We wouldn't be going to 00 but to the newly constructed Terrazas de San Michel building on La Loma de los Balsos.

Everything had changed. Apparently, there was no need to hide from anything or anybody. They didn't hand me a hat or sunglasses to disguise my features. When we entered the building, my mother and my sister, who had traveled back to Colombia two weeks before me, greeted me warmly while the Nose and Sausage brought in the luggage. Our new home had an amazing view of the city and was large and luxurious. I asked my mother about my father. I had arrived on a Wednesday, and I assumed that the visiting hours for the prison would be—as they were in every other prison in the country—limited to a few hours on Saturdays and Sundays. But my mother said that if I wanted I could spend the night or even the whole weekend with my father.

"There aren't any visiting hours there, darling. Your father has it all set up," she explained. "They bring us up there in a truck, and we can stay as long as we want. It's just like a farm."

I was startled by how comfortable my father's new life seemed to be.

Lemon picked me up early and drove to the area known as El Salado in the lower, suburban area of Envigado. I used to spend time in those mountains before my father had built the prison, so I knew the way well. We'd cook *sancocho* stew and swim in a stream of freezing-cold water below a sixty-five-foot waterfall. My father had bought a parcel of land in that area and built three hideouts on it. The first one was accessible by road, the second by mule or motorcycle, and the third only by mule or on foot. The third one, a three-bedroom cabin, took at least two hours by mule to reach, as you had to pass among marshes, chasms, and damp, mossy stones.

Halfway there, Lemon turned off toward a small farm beside the winding, muddy road and stopped in front of a sign that said "Tavern." Before me, I saw a huge parking lot full of luxury cars and a small, makeshift bar with pool tables, a jukebox, and clusters of tables and chairs. I'd never been there, but that land, which was below the La Catedral prison, was also my father's property.

I had arrived at the front set up by my father. Visitors would leave their cars in the lot and wait in the tavern for a truck to pick them up. Nobody who wasn't a visitor to the prison could enter the tavern, and nobody knew how to get up to La Catedral. The prison didn't have a telephone, but an internal communication system with underground cables ran from the tavern up the mountain to the prison. I hadn't even been to see him yet, but I'd already discovered that my father had installed what amounted to a telephone with an uninterceptable signal, which would prove very useful in the months to come.

Henchmen who didn't need to see my father to receive their orders could call him up from the tavern without even giving a password, as the system was considered infallible. The device also allowed them to organize trips to the prison, as the truck could carry only a limited number of people at a time. The truck was a dark-blue Japanese make with a secret compartment that could fit ten to fifteen people if they squeezed in.

Lemon's stop at the tavern was brief, and almost immediately I heard instructions for me to get into a private car. I was Pablo's son and didn't have to hide in a truck. It was around midday when I rode up to La Catedral in an old, red Toyota Land Cruiser with a white interior.

My father was wearing a white poncho and laughing mischievously when he came to welcome me, as if to say, "Look what I've pulled off here." We'd always greeted each other with a hug and a kiss on the cheek, and this time was no exception.

My grandmother Hermilda was already there, since she spent a lot of time visiting Roberto, her eldest son, who woke up earlier than my father. I soon saw more familiar faces than I'd imagined. Inside those prison guard uniforms were the men I'd been around all my life, the ones who'd always been by my father's side.

I felt like I was in a huge theater production where the guards and prisoners were all putting on an act. Some of the men who'd turned themselves in with my father on June 19 weren't even involved with him in any capacity. These gate crashers included John Jairo Betancur, "Polystyrene"; Juan Urquijo, a good-for-nothing from Aranjuez; Alfonso León Puerta, "Little Angel," who was unemployed in Cúcuta and asked Crud to take him to La Catedral; José Fernando Ospina; "Fatty" Lambas, whom Crud had paid to go to prison in his place; Carlos Díaz, "the Claw," a slaughterer at the La Estrella slaughterhouse; and Jorge Eduardo "Tato" Avendaño, from the La Paz neighborhood.

These men were so unimportant that on the day they were supposed to turn themselves in, they waited for more than five hours at the Oviedo shopping center for the attorney general's CTI agents to show up. They had to call several times to ask to be picked up because they didn't have money for transport.

Meanwhile, my father had already approached five guards who'd been sent from Bogotá and offered a monthly salary in exchange for their silence.

"Nobody hears anything or sees anything here. Watch what you say and don't cause trouble," my father said he'd told the guards before ushering them to a separate area of the prison, where he had no more contact with them.

Naively, I had believed that my father would stop committing crimes, and after spending a few years in prison, would come back home for good. I was quite wrong. Over the next few days, it would become clear that my father was regrouping inside La Catedral: reestablishing his military apparatus, setting up his drug-running routes, and continuing with kidnapping and extortion as a reliable source of income. And all of it right under the nose of the government, which seemed apathetic now that it had its number one enemy behind bars at last.

After a cup of coffee, I went with my father for a tour of the prison. Near the entrance were three pool tables, a ping pong table, and lots of board games scattered across the floor. Beyond were the dining room and the kitchen, with an opening in the wall through which trays of food could be passed between the two rooms. The men rarely used the dining room because the space was extremely cold, so they hired three chefs and ordered food to their cells over the intercom.

When we arrived at the health clinic section, I was surprised to find Eugenio, the doctor from the Nápoles estate, who told me he was at my service. At my father's request, he explained the symptoms of cyanide poisoning and how to use the antidote.

For a while now my father had been taking precautions because he feared his enemies from the Cali Cartel would poison his food. He'd brought with him to La Catedral two employees who would be exclusively responsible for preparing his food, which they did in a special separate kitchen.

From the clinic, we walked down fifteen steps and reached a long, partially covered terrace that provided access to all the "cells," which in reality were suites. You could see the whole city from there, and telescopes of all sizes were set up, including a fat, orange one that caught my eye.

"With that telescope we've even been able to read the license plates on the cars driving through the Pueblito Paisa. What do you think of that? Take a look, and you'll see how far you can see," my father said proudly.

I was impressed. His boast about the license plates was true.

The telescope allowed you to see many miles away with great accuracy.

To the right of the terrace was my father's cell, which was freezing like the rest of the prison. They'd installed wood on the floors and walls, but it hadn't helped. The cold was too intense—I could see why they'd needed the mountaineering jackets. My father's cell had a 250-square-foot living room and then, through a door, a bedroom with a large bathroom, also 250 square feet in size. Everything was top-of-the-line since the place had just been built. My father said he'd soon relinquish his cell to Otto, as my mother had started building him a new cell in one corner of the prison that was larger and had a better view.

I hadn't packed a change of clothes for my visit because I hadn't expected to be able to sleep over at a prison. To be honest, I was a little frightened by the idea. I thought if the authorities found me there, something bad might happen. But my father insisted that I stay and show him and his men the gifts I'd brought.

After guards carried in the ten suitcases of gifts from my trip to the United States, we met in the living room of my father's cell. His men all sat in a circle in white plastic chairs, and I took out even more coats one by one and started to pass them around. They joked around, pretending to be at a fashion show. My father also called in a few guards who didn't have warm enough clothing and gave them some of the coats.

My father thought the pen cameras would be extremely useful and stashed four of them for his lawyers. He said it wouldn't be a bad idea for them to use the pens when meeting with politicians in Bogotá: "So they don't forget the money I've given and favors I've done for them."

In New York I'd also purchased a few more personal gifts for my father. We'd spent many weekends of my childhood watching James Bond and Charlie Chaplin movies together, so I brought him the complete filmography of the famous English spy on VHS, which made him really happy. I also gave him a portable VCR that played European movies in the Pal format as well as the normal NTSC format.

"Grégory, have you ever seen a movie about John Dillinger? You know I'm fascinated by his story." My father said he was obsessed with the famous bank robber who had stayed one step ahead of American law enforcement for years. I hadn't seen the movie.

That night we went to scope out the new cell that my mother was designing for my father, taking flashlights because it was still under construction. As he was explaining where everything would go, I noticed he didn't seem convinced that the place would meet his needs. The men especially mocked a small wall that had been built just that day. "This wall is no good here," my father said and kicked it twice, knocking down a third of it. The bodyguards helped with the rest.

I remember that someone had given my father a waterbed. I slept on it with him that night, and though at first I enjoyed the rippling motion, after a while it was like spending the night in a sailboat out at sea. Every movement—my father's or mine—created waves within the bed that made me seasick. Terribly uncomfortable, I woke up with my back aching and my teeth chattering.

My mother came up to La Catedral the next day with a change of clothes and Manuela. From the size of the luggage, I knew we would be spending the weekend together as a family. That hadn't been in my plans, since I was really missing Andrea after our trip across the United States. It had been almost three weeks since I'd seen her, and I'd spent most of my time glued to my cell phone. I insisted that I needed to go down to Medellín to visit her, and my father didn't like that at all. My parents called me in to speak with them alone.

"Son, you know I never give people a hard time about money, but go easy with the travel expenses, all right? You spent a huge amount in a short period. You know we're not doing so great right now, and Kiko Moncada has been loaning me money for the war for a while. The one thing I know how to do in life is make money, so I know I'll get back on my feet, but it's time to show a little restraint right now. So go on and don't let it happen again," my father said, tousling my hair with his right hand.

I couldn't argue because they were absolutely right, but I did raise the point that I wasn't the only one who had spent all that money, since there had been fifteen of us staying in the best hotels, eating in the finest restaurants, and traveling always in first class.

That first weekend as a family at La Catedral had its ups and downs. When my mother saw that the wall of the new cell had been destroyed, she raised a stink and started scolding my father, saying it was disrespectful and that he just couldn't envision the design.

"Since you and your boys know so much about design, why don't you all work it out then? Count me out. Fix it yourselves," she said.

Whenever I could, I talked to Andrea on the phone for hours. Eventually my father couldn't take it anymore and pulled me aside.

"What's going on with you, Grégory, with that girl you're so in love with? You're awfully young to be in that kind of relationship. You've got a lot of life to live and lots of women to meet. Don't fall in love with the first one you meet. The world is full of beautiful women. You should go out with other girls and have fun. You're too young to be so in love and hung up on just one girl."

"But I don't need other women, Papá, I'm really happy with Andrea," I said. "I don't need to experience anything with anyone else. She's not my first girlfriend. You know I've had others and a number of female friends. But I've never felt so good with somebody before. So I don't need to go out looking for what I've already found."

"That's not good, son. It's not normal for you to spend all day attached to the phone, thinking about one person. She's not everything and shouldn't be everything for you. Go figure out how you're going to meet other girls, or I'll introduce you if you want."

This conversation took place in his bedroom. Manuela was already sleeping, and since it was clear we were arguing, my mother came in and asked what was going on. I didn't want to say anything. I was on the verge of tears with rage at my sudden realization that my father must be unfaithful to my mother. "Ask him," I said.

My father had been misinformed about Andrea's motives. It turned out some family members had been spreading rumors about her and had convinced him that she was with me only for the money and that the age difference between us—she was four years older—was a problem. But they were all wrong, including my father.

The following weekend, we spent another two days at La Catedral. I was in Crud's cell when suddenly, over one of the microphone receivers, we heard Dora, my uncle Roberto's wife, shouting and making a huge scene because she'd found women's lingerie in the shower.

Crud howled with laughter and rolled around on the floor: he'd been the one who planted the lingerie and the microphone in the cell. My father was aware of the prank and came to Crud's cell to listen to the marital dispute.

"Jesus, Crud, you've gotten Roberto into a heap of trouble now. He's going to kill you when he finds out. But don't worry, I'll help you smooth things over with him and Dora," my father said, dying of laughter.

The uproar was about to lead to divorce for Roberto, so my father and Crud intervened and admitted responsibility for the mischief. There were chuckles and glares. In La Catedral, the fun was always pretty mean-spirited.

With so much free time, my father often amused himself by planning pranks, and Crud always joined in on the fun. One day they decided to play a joke on Fatty Lambas.

At a meeting with several of his men, my father asked Fatty to please bring him a cup of coffee. Fatty fetched it from the kitchen, and because the meeting wasn't about anything important, my father told him to stay.

After drinking the coffee, my father pretended to be dizzy and started foaming at the mouth. "Fatty," he said, "what did you put in that coffee? Grab him and tie him up—he poisoned me! Call Eugenio and bring the cyanide antidote. Quick, I'm going to die!"

Crud picked up my father's submachine gun and trained it on Fatty while the other two accomplices tackled him and tied him up.

"You've killed me, you've killed me. If I die, he dies too, boys. Understood?" my father said dramatically.

"You poisoned the boss, you fucking sicko! What did you do, Fatty? Confess," my father's henchmen demanded as foam continued to spew from my father's mouth.

"I swear to God, boss, I didn't put anything in your coffee! Please don't do anything to me—I'm no sicko. How could you think that, boss? I was watching them when they made your coffee in the . kitchen, and they didn't put anything weird in it. Go ask the girls, but please don't kill me," Fatty begged.

Fatty wept through the entire ten minutes of my father's performance, until finally my father stood up, wiped away the foam, and showed Fatty the wrapper from the Alka-Seltzer he'd popped into his mouth. Once they untied him, Fatty hugged my father and told him he'd thought for sure they were both going to die that night.

A SOCCER FIELD WAS BEING BUILT AT LA CATEDRAL, AND LIKE all the other construction projects there, it was being financed by my father. He invested a fortune in it, installing a drainage system to make sure the playing field wouldn't get soggy and lights so powerful they were visible from a large part of Medellín.

Once the soccer field was ready, my father organized competitive matches with special guests who were brought in from Medellín. The goalie René Higuita; the players Luis Alfonso "El Bendito" Fajardo, Leonel Álvarez, Víctor Hugo Aristizábal, and Faustino Asprilla; and team manager Francisco Maturana came up a few times to play.

At one of those matches, I noticed that Leonel Álvarez was playing really aggressively against my father. He was being tougher on him than on anyone else, but my father wasn't reacting. Álvarez was obviously a very brave player—until Crud pulled him aside on the field and told him, "Ease up on the boss. The man never says anything, but he's already glaring at you."

Of course, the soccer matches at La Catedral ended only once my father's team had won. They could last up to three hours, and my father didn't have any problem stealing the best players from the opposing team to make sure he won. Although there was a referee, dressed in the standard black, the length of the game depended simply on whether my father's team was winning.

It's always been speculated that my father owned Colombian soccer teams such as Medellín, Atlético Nacional, and Envigado, and even sponsored some players. None of that is true. Soccer was always one of his passions, but he was never interested in becoming a manager or an owner.

My father continued to install luxuries and creature comforts at the so-called prison. At my father's insistence, my mother agreed to finish the new cell. You first entered into a living room with an Italian wicker sofa and a matching pair of comfortable armchairs. Then came a dining room fit for six people and a full kitchen with a stove and refrigerator. There was also a wooden counter, where my father said a little yellow bird came every day to be fed. I thought he was making it up, but one day I and many others witnessed it firsthand. The relationship between my father and the bird was incredible. It would hop down the counter, and my father would share pieces of bread or banana. The bird even let him touch it, and he almost fainted when it perched on his arm so he could stroke it. Then it hopped up to his shoulder and stayed there while my father kept talking. The bird trusted him completely.

I wasn't surprised by my father's relationship with the bird. He'd always given the birds the best care at Nápoles. At one point, when he heard they were going to be confiscated, he'd ordered Pastor, their caretaker, to open the cages so they could fly away free. At every hideout, my father always went out to the balcony, courtyard, or other outdoor space to leave food for the birds.

In the cell, my mother exhibited a couple of oil paintings and a small sculpture by a local artist who captured scenes from the lower-class neighborhoods of Medellín. There were also framed copies of the "Wanted" posters that the authorities had released when searching for the Medellín Cartel; the famous photo of my father and Gustavo dressed like Italian mobsters; and beside his desk, a rare photo of Ernesto "Che" Guevara.

My father's bedroom was accessed through a wooden door. In one corner was the bed, which had the Virgin of Mercy, protector of inmates, on the headboard and was raised on an eight-inch cement platform so you could see the city from the pillow. On the single nightstand stood a gorgeous, colorful Tiffany lamp.

A wooden bookshelf held a twenty-nine-inch Sony television and the collection of James Bond movies that we'd started watching together. Beside the window was his office area, with a desk, sofa, a zebra skin decorating the carpeted floor, and a fireplace to alleviate the cold. Then came the bathroom with a bathtub and steam room, a clothing closet, and a hiding place—of course—where he stashed money and weapons.

Soon La Catedral got a bar with a huge hot tub that would accommodate twenty people. Directly below the cells, it offered the same expansive view of Medellín. My father granted Crud permission to decorate it, and he filled it with mirrors on which were painted the logos of the major liquor and tobacco brands. He also installed a massive sound system. But because of the severe cold, the bar was always empty, and only on a couple of occasions did they use the hot tub, which was so large that it took an entire day to fill and heat.

The projects didn't end there. On one short trip to the United States, I purchased several remote-control cars that Crud had requested for the prison. (He already had several remote-control helicopters and planes, which he flew on the soccer field.) Using a pick and shovel, I helped him build a racetrack with various jumps and sharp turns for the remote-control cars. The two of us shared a love of motorcycles and technology, and we spent hours playing with the kids who came to visit the prison.

Beside the track, they built a pond ten feet across that we started using to raise trout. One day my father got furious with Juan Urquijo because he caught twenty fish in a single day. My father sent Crud to put up a sign with the following warning: "Anyone who takes more than one trout gets a fine: a bullet in the head."

Finally it was time for my father to appear before an anonymous prosecutor, who interrogated him about the true origins of his wealth and about his drug-trafficking crimes. To protect the identities of the prosecutor's staff, the interrogation took place in a building that was still on the prison grounds, but away from the main building.

My father attended the proceedings in the company of one of his lawyers. They planned to deny all accusations and force the state to prove his guilt on their own. They'd also agreed that my father would admit to the least serious of his drug-trafficking crimes and thereby fulfill the legal obligation to confess in order to receive a reduced sentence and other benefits. My father wondered why he should help the prosecution convict him.

"Please state your full name, date of birth, and identification number for our records," the faceless prosecutor said.

"My name is Pablo Emilio Escobar Gaviria, born December 1, 1949, and my ID number is 8-345-766. I'm a cattle farmer."

"If you're a cattle farmer, can you please tell me the approximate price of a head of cattle at the market this week?"

"I must request that we postpone these proceedings for another time," my father answered. "I have a terrible headache and won't be able to continue." He got to his feet and left without another word.

Back in his cell, he recounted the incident to his men, who laughed uproariously. The so-called confession process had been an utter travesty of justice.

In December 1991, six months after my father and the other prisoners arrived, there were several parties at La Catedral, but on Christmas Eve we didn't set off the usual fireworks to avoid calling attention to ourselves. Instead, they passed around large quantities of Cristal champagne. I received great gifts, like the Cartier watch from my uncle Roberto. My mother and Manuela told me their gift was a surprise and I had to go find it somewhere in La Catedral. I checked a few places, and then, hidden behind the curtains in my father's room, I found a brand-new Honda CR-125 motorcycle, perfect for motocross, one of my favorite sports. I couldn't believe they'd brought my gift up to the prison.

A few months later, I visited the prison with a newspaper clipping that reported my triumph in a freestyle motorcycle race. My father was very proud of my championship.

Not long after, the Antioquia Motorcycle League organized a car race known as a "quarter-miler," in which vehicles race in a straight line at high speed till they reach the finish line. I started practicing for the competition with several borrowed cars, including a BMW M3, a Toyota Celica, a Porsche 911, and a 1991 Ford Mustang convertible. In the days leading up to the event, when I went to register the vehicles, I met dozens of curious passersby who would come check out the cars and ask questions about the race. Amongst this crowd of people, I spotted two men who clearly were interested not in the race but in me and my bodyguards. To avoid trouble, I decided to get out of there, and the two bodyguards stayed behind to investigate.

When I left, driving the speedy Toyota Celica, I encountered something even stranger: an ambulance parked outside the main door of the Motorcycle League headquarters. It turned out to be the same ambulance I had eluded a few days earlier on the way to my private high school. I found it suspicious since it was seven in the morning and a relatively sparse area, and just as a precaution I avoided it, making a quick U-turn.

My father knew I was going to compete, and whenever that happened he always ordered his men to put extra security on me, as the risks were greater in public places. I remember my father repeatedly stating that he was tired of trying to keep the Cali Cartel from kidnapping me. He was certain that if I fell into his enemies' hands, they'd charge him a huge ransom and then kill me anyway. He also used to say that he still honored their old agreement that the cartels would not attack each other's family members. Even though he knew the movements and whereabouts of every son, daughter, father, mother, uncle, cousin, and friend of all the capos, he claimed, he would never hurt them unless they touched me or Manuela.

With my security bulked up, I continued my preparation for the race, but my father suddenly summoned me to La Catedral, saying it was urgent. "Urgent" was a term we didn't use every day, so I didn't ask any questions. I went straight to La Catedral, where my father waited, a pile of cassettes and documents stamped with the police seal on his desk. Unsure of what was happening, I greeted him.

"I have some good news and some bad news, son," he said,

looking me in the eye. It was clear he was sorry about what he was about to tell me. "The bad news is they were going to kidnap you at the upcoming race. The good news is that I found out in time and managed to track down the group that thinks it's going to grab you."

I went pale. The illusion of safety at La Catedral had just shattered.

"I need you to stay at the prison. Have someone send you some clothing. You can't go back to Medellín until I personally resolve this. I have recordings of these men. They think they're smarter than me. We've got all the details of the operation. The problem is, this time they joined forces to kidnap you. There are a number of soldiers involved in the first phase of the operation and police officers in the second phase."

"How did you find all this out? Does this mean I won't be able to race? It sucks that things have to be this way, Papá. I thought our lives would calm down, but I'm still caught in the middle. What are you going to do? Which law enforcement agency are you going to notify?" I asked.

"None of them, son. Those assholes will have to answer to me directly if anything happens to you. That's why I needed you here, so they wouldn't have the opportunity. Wait while my men confirm the last bits of information on the people who were after you. Then you can memorize their names in case they stop you one day and try to hurt you."

I went to get something to eat and called my mother to ask her to send clothing for a couple of days, but my father shouted that I needed clothing for at least ten. That made me feel even worse. My mother had no idea what was going on, and I told her not to worry, that we were fine and my father would explain everything when she visited.

When I returned to my father's room, I recognized that he was being extra cautious about the information he'd received on my kidnapping. He had only Otto and Crud with him. Popeye poked his head in the door and offered to help, but my father told him no, thank you very much, they were dealing with a very delicate matter.

"You know what, man? Why don't you give me a hand and bring us all a coffee?" my father said.

"All right, boss, I'll tell the girls to make some." Popeye turned and left, grumbling.

"Otto, please hand me the cell phone. Son, come sit next to me on the bed," he said. "Don't worry, I'm going to talk to your kidnappers and let them know what'll happen to them if they go through with their plan."

He started dialing the phone numbers of the men involved—captains, lieutenants, sergeants, and even a corporal—and gave them all the same speech.

"This is Pablo Emilio Escobar Gaviria, ID number 8-345-766. I am aware of your plans to abduct my son Juan Pablo at the quarter-miler in Medellín, with the help of the army, which will carry out an initial attack to disarm his bodyguards and then drag Juan Pablo off by the hair. But I want you to know that I know where your mother lives, and your whole family, and if anything happens to my son, you and your family will have to answer to me. So you'd best go ahead and evacuate that apartment in Antioquia, because I've already given my men the order that if they see your family around there, you know what will happen. You messed with my family, and now all bets are off, understood? You have twenty-four hours to leave Medellín. If you don't, I'll declare the apartment a military target, and you know what I'm capable of. Be grateful I'm letting you live. Or do you think that because you're a policeman or because I turned myself in I'm afraid of you or something?"

This was the fifth time they'd tried to kidnap me. In the end, I wasn't allowed to go to the race and had to stay at La Catedral for almost three weeks, until my father confirmed that the conspirators had been removed from their posts.

Meanwhile, evidence of the prison's charade continued to present itself. At around that time, a wedding was held at La Catedral for Tato Avendaño and his girlfriend, Ivonne. They were there for fifteen days and spent their honeymoon trying out the heart-shaped rotating bed that had been built for the occasion. It was a huge celebration, attended by dozens of people as if the event were taking place at a prominent hotel.

The men spent a lot of their time betting on pool and card games. They would bet fifteen hundred dollars on a five-minute hand during what they called their "skinny-cow" times. When they were flusher with cash, they'd bet fifteen thousand or more. My father would play for hours with Stud, Otto, Comanche, and Crud—and he was considered only a moderate gambler. Many others would bet up to a million dollars on the dice. Popeye never joined in, saying he wasn't going to throw his hard-earned money away on gambling. He also told the boys that it was better to buy gold bars to hide in the walls because they wouldn't decompose in the humidity the way dollar bills did.

Ironically, the prison was used as a refuge for other criminals who needed a hideout. Fidel Castaño spent two or three weeks straight there, sleeping in a room next to my father, bathing in his tub, eating at his table—my father treated him like a friend. Until one day, when his men caught Fidel spying inside the prison, and my father started becoming suspicious. That was the beginning of the rift that would lead to a deadly war between my father and the Castaño brothers.

Comanche, one of the leaders of Prisco Lopera's gang, also had a suite there to hide in whenever things got a little too hot in Medellín.

One weekend I decided to stay at La Catedral a few days extra, until midweek. The prison was comfortable and had an amazing view, and we were treated so well that nobody ever wanted to leave. While I was there, Kiko Moncada arrived and greeted me warmly as usual, since we'd met three or four times before. The first time had been at a rural estate near Yerbabuena in El Poblado, where he told us that he'd once had trouble buying a Ferrari because the people at the dealership wouldn't sell one to just anybody. He'd had to buy it through a third party. The second time had been in an office tower next to the Mónaco building after my father had already declared war on the government. At that meeting, he'd told my father, "Pablo, my man, I'm all in. We're going to give it to those bastards with everything we've got. You already know, I already told you, but I'm telling you again now so you don't think I was just saying it. I've got a hundred million dollars ready for you to use on this war. You can count on that money—I've got my family well taken care of already, so that money's extra, and it's all yours, brother. You can pay it back when you're able, no interest. That's my contribution to the fight. Tell your people to go by my office downtown and pick it up whenever you need it. Or tell me where, and I'll have it sent it right now."

"No, no worries, brother, I know, and I'm very grateful. As soon as mine runs out, I'll come ask you for it. The war is costing a fortune. I'll be bothering you for it really soon. I appreciate your support, Kiko," my father had replied.

I'd also encountered him that time at the La Isla hideout, when he, Carlos Lehder, Fidel Castaño, and my father were reading *The Man Who Made It Snow* by Max Mermelstein, an American who had worked for my father and other members of the Medellín Cartel before flipping on them.

My father rarely mentioned Moncada in front of me, but whenever he did, he referred to him fondly—you could tell they got along well, and not just because of the money. He always talked about how sincere Moncada was and what close friends they were.

Now, in La Catedral, my father filled Moncada in on the war against the Cali Cartel, since the latest phase had been funded with his money. Hours later, I was lounging on my father's bed, watching a movie, when they came in and sat down to talk at the desk in the room. I moved to leave so they could be alone, but my father told me not to worry, to keep watching my movie. Curiosity got the better of me, and I couldn't help listening to their conversation, especially the point when my father said, "So, Kiko, tell me how much I owe you at this point."

"Give me a second, Pablo. I'll call the bookkeeper, who's just outside," Moncada said.

An unfamiliar man entered, nodded hello, and set down a briefcase. Moncada opened it and removed a large piece of printer paper, but my father waved it off.

"No, Kiko, don't worry about showing me all the accounting. Relax, man, just tell me how much I owe you so we can settle up."

"Pablo, so far you owe me twenty-three point five million dollars. I want you to know that I'm not asking you to pay that back. I'm here because you asked about the money. The other seventy-six million is ready whenever you need it."

"Thanks so much for everything, Kiko. But I hope I won't have to bother you for it, because if everything goes well with the Mexico job, I'll be able to pay you everything I owe you then."

"That's great, brother. Cool. We'll pull that one off, and then we can settle things. That's the good thing about coke, right? It solves everything," Moncada said, laughing.

I watched them out of the corner of my eye, pretending to focus on the movie.

"All right, brother, we're all set. Look, I'm not trying to kick you out—if you want to stay, it's no problem, we've got everything you need here—but the last truck goes down at eight at night, and it's a quarter till right now, if you have to go. Whatever works for you," my father eventually said.

"All right, Pablo, I'd better go down. I've got a chick waiting for me. We'll be in touch."

My father said he'd walk Moncada to the truck, and they left the room. I went on watching the James Bond movie.

Over the next few days, something seemingly remarkable happened. The prison warden ordered the guards to engage in target practice at a makeshift shooting range. But the guards weren't the only ones to participate in this training. They were joined by soldiers who manned the checkpoints up to La Catedral and their superior officers, and of course by my father and his men.

Naturally, my father's team had the best, most modern weapons: gleaming Colt AR-15 rifles with laser sights, Heckler submachine guns, and Pietro Beretta and Sig Sauer pistols. The soldiers, by contrast, were practicing with their heavy, rusty, but very powerful G-3 rifles, and the guards were using their old .38 caliber revolvers. My father's arsenal was impressive, but the prison officials and military personnel didn't bat an eye.

Around the same time, my father softened his firm opposition to my relationship with Andrea and even invited her up so he could meet her. But she took refuge in her university studies in advertising and never accepted the offer.

Still, my father, sly dog that he was, always managed to send for me at the very moment that beauty queens were scheduled to visit the prison. This meant that on the two occasions that Andrea accompanied me to the tavern, she found herself surrounded by a dozen perfumed, high-heeled beauties.

The blue truck with the secret compartment would head up to La Catedral loaded with beautiful women, and fourteen-year-old me in the middle of them. I'll never forget one humorous incident that occurred when the vehicle reached the second army checkpoint before entering the prison. The soldiers at the first checkpoint had merely lifted the bar so the truck could pass through, but at the second, they noted the make and model of the truck, the license plate number, the driver information, and the report of the contents, which was obviously fake. The back of the truck had small holes that made it possible for the "cargo" to see outside, but not vice versa.

The officer detained the truck for longer than normal and started to walk around it. He'd allowed the truck to enter many times before without any inspection or question, but it appeared that curiosity was going to win out that day. Then he looked at the back of the truck and shouted, "Do me a favor and at least wear less perfume next time, goddammit!" The beauty queens and I cracked up. Nobody, not even the soldiers, could contain their laughter.

Up at La Catedral, the prisoners waited in cologne and their best clothes, prepared with gifts and flowers with which they hoped to woo the beauties, whose stay at the prison was always short but well paid.

On the other hand, the brief time my father spent in La Cate-dral served to strengthen his bond with his children. He gave Manuela a beeper so she could send messages to him all day long. He, of course, also had a beeper reserved exclusively for receiv-ing her messages, and he carried it with him in his pants pocket everywhere he went.

Only thirty feet from his room, my father had his men build a giant dollhouse for Manuela. They painted it white and pink, and the daughters of several prisoners, including Crud, would play there. My sister once complained that even though the dollhouse was supposed to be hers, all the girls got to use it. To placate her, my father put a fence around it with a sign that said "Private Prop-erty" and a padlock that only Manuela had the key to. All the house was missing was running water.

Crud's daughters complained too, which produced an amusing rivalry between the fathers. In a loud voice, to be sure my sister and father heard, Crud promised to build his daughters a bigger, pret-tier house. True to his word, he built a spectacular treehouse, which made my sister so jealous that she tried to remove the padlock from her house so she could share the new one with the other girls.

A skilled carpenter, Crud also built a massive pigeon coop because he knew how much my father loved birds. I thought it was strange to have almost two hundred pigeons in such a cold place, but I later discovered that the purpose was to raise carrier pigeons. Soon enough they had a number of trained pigeons that Juan Carlos, one of Crud's friends, would take away from the prison and then release. Incredibly, the birds would return safe and sound to La Catedral.

"What do you think of the carrier pigeons, son?" my father asked me. "Those gringos hovering above us with their flying saucers, and our pigeons cruising right past them. Who's going to catch on? Not those brainiacs," he went on, referring to US surveillance efforts.

One time he sent Juan Carlos to take the pigeons to "13," our code name for the apartment in the Terrazas de San Michel building. He asked Manuela to write him a little letter so the pigeons could deliver it to La Catedral, and they could read it together when she next visited. My father and his men's creativity was boundless, and they'd certainly use it to their advantage in the months to come.

MY FATHER DIDN'T CARRY A WEAPON IN LA CATEDRAL BECAUSE there was always a guard by his side, ready to pass him a submachine gun or a cell phone. This relaxed atmosphere suddenly evaporated, however, when the media reported that the Cali Cartel was planning to bomb the prison from an airplane.

I went up to the prison a few days later. It seemed deserted. There was nobody in the main hall, just a couple of frightened-looking guards. *Where is everybody?* I wondered as a guard signaled me to follow him down a dirt path toward the soccer field. From there, he pointed at the woods, where a few wooden cabins were hidden amid the vegetation.

I realized then that my father and all of his men had moved to shelters they'd built just inside the prison's perimeter fence. I couldn't find my father's cabin until he emerged from a thicket and showed me the way. When I asked him what was going on, he told me he'd decided to evacuate the main building because that was the area most likely to be bombed.

"Everyone's been instructed that if anyone flies over, we shoot. This airspace is off limits. I'm going to see if I can put in some antiaircraft artillery. I chose to put my cabin in this cleft in the mountain because it can't be seen from above or from within the woods. Not even you could find me, so I don't have to worry. But it's twice as cold because there's a little spring of ice-cold water that runs under it and the sun never reaches it." My father had selected the worst area for his cabin.

"So you're going to live out your sentence here? In this awful cold?" I asked.

"It's just temporary. I told your mother to have the architect draw up some anti-bombing designs, which should be here tomorrow. Do me a favor and don't go back to that building; it's too dangerous."

When we received them, the designs were futuristic, and I liked them. Each room was egg-shaped and would be protected with a huge quantity of steel and concrete and then covered with earth so it couldn't be seen from the air or detected by satellite. But my father didn't accept the architect's plan, believing that wooden cabins would be discreet enough—not to mention cheaper. A few days later, he moved to a small cabin that was better located and not so cold, but just as hard to find. Though La Catedral was never bombed, my father and his men never returned to the prison's main building.

Some time later, a number of media outlets published unconfirmed reports suggesting that Kiko Moncada and Fernando Galeano had been murdered inside La Catedral. In the ensuing panic, my father suddenly forbade anyone, including his family, to come to the prison. Something was clearly going on up there, so I called to find out why we couldn't visit. He didn't give me any reason, only reassured me that things would go back to normal very soon.

My father and his men didn't take kindly to being asked a lot of questions, so I decided not to push them. But my questions began to find answers when the media reported that the La Catedral prisoners had refused entry to a team of CTI investigators sent by the attorney general's office to inspect the prison and confirm or rebut the rumors about the disappearance of my father's two business partners.

Only a few days earlier, before we'd heard the news that Moncada might be dead, my parents and I had been walking through the prison when a mischievous smile formed on my father's face, the same one he always wore when he'd pulled off a job. Eventually he couldn't hold back any longer and said, "I'm really happy, darling. I've got really excellent news. I've just paid Kiko all of the debt I owed him after he's helped out so much with our cause. I earned a little money with him in Mexico, and the good news is that my part of the take was thirty-two million dollars. Minus the twenty-four I owed him, that leaves me eight million in the black."

Remembering how close my father and Moncada had been, it all sounded quite strange. I couldn't believe that the journalists' claims might be true.

A couple of days later, my father authorized me to visit once more. I arrived at the tavern late and found a lot of people in line to go up to La Catedral. Though they gave me priority, I had to wait a pretty long time, and Shooter and Tití came up to say hello.

"What's up, Juancho, man, how you doing? All good?" Shooter inquired.

"All good, Grasshopper, my man, how are you and the old lady?" I answered.

"All good. And what did you think of the coup?" he asked nervously.

Just then they called me to the truck, and I only managed to gesture to him that I had no idea what he was referring to. Shooter's question echoed in my mind, and it didn't take me long to connect the "coup" with the rumors about Kiko Moncada and Fernando Galeano. I took it as a sign that the order to kill them might actually have come from my father.

Still pondering Shooter's question, I was shocked by the possibility that my father could be such a terrible friend. He had always taught me the importance of loyalty, and many of his problems had stemmed from his eagerness to help friends. I can't say much about Galeano because I never met him. I first heard his name and learned that he was part of the cartel only when the gossip about his death began.

As soon as I had the chance to speak with my father, I told him I was troubled. "Papá, what is going on? I'm worried. On the news and around town, people are saying that Kiko is dead. Is that true? You and he were such good friends. So what happened to him?"

"Son, I'll tell you so they don't feed you a pack of lies," he began. "What I heard is that the Cali Cartel picked up Kiko and Galeano and released them in exchange for their promise that they wouldn't help me finance the war against Cali, that they'd cut off all economic support and pass on information about me. I didn't believe it was true at first—as you know, Kiko was a good friend of mine. But then I heard recordings of one of the Cali narcos telling Kiko off because he was still giving me money."

"But what did Kiko actually do to you?" I asked, sensing that my father seemed willing to discuss it.

"Well, I had him come up so I could show him the intelligence we'd been gathering on the Cali Cartel and tell him about a couple of operations that we'd set up to take down Gilberto Rodríguez and Pacho Herrera, but suddenly it all went awry and the police and the Cali guys arrived and engaged my men in a gunfight. The first time it happened I figured it could be a coincidence, but the second and third times I looked into it and was able to identify the person who was feeding them the information.

"I'm sure he did it because he was scared. Kiko was never one for violence. But everybody knows what happens when you do me like that. He was a dear friend, and I did everything I could to avoid that outcome, but instead of coming to tell me what was going on, he allied himself with my enemies. The same thing happened with Galeano: I sent him a message asking for money, and he told me he was broke and would no longer be able to contribute. A few days later Tití showed up and said he found one of Galeano's caches with something like twenty-three million dollars in it. Don't ask me for any more details, that's all I'm going to say. Kiko and Galeano double-crossed me with the Cali guys."

I was silent, and my father left for a meeting. When he returned, he warned me, "Careful with Fidel Castaño if you see him. I found out he's another traitor who's working with Cali and going around saying I'm killing my friends so I can take their money. So watch out. If you see him, watch out for him and Carlitos, his brother."

I later discovered that my father tried to force the same fate on the Castaño brothers as he had on Moncada and Galeano. He invited them to La Catedral together, but Fidel was suspicious and had Carlos stay down below. They never spoke again, and the Castaños would end up aligning themselves with Los Pepes, the group that would eventually bring my father down.

On the afternoon of Tuesday, July 21, 1992, my bodyguards, a few friends, my cousin Nicolás—my uncle Roberto's son—and I played soccer in a place known as the 20, in the upper section of Envigado. After the game, Nicolás invited me and a friend to a barbecue at his penthouse apartment in a building four blocks from the Oviedo shopping center in Medellín. At around six, Nicolás received a call on his cell phone from Roberto, who sounded upset: "Stay posted. Something strange is going on outside La Catedral."

Then my father came on the line. "Grégory, there are more soldiers than usual and military trucks. There are helicopters circling overhead too. Something may go down, but we don't know what."

"What should I do in the meantime, Papá?"

"Call Giovanni and tell him to go to you in case I need to talk to him."

The unexpected phone call left us extremely worried, especially Nicolás, who had the feeling his father had been saying good-bye. My father had seemed fairly relaxed, but that didn't mean too much because he amazingly was always composed, even in the worst moments.

An hour later, Roberto called again. I answered.

"Juan Pablo, go get my children and let me speak to them. I think they've come to kill us, and I want to say good-bye."

"Uncle, let me talk to my father. What should I do? Should I call the authorities?" I said.

My father got on and told me to let him talk to Giovanni, who had just arrived at Nicolás's apartment.

"Giovanni," he said, "send people to Olaya and Rionegro to check if there are any American planes at the airports there. Have everything ready to go. If there's a suspicious plane, wait for my orders to destroy it."

The first shadows of night began to fall over Medellín, and we still had no idea what was happening. But soon Roberto called again, and after that we were in constant contact with him. Through short conversations with Nicolás, Roberto reported that the army had arrived at the prison gates, but the prison guards—who in actuality were my father's men—had refused them entry and aimed their weapons at them, as they were trespassing on the territory of the National Directorate of Prisons and violating the official government accords stating that the military would be allowed only outside the perimeter.

Soon after, he told us the situation was becoming complicated, and they were afraid there might be an armed conflict with the soldiers. My father had commanded the men to ready all their weapons and barricade themselves in strategic positions throughout the prison.

By that time, Giovanni had confirmed that no foreign airplanes had landed that day in nearby airports. He also assured my father that several of his men were on the alert and reachable by cell phone.

In an effort to resolve the situation, I decided to play one of our cards. I asked Giovanni to accompany me to the home of Juan Gómez Martínez, the governor of Antioquia, who might have information on what was happening at La Catedral. On the way there, Giovanni revealed something I hadn't known at the time: my father had ordered his men to kidnap Gómez Martínez back when he was the editor of *El Colombiano,* but he had barricaded himself in his house with a .38 revolver and managed to fend off the twenty men who'd been sent after him.

This story didn't exactly fill me with optimism, but Giovanni thought we might be able to get an audience with the governor if he presented a press card from a Medellín radio station. This strategy worked, and when we arrived at the governor's residence, the police officers posted out front let us through immediately.

After we rang the bell several times, Gómez Martínez opened the door. He looked half asleep in a robe and with his hair disheveled. Giovanni spoke first: "Governor, I'm a journalist, and we've come here to see you because there's something going on at La Catedral. There is unusual activity happening, so I'm here with Juan Pablo, Pablo Escobar's son."

"Governor, they're very worried up there. The government promised it wouldn't move the prisoners," I said.

Gómez Martínez couldn't hide his surprise and some displeasure at my presence in his home, but he told us to wait while he made inquiries. He closed and bolted the door. Ten minutes later, he appeared again. He'd called the Casa de Nariño in Bogotá, the Fourth Brigade headquarters in Medellín, and several generals, and no one had given him any information. He did note that one general had shared that the operation's objective was to take my father into military custody.

When we got back to Nicolás's apartment, we were updated with several pieces of alarming information. The army had the prison surrounded, and the vice minister of justice, Eduardo Mendoza, and the director of prisons, Colonel Hernando Navas Rubio, had come from Bogotá with the news that the government was transferring my father to another prison. My father had allowed the two men to enter the prison, and he argued with the vice minister and absolutely refused to comply. The situation escalated, and Mendoza and Navas were tied up as Little Angel, Otto, and Crud trained weapons on them. In other words, the officials were being held hostage inside La Catedral, which the army was threatening to occupy by force. My father claimed that Mendoza and Navas were a sort of life insurance policy.

At that moment, Dora, my uncle Roberto's wife, arrived at the apartment and managed to reach Roberto by cell phone. They spoke for several minutes, wept bitterly, and said good-bye.

One of the people who had been present at La Catedral that night later told me that when my father recognized how nervous the guards and prisoners were, he assured them, "Boys, don't get nervous yet. When you see me tie my sneakers, then you can go ahead and worry."

Later, he did just that, placing his left foot up on a wall and tying his shoe, then doing the same with the right. It became clear to the men who were with him that night that my father was planning to escape from La Catedral.

My father was still on the line. "Look, Grégory, do you remember Álvaro's house?" he said, referring to the property by the name of its caretaker.

"Of course, Papá."

"Are you sure you've never taken anyone there?"

"I have taken a few people there, Papá, but I'm sure it'll be a good hideout for you."

"Go ahead and get it ready," he instructed me.

A few minutes after we hung up, from the living room of Nicolás's penthouse, there in the hills above Medellín we saw La Catedral suddenly go dark. On the instructions of my father, who had just reached the perimeter fence with the other fugitives, a guard shut off the lighting system for the entire prison.

Once everything was sunk into darkness, the men opened a hole in a brick wall and crawled through. My father had created this escape route during the construction phase; the section of the wall had been mortared with a very weak mix of concrete, so all it took was two kicks to break it open.

When we didn't hear anything from the fugitives for a while, Nicolás and I decided to wait at Álvaro's house.

But my father never arrived. He was already swimming in the pool at the farm known as Memo Trino in El Salado, where he and the nine men who'd fled with him, including my uncle Roberto, had taken refuge. From there they could hear the explosions and the commotion of the soldiers who'd stormed the prison to capture my father.

It would take them twelve hours to conclude that he'd escaped.

13

Worry When I Tie My Sneakers

The doorbell seemed louder than usual, and my mother, Manuela, and I jumped in our chairs in the dining room. Someone had arrived, but, strangely, our security guards hadn't called up on the intercom.

I ran to the bulletproof, bombproof door and made sure the locks were securely in place.

"Who is it?" I asked through the intercom, disguising my voice.

"It's meeeee," responded a fake female voice that somehow sounded vaguely familiar.

It turned out to be Popeye, who had come to escort us to my father's hideout. We hadn't heard from him since Tuesday, July 21, 1992, when he'd escaped from La Catedral.

We packed bags for several days along with, as usual, homemade food and desserts that my mother had always been able to prepare in a matter of minutes in this sort of circumstance.

"It's for your father," she replied when I objected that we were in a hurry and all that food wasn't going to fit in the little Renault 4 that Popeye had brought. So we headed out, my mother in the front seat and Manuela and me in the back, crammed in among the suitcases and baking dishes that threatened to shatter with each jounce of the car.

We were once again going into hiding, and none of us yet realized that this time there was no coming back. When he'd escaped from La Catedral, my father had destroyed his best option for putting his life back together—not to mention ours—and for bringing his terror campaign against the nation to an end.

As we drove to Álvaro's house, where I had waited for my father in vain after the escape, I asked Popeye why it had taken them four days to resurface. He told me my father had decided to wait until my uncle Roberto had found a safe place to hide.

After taking multiple detours to throw off any possible tails, we made it to our new shelter. As soon as he saw us, my father ran out to hug Manuela and then greeted me cheerfully with a kiss on the cheek. He gave my mother a long hug, and she couldn't help bursting into tears. As always, Popeye made a joke to relieve the tension of the moment.

"Don't worry, boss lady, Mr. Danger here"—he sometimes called my father this—"promises he'll never make you cry again from here on out."

While he ate the food we had gone to such pain to bring, my father recounted his escape. Like a good *machista*, he expressed his irritation with the army's version of events, which claimed through the media that my father had made his escape disguised as a woman. He then had Popeye call RCN Radio, as he planned to communicate to the government through the station's director, Juan Gossaín.

It was eleven at night, but within minutes my father was chatting with Gossaín, who happened to be in a meeting with his colleagues María Isabel Rueda, director of the TV news program *QAP*, and Francisco Santos Calderón, coeditor of the newspaper *El Tiempo*. Leaning on his elbows on the pool table, my father said hello and announced that he wished to refute information provided by the army regarding his escape from La Catedral. Specifically, he was referring to the Fourth Brigade's account that he had fled the prison dressed in women's apparel.

After hearing out his demands, Gossaín and the other two journalists began to ask my father questions, trying to ascertain whether he was willing to open a new negotiation with the government and attorney general to turn himself in again. My father said that he was, but on several conditions: he wanted a guarantee that he would not be transferred, a promise that he would be incarcerated somewhere in Antioquia, and the complete exclusion of the police from the process. My father and the journalists spoke several times that night, until after four in the morning, but there was no definitive response from the government, nor would there be in the months to come.

My father and I often stayed up very late and would go to bed after six in the morning. He'd lived that way most of his life, since the police rarely conducted raids after that hour. On one of those nights, as we gazed out at Medellín from Álvaro's house, I heard my father talking to Popeye about the tough times ahead if they were forced to hide out for a long period. They'd done it before, but now things would be different.

My father intended to keep Popeye with him in hiding, but Popeye's facial expression suggested he wasn't fond of the idea of being in confinement again. He turned red and rapidly burst out, "Boss, I really hate to say this, but I can't handle being locked up again. You know I go crazy being in there. I can't go with you on this one." He looked down at the floor, avoiding my father's silence and penetrating stare.

"Ha-ha-ha, don't kill me for this, boss, ha-ha," Popeye continued, pale, his voice shaking and his feet twitching as if they wanted to take off running.

"No, no. Relax, man, I understand. Being locked up is rough. You've had to go through it once already," my father said. "I don't have a choice, so I have to do it. I just need you to be patient a few days longer so I can get myself organized and find someone else to go with me as I change hideouts and cars. And after that, you can leave, no problem."

"All right, boss, you can count on it. Thanks. I want to leave the country for a while under an alias to wait for the tide to go out a bit, and then I'll come back and be at your service, boss. Whatever you need."

My father didn't say another word and went to speak with my mother alone. A few minutes later, I followed.

"Hey, Papá, what was that crap Popeye was saying? Don't you think it's wrong for him to ditch you like that?"

"Calm down, son, it's all right. We have to treat him well to make sure he's happy when he leaves here. If they don't gun him down on the street, he'll end up turning himself in faster than a rooster's crow."

My father chose Little Angel to replace Popeye. While we remained in hiding at Álvaro's house, the Search Bloc, the police unit recently established with the specific objective of apprehending my father and his associates, carried out thousands of raids across Medellín. Of course they also searched for my father's men, who started fleeing from hideout to hideout. As the days passed, many of them realized that the only safe place to be was in prison.

And so, just as my father had predicted, the mad dash began. Popeye and Otto turned themselves in again. So did my uncle Roberto, after telling my father and getting his consent. The hunt intensified further, and between October and November, my father lost two other men, Tyson and Pigeon. The media speculated that my father didn't have anyone left, but they were wrong: there were still dozens of men ready to do whatever it took for a wad of cash.

On December 1, 1992, we celebrated my father's forty-third birthday discreetly, with dinner, cake, and conversation. The carefree atmosphere of earlier periods was gone. We no longer had the massive security teams, caravans of cars, dozens of armed men, or even the whole family together in one place. Though the hideout was secure, we still thought it was necessary to take shifts monitoring the perimeter. Every four hours, Álvaro, Little Angel, my father, and I would switch off.

On December 3, a car bomb exploded near the Atanasio Girardot Stadium and killed several police officers in a patrol car. Convinced that violence would force the government to grant him the judicial concessions he'd demanded several times, my father had clearly opted to ramp up his war against it. Over the next few weeks, another dozen cars would blow up in Medellín, and the "pistol plan" against the secret police would lead to the deaths of about sixty agents in two months.

Amid this increasingly tense, grim atmosphere, on December 7 we celebrated the Day of the Little Candles, the holiday marking the eve of the Immaculate Conception. That night the four of us gathered on the rear patio of the house with the only five candles we'd been able to find. Little Angel had chosen to stay in his room, though my mother had invited him to join us, and Álvaro had taken up as guard. As we stood around a small statue of the Virgin next to the clotheslines, my mother started praying aloud. My father and I followed her with our heads bowed while Manuela played on the patio. Later we lit the five candles, one for the Virgin and the other four for each member of our family.

As we did this, I noted that my father was strangely silent, caught somewhere between uncertainty and faith. His silence wasn't all that out of the ordinary. He'd always struggled with his religious beliefs. I'd asked him only once whether he believed in God. "God is something very personal for every individual," he'd immediately replied.

My grandmother Hermilda once told me that when he was little, Pablo used to crawl under the blankets to pray because he didn't like people to watch him. I realized then what he'd been doing all those times when I would pull off the blanket to wake him up and find him with his eyes open and his hands crossed on his chest. He was praying.

Because of our isolation and the troubling rumors that my mother's family was at risk of being attacked, my father suggested that we separate for a while. We reluctantly agreed, and my mother, Manuela, and I went to the Altos building while my father headed for yet another hideout—the identity of which he refused to reveal.

"Tell your brothers and sisters to move or leave the country; things are going to keep getting more and more dangerous for them," my father instructed my mother when we said good-bye. And once again he'd be proven right. On the night of December 18, as we recited the Advent novena in the common area of the Altos building with the Henaos, one of the bodyguards suddenly appeared and warned that Search Bloc agents had arrived. I headed toward the rear of the building, toward a little path that led to a garage next door where we always had a car ready. But as I tried to escape, I came face-to-face with several rifles. The novena celebration came to a halt. Men, women, and children—some thirty children in total—all in attendance were split into groups. After searching us thoroughly, they asked for our documents, and I decided to identify myself.

"My name is Juan Pablo Escobar Henao. I'm fifteen years old, and my father is Pablo Escobar. I live in this building, and my papers are upstairs in my room."

The agent immediately called over his commanding officer, a police colonel, and informed him of my presence. The colonel pulled me aside, waved over two of his men, and said, "If he even blinks, shoot him." Then, over the radiotelephone to the Carlos Holguín School, the Search Bloc's center of operations, he announced that they had captured me and would bring me in for interrogation.

Luckily, our guests included the wife and one of the sons of Álvaro Villegas Moreno, a former governor of Antioquia, who also lived in the building. When he learned of what was happening, he came down in his pajamas and slippers to speak with the colonel and make sure that the raid was being carried out in accordance with the law. It had been going on for two hours by that point, and the more than one hundred elegantly dressed guests were still standing under the watchful eyes of the Search Bloc.

The former governor's presence reassured the parents, who objected to how their children were being treated and demanded that they at least be given something to eat. The police consented, but they didn't give the men anything. I was with the men, even though I was only fifteen.

"Those little friends you were hanging out with a few days back are going to show up tomorrow," the officer said, but I had no idea what he was talking about.

"This way! Follow me!" he shouted.

"Where are you taking me, Colonel?" I asked.

"No questions. I'm not telling you anything. Follow me or I'll drag you myself. Come on, let's move."

Then the two officers who had been training their guns on me prodded me in the stomach as an indication to start walking. I'll never forget the anguished looks on the faces of my mother and relatives as they wondered what kind of fate I was being marched off to.

When we reached the building's foyer, the colonel, who was walking ahead of me, told me to stop. At least thirty hooded men appeared and aimed their rifles at me. I was positive they were going to shoot me.

"Two steps forward. Turn right, now left, now turn your back. State your full name—speak up!" ordered one of the hooded figures, a short man with a hoarse voice.*

---

*At the end of 1994, Carlos Castaño revealed to my mother that he had been one of the hooded men who came to the Altos building that night. According to him, the others were his brother, Fidel Castaño, and other men who would later become members of Los Pepes.

Then they pushed me aside, and the man with the hoarse voice repeated the same line to each man who had attended the party. Only two females were subjected to the same treatment: my mother and Manuela.

A few minutes later, the colonel gave orders to transfer me to the Carlos Holguín School. I asked him why they were arresting me when they hadn't found anything illegal. All he said was that the Search Bloc was going to have a little fun with "Pablo's son" back at headquarters.

Now three in the morning, they were leading me toward a Search Bloc vehicle when a representative from the inspector general's office arrived. He told them they couldn't arrest a minor and demanded that they remove my handcuffs. I was lucky he showed up when he did. After a shouting match between the official and the head of the police operation, the Search Bloc left the building.

It was seven in the morning on December 19. The police were gone, but my mother, Manuela, and I were still terrified. We had become the main targets of my father's enemies.

On December 21, one of my father's bodyguards came to check in on us and shared staggering news. My father had personally engaged in several military actions. He had two objectives: to demonstrate that he hadn't been beaten yet and to inspire the men who were still part of his military apparatus. According to the bodyguard's account, my father had headed up a group of fifty men and established two checkpoints on the Vía Las Palmas highway. The goal was to draw out the Search Bloc and blow up its trucks by loading vehicles with dynamite and parking them on either side of the road. My father and his henchmen wore DAS armbands and stopped dozens of cars that were coming down from José María Córdova Airport; after examining their documents, they'd let the travelers continue on their way.

We also learned that at dawn on December 20, my father had led an armed group to blow up the house in the Las Acacias neighborhood from which Captain Fernando Posada Hoyos, head of intelligence for the police in Medellín, carried out operations against the Medellín Cartel. The procession of vehicles surrounded the house, the bodyguard reported, and one of my father's men placed a powerful charge of dynamite next to the bedroom where the officer was sleeping. When it went off, they searched for him amid the rubble and finished him off.*

On December 23, my father sent for us so we could spend Christmas and New Year's together. We went to a farm in Belén, on the outskirts of Medellín, and stayed in what appeared to be the butler's house. My father ordered fireworks, Manuela and I released helium balloons, and my mother made custard and sweet fritters on a makeshift bonfire.

We spent hours in the breezeway of the house, a rustic structure perched on the edge of a ravine. When I noticed that there was freshly disturbed soil beneath us, I asked my father what was hidden there. He couldn't conceal his naughty smile, but he didn't answer. Afterward I heard him ask Little Angel to move the explosives to a safer place.

THE BEGINNING OF 1993, THE LAST YEAR OF MY FATHER'S LIFE, WAS hectic and intense. And extremely violent. After spending New Year's together, we traveled to a beautiful estate that my mother had given me in the town of San Jerónimo, two hours west of Medellín.

---

* Not long after Captain Posada's death, my father's enemies tried to implicate me in that incident. A purported eyewitness told the prosecutor that he'd seen me with my father that night in a bar in Envigado, but the murder took place far from there. I went to a juvenile court judge to give my version of events and asked him to issue subpoenas to a dozen neighbors and employees at the Altos building who'd seen me there throughout that night. In addition, a few hours earlier, the Search Bloc had conducted a raid at the Altos building that lasted more than ten hours. The supposed witness sent the court a letter saying he'd been tortured to make him finger me.

My mother had remodeled it, and it pained us to tell my father not to come because it wasn't secure. We were at that estate when we found out that my father had set one of his plans in motion: to get the government to treat him as a political criminal. He'd been contemplating this possibility ever since he'd forged a close relationship with the M-19 in 1981. My father sent a message to Attorney General De Greiff announcing the establishment of the armed group Rebel Antioquia and condemning the violence, murder, and torture perpetrated by the Search Bloc. He added, that, given the arrests and raids on his lawyers' offices, he had "no alternative but to abandon his legal battle and take up an organized armed struggle."

While his new endeavor was being hotly debated in the media, my mother's sister Luz Marina and Martha Ligia, an old friend of the family and the wife of a notorious Medellín drug lord, arrived unexpectedly.

Inconsolable, Luz told us that at around noon she'd been in her shop in El Vivero talking with Martha when Carlos Castaño had appeared, heavily armed and accompanied by two dozen men in several trucks. Castaño, who had by then left the Medellín Cartel and become a paramilitary leader, had intended to kidnap her, but he stopped short, surprised, when he saw Martha Ligia. He'd had no choice but to say hello and walk away.

According to my aunt, who was still flustered, they then saw a column of smoke rising from a spot not far away. Terrified, they immediately fled to us in San Jerónimo. Later she'd discover that the smoke had been coming from her own house in El Diamante. That afternoon, my aunt and her two young children were left without home or job.

Before setting the house on fire, we'd later learn, Castaño's men had taken one of my mother's most prized pieces of art, which had been moved to Luz's house after the Mónaco car-bomb attack: the painting *Rock and Roll* by the Spanish genius Salvador Dalí. It wasn't a large painting, but it was worth a fortune. It was that artwork that Castaño would offer to return to my mother after my father's death, when we'd negotiate peace with my father's enemies.

On the walls and in the ruins of my aunt Luz Marina's house, you could still see the outlines of numerous works of art that could not be saved from the fire: a priceless painting by Claudio Bravo and sculptures by the masters Igor Mitoraj, Fernando Botero, and Édgar Negret.

"I couldn't even rescue my underwear," she moaned when I tried unsuccessfully to soothe her.

"Watch out, that man is capable of anything," Martha Ligia warned, referring to Carlos Castaño, before she said good-bye and headed back to Medellín.

The future seemed bleak. Not only had the family been targeted, but my father's military apparatus had also suffered a serious blow with the deaths of Juan Carlos Ospina, Socket, and Víctor "Blue Eyes" Granada. The war was heating up, and in response, my father ordered his men to set off car bombs in three different areas of Bogotá. The gruesome attacks galvanized a group that would eventually prove lethal for my father: Los Pepes.

Los Pepes formed in 1993 as a group of anonymous vigilantes who claimed to have been "persecuted by Pablo Escobar." It was led by former Medellín Cartel members Fidel and Carlos Castaño as well as Diego "Don Berna" Murillo and received significant financing from the Cali Cartel. The group made its debut with two attacks clearly intended to send the message that my father's family would be in its sights from then on. On January 31, it dynamited my grandmother Hermilda's country house in El Peñol and detonated car bombs at the entrances of the Abedules and Arcos buildings, where a significant portion of the Escobar Gaviria and Escobar Henao families lived.

The attacks sent us on the run again, and my father quickly located a new hideout for us. Little Angel took us to an apartment on

Avenida La Playa, a couple of blocks from Avenida Oriental in downtown Medellín.

My father was waiting for us there, and as soon as he saw us he insisted, for the first time, that we leave the country.

My father suggested that I could travel to the United States with Manuela; Marta, my uncle Fernando's wife; and their two children. Oh, and Snowflake and Cottonball, Manuela's pair of French poodle puppies, whom she refused to leave behind. He noted that if I wanted, I could bring my girlfriend too, but that we'd have to speak with her and her family first.

"Tomorrow night, you go get Andrea, so I can meet her and talk to her here. Make extra certain nobody follows you," my father said.

Accompanied by Little Angel, I raced to Andrea's house without prior warning. For the first time, I showed up with only one bodyguard and in a Mazda that Andrea didn't recognize. She wasn't worried that my father wanted to talk to her, and as we drove back to the hideout, I asked her to keep her eyes closed the whole way.

"What have you done to my family, kid?" my father joked with Andrea, who attempted without much success to mask her fear at his ominous-sounding question. "Neither of my two children wants to go to the United States unless you go with them," he added to ease the tension.

There was no time for debate or delay, so that same night I went with my mother to talk to Trinidad, Andrea's mother. After a twenty-minute discussion, my future mother-in-law had no objection to the trip.

As she and Andrea parted ways, her mother privately uttered a prophetic statement: "Daughter, you're going off to suffer now."

On the afternoon of February 18, we had everything ready for the trip to Miami, which was scheduled for ten in the morning the next day. My father advised us to set out five hours before the flight, but that left two logistical questions: since we were arriving at the airport so early, where should we hide so that nobody saw us? And how could we get to the airport without being spotted?

To address the first problem, we decided that one of my father's men would drive the Mazda that nobody recognized and leave it parked in the airport lot, where it would stay until it was time to check in for the flight. That also solved another issue: the luggage. We called one of my father's contacts at the airport, who agreed to retrieve the bags from the car and store them until we got there.

The second problem was trickier. There was some risk that Los Pepes would follow us and try something on the road, even if we had escorts. So we came up with another approach: Andrea and I would hail a taxi on the street, take it to the rear of the Nutibara Hotel in downtown Medellín, and climb into a shuttle that would make the trip to the airport in an hour via the Medellín–Bogotá highway. Manuela, our two cousins, and Marta would leave later with two bodyguards.

That's the plan we stuck by. Once at the hotel, not many passengers boarded the shuttle with us, but I had my heart in my throat the entire trip anyway because the guy drove like a maniac, not seeming to care much about either his life or those of his helpless passengers. Frustratingly, I couldn't say anything to him for fear of drawing attention to myself. Behind the shuttle, at a prudent distance, the Nose and the Jap followed us.

As planned, we arrived quite early and headed straight to the Mazda that had been parked in the lot the day before. As an additional precaution, I gave the Jap a list with the names and direct phone numbers of the regional inspector general's office, the local and national news media, and the personal phone numbers of a number of prominent journalists. The bodyguard would start dialing if things got out of hand. We agreed that he would watch me at all times, alert for my signal. That was our plan B.

Andrea and I closed our eyes for a while, unable to sleep. Almost three hours passed, and at last it was time to enter the airport. We rubbed our eyes, stretched, and got out of the car. Immediately I felt unsafe.

"We've been made, we've been made!" I said to Andrea, who looked at me in confusion, not understanding my panic. For her, who hadn't grown up surrounded by fear, it was just another morning at the Rionegro airport.

But I wasn't imagining things. I saw strange movements, people who clearly weren't waiting for a relative or who were out of place. Parked in a no-parking zone near two airport police officers, I spotted a white double-cab Chevrolet LUV pickup truck that my father had mentioned as being associated with Los Pepes.

"Baby, let's go in right now. I don't like the people I'm seeing out here. If we get through passport control, we'll be in a safer area. Hurry!" I told Andrea.

We practically plowed down those waiting in line, and they protested as we entered the first passport booth. The DAS agent reviewed my passport page by page, carefully examined my signature and fingerprint, looked and looked several times at the tourist visa to the United States and, since I was still a minor, the authorization to leave the country signed and authenticated several days earlier by my father, who had registered his signature with a civil-law notary so he didn't have to come out of hiding.

The immigration agent stared at me with contempt. He wanted to find a reason to prevent me from getting through but clearly couldn't, so he had no choice but to grit his teeth and stamp both passports.

In the public hall of the airport, beyond the dark-tinted glass, I could make out men in civilian dress wearing hoods and armed with rifles and submachine guns. They were patrolling in groups of six as if they were security forces. I counted more than twenty men all through the area. Travelers, airline employees, food service workers, and janitors glanced at each other uneasily. Nobody knew who they were or why they were there. They didn't have official identification, and no law enforcement officer even went near them. A somber silence settled in the airport.

With all our papers in order, we passed through the metal detector, x-ray machine, drug-sniffing dogs, police pat-down, everything. My sister and our cousins and aunt were in line too. They got delayed at first, and only once everyone made it through did I start to breathe easier.

But almost immediately several agents from the Elite Antiterrorist Unit appeared, followed by several young men who were carrying our suitcases and started opening them all up.

"No, no, no, hang on a minute, hang on a minute," I said, alarmed. "Please wait. You can't open my family's luggage like that. I'm happy to let you search them, but just one at a time so I can watch you. I take personal responsibility for the contents of each bag. But please hurry, the plane's about to take off."

A crowd of travelers spectated, but the agents deliberately took ages to go through the suitcases, which had already been searched several times. It was obvious they wanted us to miss our flight. Realizing that terrible things might happen, I pretended my ear was itching as I searched for the Jap among the crowd pressed against the tinted glass. I wanted to give him the sign we'd established to activate our plan B. When I found him, I subtly changed the movement of my fingers and imitated the shape of a telephone. He got the message and disappeared.

One of the agents saw me making the signal and scanned the crowd, trying to identify the person I'd been communicating with. Luckily he was unsuccessful and angrily asked me, "Who the hell were you talking to?"

"Nobody, my ear was itching," I lied rather lamely.

That led to an argument with the agents. I told them their actions were out of line, that we had to catch our plane, and I showed them my passport with the exit stamp and valid visa. The officer in charge said they were just carrying out their inspection duties.

But their delay tactics succeeded. The airplane left without us, and no others were departing that day. I felt completely alone at that moment, responsible for the safety and lives of three young girls and an adult woman.

A few minutes later, the head of the airport police walked over to us: "All right, I need you to clear the area quickly. You've missed your flight, so you need to leave now."

"I'm sorry to tell you this, sir, but we're not going anywhere. You made us miss that flight on purpose, and Los Pepes are waiting outside to abduct us. You can see them from here, right?" I pointed at the armed men outside. "You want us to go out so they can kill us all? I'm terribly sorry, but I'm making you responsible for ensuring our safety and our lives, and you'll have to answer to my father for anything that happens to us from now on."

The man was completely rattled. Suddenly several journalists arrived; it was a relief to see the lights and the flashes coming through that dark glass between the main hall and the security area. The reporters' presence scared off the hooded men, who disappeared. But that didn't mean they were gone.

In the chaos, a savior appeared before me: a fifty-year-old man I'd never seen before. His name was Dionisio, and he worked for a local airline. "Sir," he said, "I know you're in a tight spot. If there is anything I can do to assist, you can count on me."

I thought for a moment and then quietly asked him to help me get access to an office with a telephone and a Yellow Pages directory.

"All right, no problem, let me look for the keys. When I signal to you from the end of the hall, tell the police you're going to the bathroom. They know you're not leaving here anyway."

It worked. The good man came through, and I soon found myself in an office, with no idea what to do next. We'd carefully planned how to get into the airport, but never how to escape it. The first thing I did was look up Aeroes, an airline belonging to my father. *They can send one of my father's choppers,* I thought. *It doesn't matter if it's caught on film and the government confiscates the aircraft afterward. This is about staying alive.* But I couldn't find their number in the directory.

I was about to give up when, through a small window, I spotted a helicopter from the company Helicol landing. "Who's that chopper for, the one that's landing right now? I need it," I told Dionisio.

"No, sir, it's for some executives who've been waiting a while and already have a flight plan set up, so that's not possible," he said.

I picked up the telephone directory, dialed Helicol's number, and asked Dionisio to request helicopter service in his name. They agreed to send a chopper as soon as one was available.

After a while, when the chopper was about to arrive, we headed to the exit for the helipads. The agents blocked our path. Things could have gotten messy again, but just then an official from the inspector general's office appeared. The Jap had called the inspector general. They had no choice but to let us go.

It seemed like we were waiting out on the platform for the helicopter forever. We had to leave our luggage behind because it weighed too much. As we were getting ready to board the aircraft, a colonel who was clearly from the Search Bloc arrived.

"We're looking for that bastard father of yours so we can kill him," he said.

"I wish you luck, Colonel."

"Next time you're not going to get away. And if I see you or your father again, I'll kill you," he replied, clenching his fist with rage. It was clear he was tempted to punch me, but he refrained when he scanned the area and saw several cameramen on the other side of the platform's security bars.

The agent left, and Andrea, Catalina, Marcela, Marta, Manuela and her nanny, Nubia, and I climbed onto the helicopter and headed to Medellín's Olaya Herrera Airport. With Snowflake and Cottonball, of course. There, an employee of the inspector general's office was waiting for us. I had to pay his taxi fare because he didn't have any money. Moments later, a reporter from the regional TV channel Teleantioquia showed up.

I told everybody to wait and went into an office to figure out what to do next. The clock was ticking, and I was sure that it was only a matter of time before Los Pepes came after us again. Then I thought of a plan.

"Look, here's the thing," I told the reporters. "They were going to kill us back at the airport, and my family and I barely managed to escape. I promise I'll give you an interview, but I need your help."

"Whatever you need," they answered.

"We're going to go somewhere. You can follow in your car, but you have to keep filming the entire time in case something happens to us."

They agreed, and we headed for the Altos building at top speed. My plan seemed like madness because the building had just been raided by the Search Bloc two months earlier and we were easy targets there. But I had to take them to a territory I knew like the back of my hand.

Down in the basement of the Altos building, I gave the taxi driver a seven-hundred-dollar tip for the high-speed trip from the airport. I talked to a reporter and gave the first interview of my life. I explained what had happened and discussed whether my father was going to turn himself in. I answered the questions as best as I could and then left, running up the stairs to the building's outdoor swimming pool. A small creek ran along one side of the property, and we'd always left a gap in the boundary along the property line there so we could escape into the yard of the building next door, where we had an apartment and kept a vehicle with the keys in the ignition and a full tank of gas in the parking garage. That's where I had tried go when the Search Bloc had raided our party months before.

My sister and the others had already gone next door and were waiting for me beside a Mitsubishi SUV. That was how we got away. According to what I was told afterward, five trucks full of hooded men occupied the building and turned it inside out looking for us. But we were already in 00, where we quickly changed into clean clothes and kept moving, since we knew Los Pepes had the place on their radar.

We went down to the basement of 00 and got into a Renault 4 before heading to the apartment on Avenida La Playa, the one we'd just left that morning. There we found my mother, who was weeping at the radio reports of our thwarted trip to the United States.

We shared a long hug, and then I explained that the apartment didn't seem safe anymore because Snowflake and Cottonball had now been on the television reports, and it was only a matter of time before the neighbors made the connection and notified the police that Pablo's family lived here. I'd hardly finished speaking when the doorbell rang. It was Little Angel.

"Good afternoon, the boss sent me to fetch you. We have to move; this hideout isn't safe. Juancho, the boss wanted me to tell you to retrieve the money from the stash here. We're done with this apartment," he said.

"All right, come help me with that. We'll need a Phillips-head screwdriver to open that up," I replied, pointing to the wardrobe where it was hidden.

We struggled with the piece of furniture for several minutes in vain. The screws were stuck tight.

"Ramón"—another of our names for Little Angel—"we're going to have to break it open."

"Aren't you worried about making too much noise?" he asked.

"I'm more worried about leaving that money behind and about wasting time trying to get it out. By the time the neighbors complain, we'll already be gone and they'll never see us again."

We kicked at the furniture over and over, with little success but a great deal of noise. Then we brought in a huge hammer from the kitchen and managed to break through the wood. With every blow, we felt as if the police were one step closer and might burst in at any moment.

At last we were able to stuff the money in a briefcase and make our escape. The La Playa apartment was raided that very afternoon. The police were nipping at our heels.

We kept our eyes closed throughout the journey, and Little Angel made several extra turns on our way to a nearby hideout, a house I'd guess was near Medellín's Pablo Tobón Uribe Theater.

Once he'd closed the garage door and we could open our eyes, we saw my father. Manuela clambered out and kissed him on the cheek, and my mother caught the two of them in a hug.

"Hi, Papá, I didn't think I'd see you again so soon. It's good to be here. You can't imagine the jam we were in. It was a miracle we made it," I said as I hugged and kissed him.

"Don't worry, son, the important thing is that you're all OK and here with me. I saw some of it on TV and heard it on the radio. You did a great job with that helicopter maneuver, you outsmarted them all." He smiled and patted me on the shoulder several times.

Andrea and I spent the night in a room that had only a twin bed. We'd sleep close together from that day on.

I prayed for a long time before going to bed, filling myself with peace and tranquility so I'd be able to fall asleep. I left my fear in God's hands.

After six in the evening on Saturday, February 20, 1993, we turned on the television set in a small den. We were watching the cable channel Univisión when a report revealed that our visas had been canceled by the American ambassador, Morris Busby.

"Don't worry, the world's a big place. There's Europe and Asia . . . Australia would be a good place for you. Leave it to me. You'll see, I'll get you those visas. Or you can travel under false identities, and I'll meet up with you afterward. I'll get on a boat and show up there," my father said loudly to cheer us up. There was a short silence, and he offered another option: "Or there's another alternative. We can hide together—you can stay with me, and we'll go to the jungle for a while. Now, with the support of the ELN guerrilla group, I'm going to get back a lot of my power."

The conversation ended there. My mother stayed in her room, crying in bed. She was willing to go into the jungle with her husband, but not to endanger the lives of her children. She didn't see the jungle as a viable option.

All that week, my mother, Andrea, and I wore my father's clothing because we didn't have any of our own with us.

"Careful someone doesn't mistake you for me out there!" my father would joke when he saw us in his clothes.

And so, in someone else's clothing, on February 24 I celebrated my sixteenth birthday. There were no photos or videos, just a homemade dessert—no comparison to my fifteenth birthday party at the Altos building, with more than one hundred twenty guests in black tie attire, three bands, a buffet, an artificial island in the swimming pool, and other extravagance.

On the seven o'clock news the next evening, my father received more grim tidings: earlier that day, without consulting anyone, Giovanni Lopera, "the Supermodel," had turned himself in to the Antioquian prosecutor's office. My father was dumbfounded; he had just lost Pinina's successor.

Over the next several days, Los Pepes struck hard at those who had been aligned with my father in legal or political matters. On February 27, they destroyed the Corona estate belonging to Diego Londoño White; on March 1, they took out his brother, Luis Guillermo; on March 2, they assassinated Hernán Darío Henao, "HH," manager of the Nápoles estate, whom the authorities and the media claimed was a relative of my mother. (Actually, they weren't related at all.) On March 4, they murdered my father's lawyer, Raúl Zapata Vergara.

From the news we also heard that Shooter had died. It had gone down at Shooter's apartment in the Banco Comercial Antioqueño building, right in downtown Medellín, where he and my father had met only a few days earlier. That's when we knew they'd given my father his death sentence.

When the news reported on it, my father already had an explanation for what must have transpired: "Juan Caca turned him in. The police picked Juan up and tortured him, and he gave them the keys to the apartment. That's how they caught Shooter so easily. He was sleeping soundly, thinking there was no way Juan would reveal where he was. A mistake that cost him his life," my father said as the news program showed images of the apartment of one of his few loyal henchmen, one of the few who called my father by his first name, who hadn't abandoned my father or turned himself in. Shooter was a fearless man who took great pleasure in defying the law.

"Papá, what are you going to do now that you don't have anybody out here to protect you? What's going to happen now? You're practically alone, without anybody," I asked anxiously.

"We'll see, son," he said pensively.

"Papá, you don't have anyone to take care of you. I think the best move would be for us to split up, with the men in one hideout and the women in another, for their safety. If they come for you at any moment and the women are there, imagine the bloodbath. We have to protect them. I'll stay with you, no matter what," I said, shaking with fear. He looked at me in silence.

"I think that's the best thing for the moment, until we see what happens. Little Angel is more useful out there, fighting, but he can't do that while also protecting us," he replied in agreement.

For the first time, my father had accepted one of my suggestions. His admission that he needed me by his side made it clear that we were in a free fall. There was no one else to turn to. Little Angel would now also become my father's link to the outside world, an enormous risk because he had to go out for long periods of time, and my father wouldn't have control over him.

So Little Angel got ready to go out to a meeting, and my father gave him three hours to return. It seemed like an eternity. It was a huge risk to stay in the house waiting for him, but also a risk to change location, burning a good hideout for no reason. Little Angel had just left when my father turned to me. "Grégory, how long do you take in the shower? I imagine you'll take an hour, and I can't wait that long. Let's go take a drive in the car until Little Angel gets back. Skip the shower and come with me. Or should I go on my own?"

"Papá, I promise I'll be out, showered and dressed, in ten minutes, and we can go wherever you want. But let me get ready."

"All right, then, move it."

Fifteen minutes later, we got into the Renault 4 parked in the garage. My father was wearing a polo shirt, jeans, and a dark cap, and had a thick beard. As he instructed, I closed my eyes as we left. I was consumed with anguish, imagining what would happen if they arrested Little Angel and forced him to give up my father's location. Though I always disagreed with his violent methods, I never even contemplated leaving my father on his own. Yet I was distressed that this meant leaving the rest of the family behind.

"Papá, is it OK to leave the women by themselves?" I asked uncertainly.

"We have to spend time out of the house, for safety reasons. Don't worry. We're going to go out for a drive through the city while we wait. It's better to keep moving. I'll let you know when you can open your eyes."

Go for a drive? How could my father go out and drive through a city teeming with policemen and checkpoints set up to catch the world's most wanted man? Going out with him in the suburbs of northeastern Medellín was gambling with my own life. But I couldn't help but feel it was the least risky option. When it was time for me to open my eyes, the first thing I saw was the La Milagrosa bus station, which I used to pass on my way to school.

My father drove calmly, respecting the stoplights and traffic signs so he'd blend in with the other drivers. We continued driving for close to two and a half hours, and then he asked me to close my eyes as we headed back.

To keep me distracted from my worry, he told me what he was seeing on the street: we were near the hideout, he didn't see any strange activity, everything seemed fine. He said we'd take another turn around the neighborhood and then enter the house. Once we did, we found out Little Angel had already returned. I breathed a sigh of relief.

DORALBA, THE HOUSEKEEPER AT THE HIDEOUT, WAS AN EXCELLENT seamstress and made her own clothing. Since my father's favorite New Man–brand jeans were wearing out, she offered to make him similar ones so he'd have backups. He loved the idea.

"It'll be great to get your help with the jeans. And let me ask you something—do you think you could make me a few police uniforms?" he asked, clearly plotting his next move.

A couple of days later, my father announced that because of the search operations in the city center, it would be safer for him to leave. He said he would meet us at a new hiding spot.

Little Angel took my father away and two days later came back for us. He brought us to two small houses in Belén Aguas Frías, which my father had dubbed "Aburrilandia"—"Boredomland." Bored out of our minds, we spent Easter week there, unable to do anything in fear that we might be discovered.

Our situation was already difficult, but my father made it even more complicated on April 15, when a car bomb detonated on the corner of Calle 93 and Carrera 15 in Bogotá, killing several people and causing serious damage. Far from bringing the government to its knees, as my father had hoped, that attack made Los Pepes redouble their offensive against him and the rest of the cartel.

After seeing the dramatic images of the victims and the destruction of a large commercial district on the news, one night I told my father that I didn't agree with his indiscriminate violence and the unjust deaths of innocent people.

"Don't forget, the first victims of so-called narcoterrorism in Colombia were your mother, your little sister, and you when they bombed the Mónaco building," he responded. "I didn't invent this. I am using the same weapon they used to try to destroy what I love most, which is all of you."

"Well, I don't like violence, Papá. It makes things worse, gets us further from finding a solution. How can anyone support attacks that kill innocent children? I don't think violence is the way out. You should look for another way," I said.

"Do you think you and your little sister weren't innocent children when they set off that bomb? How would you rather I wage war against a government that's just as terroristic as me, if not more so? What should I do to fight a corrupt police force and government that are allied with Los Pepes? Haven't you noticed that I'm the only narco they're going after? At least I chose to be a bandit, and that's what I am. Not like them, who wear a uniform by day and then put on their hoods at night."

"Papá, nobody wins wars against institutions. We all lose."

Not long afterward, my father decided it was time to leave Aburrilandia, and we headed to a larger, more comfortable farmhouse in nearby Belén. Located at the end of the highway, the house had wide porches where my father spent hours and hours looking out at the impressive view of Medellín.

At the rear of the house were stables and a small, run-down pigsty. The caretaker, nicknamed "Blondie," communicated with the neighbors so they wouldn't become suspicious. He also took care of feeding four cows that my father purchased to give the appearance of normality. Those animals were a source of great pleasure for us. My father would bring in fresh milk, and we would drink it while it was still warm. In those small moments, we forgot about our uncertain future and the dire straits we were in.

While in Belén, we tried to entertain ourselves as best as we could. One day we started repairing a dilapidated little cabin that my father dubbed "the Pit." It was a fifteen-minute walk from the main house, inaccessible by road. Little Angel worked to fix the numerous leaks in the roof, I started painting the house, and Manuela and my father quickly joined in. Several days went by in which we were grateful simply to have a way to pass the time.

We still had to solve the electricity problem. The supply in the house was so weak that we had to turn out all the lights if we wanted to watch the news on a small television set. One time the television went out because Andrea went to the bathroom.

"Turn off the light, we're watching the news!" my father and I shouted in unison.

"Sorry, sorry, I forgot," she answered. "Sweetheart, bring me a flashlight, would you?"

One time, Snowflake, the little white puppy, got lost. We called his name everywhere and eventually spotted him across the street, socializing with the other dogs and leaping in the shrubbery. Though she knew Snowflake would come back when he felt like it, my sister watched him closely from across the street, praying that nobody would steal him because she knew we wouldn't be able to rescue him.

While in hiding, my parents were both able to communicate with family, associates, and a few friends through a coordinated system they'd developed. Little Angel would collect my father's correspondence from the designated message bearer, and Andrea would collect my mother's. They usually went down to Medellín together, split up, and then met up again for the return journey at an established time. Not a minute sooner or a minute later. Strict punctuality was essential due to the risk that one of them might be kidnapped and reveal the chain by which correspondence reached my father.

On May 25, 1993, my sister turned nine, and she, Andrea, and Blondie opted to go horseback riding nearby. When a couple of men in Medellín employee uniforms approached Andrea and asked if she was Fabio Ochoa Vásquez's wife, she said no, and the three returned immediately to alert my father. Our presence was becoming suspicious.

"Pack up just the things you need, we're leaving. The birthday party's canceled. We'll saddle up all the animals and load the luggage on them. We can go through the mountains back to Aburrilandia, which is on the other side of that peak. I know the bridle path that goes there," my father said, careful not to let Manuela hear him.

"Sweetie, I have a surprise adventure for your birthday. We're going to ride horses and walk a bit to see the forest flowers. I know you're going to love it," my father improvised, transforming an escape into an excursion.

Blondie and Little Angel loaded a white horse with a large bag of fruits and vegetables and some cash in a large briefcase along with three pistols, three AK-47s, and extra ammunition. My mother wanted to bring the birthday cake, which had taken a lot of trouble to get to the hideout, so the cake, too, was loaded onto one of the horses.

A half hour after my father first announced our hasty departure, we started hiking up into the hills. We soon lost sight of my father, who told Blondie he'd wait for us farther ahead with Manuela, Snowflake, and Cottonball. We continued along the bridle path, which grew ever more slippery as a drizzle turned into a downpour.

My mother was walking a few feet behind the horse, then came me, then Andrea. Suddenly we heard the loud noise of horseshoes scraping against the stone banks of the path. The white horse was startled and reared up on its hind legs, and the weight of its load caused it to flip over. Now on its back, the animal began to slide down toward us.

Andrea started running downhill, I followed, and my mother pushed and shouted behind me. The path had a small, elevated bank with a barbed wire border fence running along it. Andrea squeezed onto the bank as best as she could. Though she barely fit, in a moment of desperation I thought to myself, "If one person can fit, two will fit," and squeezed next to her, careful to avoid the barbed wire. My mother must have thought, "If two people can fit, three will fit," and if she hadn't jumped up with us, the horse would have severely injured her.

That incident behind us, we pulled ourselves together and walked all day. About ten minutes from the house, we caught up with my father, who was cheerfully playing with Manuela.

"How much longer, Papá?" I asked, worn out.

"We're almost there. We've passed the worst part, the uphill climb. Look, it's that little house you can see down there. See the roof? And some cows?"

When we arrived, on the verge of hypothermia, we traded our wet clothes for showers in water that was even colder than the rain had been. Once we were again dressed, we started to warm up. My mother prepared something to eat while we struggled to light a fire outdoors.

Bedtime came, and we went into the unfinished house, which was infested with all kinds of beetles that had been attracted to the light Blondie had left on. There was no way to get rid of them. Andrea and I couldn't sleep because of the intense cold. Despite the double layer of clothing we were wearing, we just couldn't get warm. Eventually we had to use her hair dryer to heat up the bed.

Acknowledging the blatant deterioration of our situation, my father told us one day that he was still working on his old idea of fighting alongside the ELN guerrilla group.

"I already have direct contact with them. They're going to give me a front to command. I'm going to buy it for a million dollars," he said. "Nobody will be able to catch me in the jungle. I can hide out there for a while, work on building my business back up, gain strength, and start moving ahead with the Rebel Antioquia project. I don't see any other way out of this. The government has already said it won't negotiate with me. It wants me dead."

I was silent. I didn't know how to respond to this pipe dream. My father had proven himself capable of escaping any danger, but we were living a different reality now. Our stay in that hide-out was so tedious and uncomfortable that my father eventually suggested we go back to the Pit. We happily took our leave of Aburrilandia.

It was June 3, 1993, and my turn to keep watch. I turned on the radio, and that's when I heard the announcement: my uncle Carlos Arturo Henao had died.

Terribly sad, I ran to tell my father and found him hugging my mother, who was weeping in front of the television. In striking out at my father, Los Pepes had murdered one of my mother's brothers, a man who had never participated in any violence and made his living selling mops in Cartagena. But he'd made the mistake of traveling to Medellín to visit his wife and children at a time when Los Pepes had controlled the Rionegro airport. That night, my mother lost her second brother. Mario and Carlos had been taken by violence, and Fernando would later be taken by cigarettes, drug abuse, and heartbreak.

MY FATHER WAS ALMOST COMPLETELY ISOLATED FROM THE outside world. Maybe that's why we didn't detect the presence of the authorities monitoring us for several weeks. My father couldn't stand staying in one place for too long, and he decided to move.

Over the next few months, we changed hideouts frequently. We left the Pit for a cabin in La Cristalina, a beautiful place in Magdalena Medio. From there, we went to an apartment near the Fourth Brigade's headquarters in Medellín, and from there to the Suramericana complex near the La Macarena bullring.

Now that I've set myself the task of accurately recalling the details of our life at that time, it's hard to say exactly how long we stayed at each place. We didn't count the days that year. It didn't matter whether it was Sunday, Monday, or Friday; there was no difference. All that we thought about was our safety. What we did learn was that the best way to move from one place to another was in the rain.

"The police don't like getting wet. So if it rains, that's the ideal time to move. There aren't any checkpoints when it rains," my father said.

Our relationship with the rain was different from that of most people. For us, the rain was a protective blanket that allowed us to move through the city. In the rain, we traveled more easily. Often, rain became a signal that it was time to leave.

So it was during a torrential downpour that we arrived at the Suramericana complex, entered through the basement, and went up to a tenth-floor apartment. The apartment had three bedrooms, a utility room where Little Angel slept, and a lovely view of the city. The people who took care of the hideout were waiting for us. My father explained to me that they were a newly married couple with a young baby who'd lost their jobs and didn't have a place to live. They were facing an uncertain future.

"I promised them I'd give them this apartment and the car when we didn't need them anymore. In fact, they're already in their name. They're really happy about it. Even though it's hard to live in secrecy, it's provided them with a nice little sum of money," he went on.

The best spot in the apartment was a small balcony that offered a view of the city and of the movements of the Search Bloc and military convoys. We spent many hours there.

One night on the balcony my father started to light a joint of marijuana. My mother made a disapproving face and shut herself in the room where Manuela was sleeping soundly. Andrea watched the scene from the living room and stayed quiet, flipping through some magazines. I was sitting between my father and Little Angel, who was also smoking. It was the first time I'd seen my father smoke, but I wasn't surprised. He had never lied to me about his vice, and I didn't judge him harshly for it. He once confessed that when I used to see him walk off from the house on the Nápoles estate, it was because he was going to smoke marijuana.

On that occasion, he'd given me a master class on the dangers of drug use, the differences between various drugs, and their effects and degrees of addictiveness. He told me that if I ever wanted to try one, I should do it not with my friends but with him.

In most of the hideouts, Andrea and my mother acted as Manuela's teacher. My mother had arranged to have her school assignments sent to us, and so Manuela had a daily school routine, whether in the city or in the jungle. It also helped pass the time. During prolonged confinement, boredom strikes sooner if you don't figure out ways to occupy your mind and body. So as not to derail my last year of high school, I, too, got homework from photocopies of the most diligent students' notebooks. I completed the assignments grudgingly for months. I found it difficult to concentrate.

To top off the uneasy atmosphere of our day-to-day life, the renowned astrologist Mauricio Puerta published his prediction that my father would die that very year. "It may be," he proclaimed, "that during this planetary transit, Escobar will have his appointment with death."

"Try to track that guy down and find out who he is so we can see what he says about you, Tata," my father suggested, which surprised us since he'd always been skeptical about fortunetelling and that sort of thing.

My mother managed to reach Puerta and sent him everybody's names and dates and times of birth. In return, we got cassette tapes with his predictions, which would later shock us when they came true. For example, he claimed that we'd live for many years in a city beside one of the largest rivers in the world without specifying which. Later we would settle in Buenos Aires, a city whose shores are lapped by the waters of the wide Río de la Plata. It wouldn't be until after my father's death that we would meet Puerta in person in Bogotá, but when it comes to our lives, he hasn't been wrong yet.

As always, the time came to move again. We waited for night-fall and, eyes closed, traveled to an old house in the city. It was dubbed "Little Blondie's house" in reference to a seven-year-old boy who lived there with his parents, the caretakers for the hideout. The house had a small courtyard next to the dining and living rooms, and you could look at the sky through the house's security bars. We celebrated Father's Day there. Each of us wrote my father a card, as was our custom on special occasions.

A few days later, my father agreed to let my mother, my sister, and Andrea spend a couple of days in the home of Alba Lía Londoño, a teacher, so that Manuela could get a change of scenery, see other people, learn a little about art, and have her spirits lifted. I chose to stay back with my father. At about five in the afternoon, as the couple who took care of the hideout tried to go do some shopping, they realized that the police were setting up a checkpoint on the street right in front of the house.

"We're going to have to postpone the shopping trip until these people leave. We have to hunker down here and keep quiet. Don't turn on any lights or the TV or the radio or anything. And Little Blondie can't make any noise—if he wants to play, he should go to the back, in the kitchen. Don't make noise until I say you can," my father instructed Little Blondie's father after confirming through a gap in the window frame that the police were still setting up the roadblock. "They aren't looking for me, but I don't want them to catch me here by pure chance."

It was a tense situation. My father said we should give the impression that the house was unoccupied so the police would ignore it. He spent a lot of time peering out the peephole in the front door and sometimes directed me to keep an eye on the movements of a police officer who was standing mere inches away. The officer's silhouette was perfectly visible, his rifle in his hands, the barrel pointing skyward, and his green hat with one side of the brim folded up.

The days passed, and the roadblock remained. The agents were replaced by new ones. Our food had run out, and all that was left to eat was an old pot of *mondongo* soup, which they boiled again, adding more water and a cube of chicken bouillon. There was nothing else.

For several days I felt overcome with fear. I went through periods of optimism, acceptance, denial, despair, and terror just imagining the hail of bullets if the police forced their way in and my father tried to face them down.

"Papá, what if those men stay a month? How are we going to leave if they think the house is empty?"

"Don't worry, son. They're going to leave any minute now. Relax, this is a great weight-loss plan," he said, smiling, as if we were on an exciting camping trip.

We spent those days in profound silence, compelled to absolute discretion to avoid detection. We hardly even talked. It was lucky, I thought, that my mother, Manuela, and Andrea weren't there, or things would have been even worse.

We had a little over two million dollars in cash sitting on the table. We could have bought the whole supermarket if we'd wanted to. But our hands were tied because nobody could leave the house. The feeling of powerlessness was overwhelming.

Finally, after eight days, our strength drained, the police cleared the roadblock and everything returned to normal.

Later that day, the refrigerator was full again. Then my mother, Manuela, and Andrea came back. We didn't tell them about the horrible experience we'd had in their absence.

Our movement from hideout to hideout never ceased. Next we went to the blue house. Though Los Pepes were threatening my father's lawyers more and more, one of them, Roberto Uribe, agreed to receive messages that my father sent with Little Angel. The contents of his letters had been all over the place as of late. Now, my father had raised the possibility of sending us out of the country, but he didn't trust the attorney general's office.

"Don't worry, Ula," my father said. "Ula" was my father's new nickname for my mother, his way of teasing her because she now had to cook, clean, and iron like Eulalia, a former housekeeper of ours. Having domestic help was no longer a luxury we could enjoy. "Roberto Uribe is helping to get you all out of the country. That's one of the conditions for my surrender. Attorney General De Greiff has promised to find you refuge in another country, and then I'll turn myself in."

Manuela and I started to notice that our parents were spending a lot of time discussing our future. Their conversations always quickly turned to the need to split up the family for everyone's sake.

"I know nothing's going to happen to you once you're out of the country," my father told me. "They already promised they'll find you a country to go to. In the meantime, I'll hide out in the jungle with the ELN, and you won't see me for a while as I prepare to turn myself in. Now, nothing would happen to you if you were in the jungle with me either—that's an option too—but you need to go to school, and you won't be able to do that there. The two of you are our priority, so I've decided our best move is for you to stay in the Altos building under the attorney general's protection, though your mother has her doubts. I've authorized the CTI to move into apartment 401 and organize your arrival, but you don't have to go there immediately. We'll spend your mother's birthday here together—it's coming up soon."

Hearing the news of our eventual separation was like having a bucket of ice water dumped on me. I thought about my future, but also about my father. Both were important to me, and I found myself at a major crossroads. I was sure his second surrender would bring peace to Colombia. I was confident he wouldn't waste this new opportunity. Allying with the ELN guerillas was a leap into the void. The only way I could be loyal to my father was to advise him to turn himself in without making further demands.

Those were gray and silent days. Our spirits were low, and a constant anguish permeated our lives. On September 3, 1993, my mother turned thirty-three. We celebrated, more out of habit than because anyone was in the mood for a party. For the first time, a special occasion went by without a fuss, and the food tasted like uncertainty.

Two days later, on September 5, we were able to forget our sorrows for a short time. The Colombian soccer team had defeated the visiting Argentine team 5–0 in the final classification match for the World Cup to be held in the United States in 1994. There in the blue house's small den, we cheered with every goal. I'll never forget that day, not simply because of the game, but because it had been years since I'd seen my father so happy.

But time marches on, and the day of our departure arrived. That was the first and only time my father let me see him cry. I wanted to cry too, but I managed to hold back and instead comforted him as he looked down with glistening eyes. It was September 18, 1993.

Though also deeply moved by our parting, I was now the one who had to encourage him to keep his head up, assuring him that everything would turn out OK. I was aware of the challenges, but I never doubted that my father would find a way to turn himself in. Life forced us to either choose certain death somewhere in the Colombian jungle or take a gamble on exile and surrender.

My father gave Manuela and then my mother a long hug. Andrea was the last one to say good-bye, and by that point he couldn't speak through his tears. I was still suffused with optimism.

"Well, unfortunately we have to go," I said, my voice breaking, and then gave him a final hug and kiss on the cheek. Recovered, my father said he continued to trust that the attorney general's agents were "good people" who would keep their word to prosecute Los Pepes. His words were reassuring—it was the first time he'd ever expressed faith in a government institution.

The one he truly didn't trust was his brother Roberto.

"Juancho and Tata, take good care of Manuela. If something happens to me, and Roberto still has money, he might help you out, but if he doesn't, protect Manuela. He wouldn't be above kidnapping her," my father said. "Give the attorney general the information I've got on Los Pepes. Take these addresses so you can hand them over. They say they haven't gone after Los Pepes because they don't have good information. Now they'll have it. All right, go on then. I'll follow you for a few blocks to make sure everything's OK. Don't forget to let me know when you've arrived safely."

We left the blue house, and I drove a green Chevrolet Sprint to the Altos building. I continuously glanced in the rearview mirror and saw my father and Little Angel behind us in another vehicle.

I felt that we were safe, but it seemed awfully risky for him to follow us practically to the door of the building where we would live. It was almost eleven o'clock at night when I turned left to pull up to the building's gate. My father honked twice and drove off. Once we were inside, we went up to the third floor, where the CTI agents were waiting. My father had told us they would arrive in small groups so nobody would realize they were there—and that they had something to protect. Everything was supposed to be handled very discreetly for security reasons.

I knocked on the door several times, but nobody answered. I rang the doorbell—nothing. I was starting to worry when I heard a voice: "Who is it? Identify yourself."

"I'm Juan Pablo Escobar Henao, Pablo Escobar's son. We're here on my father's instructions to be placed under the protection of the attorney general. Please open the door. I'm with my family."

"Are you armed?"

"Armed? What for, man? Jesus," I said.

They opened the door slowly and without a word. Two armed agents looked us up and down, their expressions conveying that they'd been expecting to confront fierce beasts. Inside the apartment, at the end of the hallway, several men were aiming R-15 rifles and MP5 submachine guns at us.

"Relax, guys, it's just us. Sorry for waking you. Go to sleep, and we'll talk tomorrow. We're going to go up to our apartment, number 401, and sleep there," I said.

"No, wait, at least two people have to be with you, for your safety," said "Alpha," one of the agents who seemed to be in charge.

"Well, come on then. Let's go and see how things are up there. There isn't a lot of furniture in that apartment."

As a matter of fact, the place was practically empty. There were only three mattresses and nothing in the kitchen, much less anything to eat or drink. We'd have to wait till the next day to address these issues. It was late.

The following day, my mother spoke with a neighbor, who loaned us some of her dishes, a few pots and pans, and even her housekeeper, who appeared a minute later with a tray full of food.

Two days later, Juan Carlos "the Nose" Herrera Puerta showed up. He was a childhood friend of mine who over time had become my personal bodyguard. I'd asked him to stay with me because I had a feeling we needed extra protection. He had an eight-round shotgun and a valid letter of safe-conduct. The CTI agents found his presence suspicious, as the only people authorized to have direct contact with me were Alpha and the agents known as "A1," "Empire," and "Panther."

As we slowly began to figure out our new life together, A1 informed me that the Nose was going to have to leave.

"Look, A1. As I understand it, you are looking out for us because that's the arrangement my father made with the attorney general and the government as part of his surrender negotiations. I don't have to ask your permission to invite someone to my own home. If I'm not mistaken, I'm under your protection, not under house arrest. Or have I misunderstood something?" I said.

The Nose stayed. With Empire's intervention, our relationship with A1 improved over the next few days, and we even started to play pick-up soccer games in the basement.

The calm period we experienced in the Altos building would be shattered after five one evening, when we heard explosions that sounded like firecrackers. I cautiously peeked out a window and saw four private vehicles stopped in the middle of the intersection of Transversal Inferior and Loma del Campestre. Armed men in civilian dress got out of each vehicle, and what sounded like a bunch of young people playing around with fireworks turned out to be a hail of bullets against the façade of the Altos building.

We hid in the dressing room of the master suite, and the Nose, who had taken shelter behind a large planter, said it was no use trying to fight back because he didn't have a long-range weapon. A few minutes later, A1 and Alpha arrived, nervous, weapons drawn.

"Listen, A1, why don't you go after those people and catch them? They're right there on the corner shooting right and left," I said, desperate.

"Don't you see I can't? My mission is to protect you, not to go out and arrest people," he tried to justify himself.

"So why are there more than twenty agents here looking after us if you're not going to do anything when we get attacked?" I insisted.

Eventually the four vehicles drove off.

The surprise attack made it even harder for Manuela to fall asleep each night. Andrea lost her appetite from nerves, and a few days later she ended up passing out. We had to take her to a clinic, escorted by the Nose and fifteen CTI agents.

The Altos building was gradually converted into a fortress. The agents used dozens of sandbags to build three barricades, one on top of the roof of the guard post at the entrance, where one agent stood watch twenty-four hours a day, and two others at the corners of the property that faced the street. At the same time, more men came from Bogotá, and the number of CTI agents grew to forty; they were armed with rifles, pistols, and submachine guns. There were constant patrols inside the building, and a massive, ear-splitting siren was installed on the building's roof to alert us of any danger.

We soon had the chance to try out the siren when we heard gunshots, and everyone ran to take their positions. We hurried to hide in the far corner of the dressing room in the master suite, and the Nose stood guard so no one could get in. The minutes dragged on forever. My mother, my sister, and Andrea prayed while I talked with the Nose through the doors.

When things quieted down again, a CTI agent known as "Car Bomb" explained that three men had jumped out of two cars and started shooting. One of them had fired a rifle grenade that hit the façade of the building's fifth floor.

Panther arrived a few hours later with news from the attorney general in Bogotá: "De Greiff wants you to know that he's looking for a country for you all. He's not holding things up—it's a delicate matter and has to be dealt with carefully. That's why things are moving so slowly. He says to trust that he wants your father to turn himself in."

Wanting to inform my father of everything that was happening, I began recording all of these events with a small video camera. I spent hours on the balcony recording the vehicles I found suspicious. It was like a video diary of every anomaly, of each attack.

One day we got a horrible scare when Empire told me the Search Bloc was currently conducting a massive operation against my father in Belén Aguas Frías—Aburrilandia. Apparently they'd nearly located him by triangulating a radiotelephone conversation between the two of us. The agent's real motive, it turned out, was to observe my reaction to confirm whether the location might be correct.

A few days later we received a letter from my father that described the bloodcurdling details of his miraculous escape. He said that when he saw the police coming, he knew the radiotelephone had given him away. He added that he had an advantage because the mountain was really steep, so when he saw the law, he went running along some dangerous cliffs. Along the way he lost his radio and flashlight. He was frightened and thought he'd met his end at last as his energy began to dwindle in the cold and rain. He finally emerged in a neighborhood in Belén, where people stared at him because he was covered in mud. Luckily, nobody recognized him with his beard. There, he hailed a taxi to a cousin's house.

The agents watching us couldn't understand how I'd managed to stay in epistolary contact with my father even though they searched everyone going in and out of the building. They didn't understand how I'd been able to pass on De Greiff's messages to my father, especially when none of us ever left the apartment.

They failed to realize that, right under their noses, several people had been generously aiding us. For example, Alicia Vásquez, one of the building managers, offered to help us in any way she could, since we couldn't leave even just to go out to the visitors' parking lot. The agents never searched Alicia, so she'd receive correspondence from various relatives at her home and then bring it into the building. Another person who ferried our correspondence was Nubia Jiménez, Manuela's nanny. She would retrieve letters from Alba Lía Londoño, our teacher, who would have received them from Little Angel.

After his close escape from Aburrilandia, I lost contact with my father again until October 6, 1993, when Empire came running into the apartment. "I heard they nabbed a guy called Little Angel. Do you know him? Who was he? They told me he and his brother died in a shootout with the police here in Medellín."

"I don't know much about him. He wasn't anybody important—I saw him around in La Catedral, but he wasn't really anybody," I replied, holding back tears. I knew this news meant they were very close to catching my father.

And so we spent October 31 masking our fear and worry with the makeup applied by a woman my mother hired to help Manuela with her costume. The building held a small Halloween gathering with several of the neighbors—nothing special like in the past. The Nose lamented that he couldn't see his little son's costume as he was busy taking care of me.

The secret of how I'd been communicating with my father would soon be discovered, and involvement became riskier. When the Nose requested permission to go see his son, I asked him to leave by crossing the little creek beside the pool, the same exit we'd used to evade Los Pepes on the day of our thwarted trip to the United States.

"No, Juancho, don't make me get my shoes wet tromping through that ditch. The CTI guys are going to help me out—I already asked them and they said they would. Don't worry, I'll grab a taxi out there. I won't lead them to my house."

Ignoring my pleas, the Nose told me to relax; Alpha, A1, and

Empire would take him to the main road in El Poblado in the same Chevrolet Sprint we'd arrived in several weeks earlier. A few days later, my worst fears were borne out. The Nose was to return on Sunday, November 7, late in the afternoon. But he never arrived, and his body was never found. Los Pepes had disappeared him.

Two days later, on Tuesday, November 9, heavily armed men in hoods swarmed the Los Almendros housing development, battered down the door, and dragged out our teacher, Alba Lía Londoño. We never heard from her again either.

When I learned of Alba Lía's death, I knew I had to make an urgent call to save Nubia Jiménez, Manuela's nanny. She and Alba Lía were each links in the chain of family communication, so she would surely be targeted next. I rushed into an empty apartment and dialed as fast as I could. The phone rang several times, and when Nubia's son finally answered, he told me his mother had just gone down to meet a taxi.

"Please run after her, don't let her get in that taxi. They're going to kill her. Run now—now, now!" I shouted, and the boy dropped the phone and raced after her.

I was shaking and praying, the telephone pressed to my ear, hoping he'd reach his mother in time. I waited impatiently until I once again heard the boy's footsteps. He picked up the phone, very upset, and told me he hadn't managed to stop her. She'd been tricked into going out for a fake appointment with the teacher, who I knew had already been disappeared.

A new stage in the hunt for my father had begun. Los Pepes knew that tracking down each communication link would eventually bring them to Pablo Escobar. And since that was their one purpose, no other life mattered. Just as the lives of many people had not mattered to my father.

I thought about who else Nubia might implicate if Los Pepes tortured her, and I suggested to Andrea that we do a head count. Though most of the people associated with us who were still alive had gone into hiding, we found that one was still in his usual residence in Envigado: "Tribilín," one of my father's bodyguards.

We knew Tribi would be the next victim since he was easy to locate. We didn't know exactly where he lived, but someone at the Altos building supplied the address, and we sent a housecleaner to warn him. She came back forty minutes later, in tears.

"I'd almost gotten there when several cars appeared with armed men in hoods," she said, distraught. But there was nothing that could be done. Tribilín was wounded in a shootout trying to defend himself, and Los Pepes carried him off.

After that night, I never let go of the weapon the Nose had left behind in our apartment. I knew there were very few people remaining on Los Pepes' list. Almost everyone involved with my father was dead, and the few who weren't had fled or were rotting in prison. We, his family, were the only ones my father had left. So my mother, my sister, and the teacher's two children, who had arrived that afternoon, slept on mattresses in the dressing room. Andrea, brave and supportive, stayed by my side out in the apartment.

Those were the most agonizing nights of my life. I would close one eye so the other could rest. The chaotic situation and the broken communication with my father made it more difficult for us to leave the country, and the process seemed to have stalled. That became all the more clear when Panther brought us a message from Ana Montes, the national director of the attorney general's office and Attorney General De Greiff's right hand, demanding that my father turn himself in before they find a country to take us. They were no longer interested in helping us leave. Now it was blackmail. We were literally sleeping with the enemy.

GIVEN THIS HOSTILE ATMOSPHERE AND THE LOOMING THREAT OF death, we decided to travel to Germany without consulting anybody, having had a third party buy our tickets. But it'd turn out that the government was keeping an eye out and had quickly learned of our destination: Frankfurt.

As we awaited the day of our departure, Ana Montes icily told me that the attorney general's office was bringing two charges against me: for the alleged rapes of several young women in El Poblado and for the transport of illegal goods. It was clear they were going to try anything to keep us from leaving the country.

"Look, ma'am," I said, staring her right in the eyes, "your accusation that I raped women is unbelievable. I'd never do such a thing. Forgive me, but it would be more likely for them to rape me than the other way around. I don't want to exaggerate here, but I often have to push the women off me. They'll do anything to be with Pablo's son. So I don't need to rape anybody, I assure you."

"Well, we haven't confirmed this information yet, but several girls have talked and said that one of the rapists claimed to be related to Pablo Escobar and had blond hair, so we assumed they were talking about you. I believe you, but what about the box of guns you brought into the building?" she probed, sure that she had me now.

"Guns? Who saw any guns? I'm going to make a suggestion, ma'am. If you want, I'll stay here while you take as many men as you like and search this apartment from top to bottom. Take apart the whole building while you're at it so you can find that box you're so worried about. You don't need a warrant, you have my permission."

"All right, I believe you, I believe you. You'd better not be lying to me. I'm going back to Bogotá to keep working. There's no need to search the building. But tell your father to turn himself in, and we'll get you out of the country. Oh, and tell him not to take too long with his decision. We're going to have to call off your protection in the next few days, and you'll be left with the same level of protection that the Colombian government offers all its citizens."

"How could you do such a thing? Why?" my mother exclaimed.

"My God, how could you leave my children and me unprotected? You have no right! We're here because that's what you wanted, because you promised to get us out of the country and offer us refuge in exchange for my husband's surrender. And now you're threatening to remove our protection!"

Finally, on a sunny morning in late November, we left for Bogotá to catch a direct flight to Frankfurt. But just as we'd foreseen, Germany refused us entry even though we had all our papers in order. They forced us to return to Colombia at the request of the government and the attorney general's office.

Back in Colombia again, on November 29, officials from the attorney general's office met us at the airport and informed us that the only place they could guarantee our safety was in Residencias Tequendama, an exclusive apartment hotel in downtown Bogotá. We spent the next few hours there, with no idea as to my father's whereabouts. We only hoped he'd get in touch soon.

On December 2, my father woke up a little earlier than usual and turned on the radio he used to get news about us. Meanwhile, though still exhausted from traveling to Europe and back in less than forty-eight hours, we got up at seven in the morning. I received several phone calls requesting interviews with the media, both local outlets and some of the most prominent ones in Europe, Asia, and the United States, and I responded to all that we would not be issuing any statements. The day before, I'd said a few brief words on the radio to let my father know, in my own voice, that we were OK and to send him a birthday greeting.

At about one in the afternoon, after we'd had lunch sent up to our room, we got a call to inform us that four army generals would be coming to speak with the family. There was no way to refuse the meeting. After a few pleasantries, they assured us that one hundred soldiers were protecting the building and that they were ordering the evacuation of the rest of the twenty-ninth floor.

As we were talking, the telephone rang, and I answered as usual. It was the receptionist.

"Sir, good afternoon, I have Mr. Pablo Escobar on the line, and he wishes to speak with you."

"Hi, Grandma, how are you doing? Don't worry, we're fine, we're doing OK," I told my father, knowing he would understand that I wasn't alone. I reluctantly hung up even though I was desperate to talk to him.

As we continued our conversation with the generals, I was afraid my father wouldn't call back, yet five minutes later the phone rang again.

"Grandma, please don't call again, we're fine," I repeated, but he told me not to hang up and asked for my mother, who hurried into the next room.

I showed the generals to the door and went to warn my mother not to take too long on the phone since the call was surely being traced. She nodded and said good-bye to my father: "Take good care of yourself, you know we all need you," she said, sobbing.

"Don't worry, my love, my only incentive in life is to fight for all of you. I'm in a cave here. I'm very, very safe. We've gotten through the hard part now."

In a third phone call, I explained to him that the previous day I'd spoken with the journalist Jorge Lesmes from *Semana* magazine, who had offered to send an envelope with several questions about our situation. I told my father that I liked the idea because we could think about the answers carefully; the other reporters, every single one of them, wanted live interviews.

"Tell him yes, and to send the questions when he has them ready," my father said.

Surprisingly, my father seemed to have abandoned his old precautions regarding the length of phone calls. His main protection during the nearly twenty years of his criminal career had been to keep all communications brief, but now it seemed not to matter. It's as if he didn't care that the Search Bloc and Los Pepes would be tracking the location he was calling from, as had happened recently and only by a miracle had he escaped.

"Papá, don't call anymore. They're going to kill you," I said anxiously.

But he ignored me.

Lesmes's list of questions arrived sometime after two in the afternoon. When my father called again, I let him know, and he asked me to read the questions out while Lemon wrote them down in a notebook. He had the phone on speaker. I read the first five, and then he broke in and said he'd call back in twenty minutes.

He called at the appointed time, and I started writing down his answers. I wished I had a doctor's handwriting so I could scribble faster.

"I'll call you right back," my father said when we were halfway through.

I idly flipped through a magazine for what felt like only a minute, and then the phone rang again. I thought it was him.

"Juan Pablo, this is Gloria Congote from QAP. The police have confirmed that your father was just taken down at Medellín's Obelisco shopping center."

I was silent, stunned—it wasn't possible. I had talked to him just seven minutes earlier.

"At the Obelisco shopping center? What was my father doing there? That seems really strange to me."

"It's been confirmed."

I signaled to Andrea to turn on the radio, where they were already speculating about the possibility that my father had died in a police operation. When we'd confirmed the news from the radio, the journalist, still on the line, asked for a statement. She got it, and it's one I regret to this day: "We don't want to talk right now. But yes, I'll kill the fuckers who killed him myself. I'll kill them my-self, the bastards."

I hung up the telephone and wept disconsolately. We all wept. I quickly pushed aside my sadness and started visualizing how I could seek revenge. My desire for vengeance was overwhelming. But then I experienced a moment of reflection that turned out to be life-changing. Two paths appeared before me: becoming a dead-lier version of my father, or setting aside his bad example forever. In that instant, I recalled the many moments of depression and tedium we'd experienced while living with my father in hiding. I knew I could not take the path I had so often criticized.

I decided to retract my statement. I immediately called the jour-nalist Yamid Amat, director of the TV news program *CM&*, and explained what had happened with Gloria Congote. I said, "I want to make it very clear that I will not seek revenge. I will not avenge my father's death. The only thing I care about now is the future of my family, who have suffered so much. I'm going to work hard to help us move forward so we can pursue education and be respect-able people, and anything I can do to promote peace in this coun-try, I will do."

The events that followed are now history. My father died on December 2, 1993, at three in the afternoon, and many aspects of his life—as well as his death—continue to be subject to investigation and debate.

Over the course of these twenty-one years, many different claims have been made about the identity of the person who was actually responsible for the bullet that killed my father. There are numerous versions, the latest of which appeared in September 2014, as I was giving this manuscript a final polish. In his book *How We Killed the Boss,* the extradited ex-paramilitary leader Diego Murillo

Bejarano, known as Don Berna, claimed that his brother Rodolfo, known as "Seed," had been the one who fired the shot that killed my father.

Who killed him? It doesn't really matter. What does matter—and what I would like to emphasize—is that the forensic exam performed at six that Thursday evening by the specialists John Jairo Duque Alzate and Javier Martínez Medina indicates that he was shot three times, once fatally.

One bullet came from a gun of unknown caliber, fired by a person who was covering the rear entrance of the house where my father was hiding. When he climbed out onto the roof and then, seeing that the area was surrounded, tried to rush back in, the bullet hit him in the back of his shoulder and traveled from there into his lower jaw, where it lodged between teeth 35 and 36.

The forensic report mentions a second bullet that hit his left thigh and created a hole an inch in diameter. But in the photos from moments after his death, there is no trace of blood on his pants. In those photos taken when they laid his naked corpse on a steel table to perform the autopsy, no wounds are visible on his left leg.

There is no doubt that when he was hit in the shoulder, my father fell onto the roof and was injured. Escape was impossible. And so I want to focus on the third gunshot, the one that killed him instantly. The bullet hit him in "the upper section of the concha of the right auricle, with an irregularly shaped exit wound with everted edges in the lower left preauricular region." The bullet, whose caliber the report does not mention, entered through the right side and exited through the left. I have no wish to stir up new controversy, but I am absolutely certain that my father was the one who fired that bullet, exactly where he always said he would shoot himself in the event he was about to be captured: in the right ear.

On several occasions throughout the relentless hunt, my father told me that the day he came face-to-face with his enemies, he would fire only fourteen of the fifteen rounds in his Sig Sauer pistol at them, saving the last one for himself. In the photo that shows my father's body on the roof, you can see that the Glock pistol is in its holster, but his Sig Sauer is lying nearby and has clearly been fired.

I remember one of the times my father mentioned the possibility of taking his own life. He was talking with one of his men over the radiophone during a raid. I never forgot what he said. Nor did I know that it had been recorded by the Search Bloc and that I would hear it again long after his death: "Those bastards will never fucking take me alive."

14

Peace with the Cartels

At midday on December 5, 1993, barely forty-eight hours after my father's funeral in Medellín, we were pulled out of our sadness and uncertainty by the announcement that the horse enthusiast Fabio Ochoa Restrepo had arrived to see us at Residencias Tequendama.

We'd known Don Fabio since the early 1980s, after meeting his sons, the Ochoa brothers, at the 1979 Renault Cup. As he entered, we were amazed to discover that he'd brought dozens of containers of all sizes, all of them full of food, as if he'd emptied out his entire restaurant: something like a hundred fifty *bandejas paisas*, the favorite dish of the Antioquia region, enough food for us and all the soldiers, police officers, DAS detectives, and CTI, DIJIN, and SIJIN agents who were guarding us. It was completely over the top, in true Medellín fashion, and of course most welcome, our feast of beans, arepas, ground beef, sausage, pork rinds, eggs, and plantains, but it was the only good news the Ochoa patriarch had brought. At the end of the visit, at around five in the afternoon, he told us in a calm but solemn voice that he'd heard that Fidel Castaño, the leader of Los Pepes, still had a hit out on my mother, my sister, and me.

"Fidel Castaño says that Pablo Escobar was a warrior but that he made the mistake of having a family. That's why he doesn't have anybody, so nothing can hurt him," Don Fabio Ochoa added.

The information Don Fabio Ochoa had just shared felt like a death sentence. We were all too familiar with the immense power of Castaño, the head of the group that had hunted down my father. From that day on until we left Colombia nine months later, we'd maintain a much closer relationship with Fabio Ochoa Restrepo than we had when my father was still alive. He'd constantly send us food from his restaurant, and my sister Manuela would frequently visit him to ride his best horses.

Once we'd learned that Castaño was still determined to have us killed, we decided to make a desperate play: we sent a message from my mother, begging him to spare her children and stressing that she had never been involved in the war and was ready to make peace with her dead husband's enemies. Castaño had once been a close friend of my father's, and they'd had some success trafficking cocaine together. My mother was somewhat optimistic because, as she recalled, she and Fidel Castaño shared an interest in art. Castaño often traveled to Europe, especially Paris—where he was said to own a luxurious apartment that held a large portion of his art collection—to visit museums and buy artwork. Once, my mother showed him her collection of paintings and sculptures, which was scattered throughout the two floors of the 16,000-square-foot penthouse of the Mónaco building. There wasn't a bare wall in the place. She was very proud when a famous gallery owner told her that hers was the largest art collection in Latin America.

Fidel Castaño had been impressed by the quality of the works my mother had acquired by artists such as Fernando Botero, Édgar Negret, Darío Morales, Enrique Grau, Francisco Antonio Cano, Alejandro Obregón, Débora Arango, Claudio Bravo, Oswaldo Guayasamín, Salvador Dalí, Igor Mitoraj, and Auguste Rodin, along with valuable antiques such as Chinese vases and pre-Columbian pieces made of gold and clay. In return, a few weeks later Castaño invited my parents to dinner at his enormous mansion, Montecasino, a veritable fortress surrounded by high walls, where Los Pepes would later be born and within which the group's biggest crimes would be plotted.

The evening was a tense one. My father felt very uncomfortable at Castaño's place. He wasn't used to such ostentatious displays, by both the waiters and even Fidel himself, who greeted them in a tuxedo and had the table set with elegant silver dishware and five forks each. When it was time to eat, my father whispered to my mother for instructions on how to crack open the crab claws without making a fool of himself at the table.

Once dinner was over, Fidel showed them the house and his collection of French wines, informing them that he'd directed his staff to ready a Turkish steam bath and a hot tub.

"So we can relax, Pablo," he'd said.

My father struggled to conceal his irritation and rejected the invitation, offering the lame excuse that he had an appointment. I always thought Fidel Castaño fancied my mother, and that's why my father was so upset. Ultimately, he was jealous, and he even forbade Castaño to visit my mother at the Mónaco penthouse.

The cautious optimism we felt after sending Castaño the message turned to relief when we got his reply, a three-paragraph letter in which he said he bore us no ill will and that in fact he'd commanded Los Pepes to return a number of works of art they'd stolen from us, including the valuable painting *Rock and Roll* by the Spanish artist Salvador Dalí.

For the moment, we'd gotten Fidel Castaño off our backs. Little did we realize there was a long road ahead of us still. In the months to come, we'd have to face some of the most powerful and dangerous capos and paramilitary leaders in the country—and they'd be less understanding.

As the days passed, we began to receive visits at Residencias Tequendama from the wives and girlfriends of my father's most important lieutenants, the men who'd surrendered to the authorities after escaping from the La Catedral prison. Among them were

Otoniel González, known as Otto; Carlos Mario Urquijo, known as Stud; and Luis Carlos Aguilar, known as Crud. It was well known that my father was generous with his men, paying them large sums of money for their work, such as kidnappings, murders, and assassinations. They received money for everything they did.

The women, who sometimes stayed with us for several days, delivered messages from the capos of the cartels that had opposed my father, demanding money as compensation for the war. Ángela, Popeye's girlfriend, asked us to go to La Modelo prison to meet with the drug trafficker Iván Urdinola, as he had a message from the Cali Cartel capos. Urdinola's name was familiar to us. At some point, my father had shown us letters in which Urdinola had assured him that he wasn't allied with the Cali Cartel and expressed solidarity with my father. Though Urdinola's request, especially sent through Popeye's girlfriend, seemed strange, at the time we were unaware that we were about to embark on one of the most difficult periods of our lives, even more dangerous than the worst moments we'd spent in hiding with my father. We were about to enter the inconceivable process of seeking peace with the various drug trafficking cartels. I would turn seventeen soon, and I was quite frightened about reaching adulthood, which I couldn't avoid however much I wanted. Ultimately, I was Pablo Escobar's son, and with him dead, his enemies would turn their gaze to me.

While we were contemplating whether to go see Urdinola, my mother and I began visiting my father's men in the prisons with the permission of the attorney general's office, which not only protected us but also secured visitor's passes. Though we had bodyguards, we opted to make separate trips to the prisons to avoid offering up an easy target for an attack. Our intention was to talk with all of my father's men about the possibility of negotiating peace with the cartels. It wasn't hard to persuade them to set aside any hostility they harbored toward the other cartels, as none of them had any military power and going back to war would have been suicidal. Many of them clearly had turned themselves back in after the La Catedral raid without even consulting with my father because they were tired of all the violence.

One day I went to La Picota prison, where Stud, Tití, and Crud were incarcerated. In the distance, I also spotted Leonidas Vargas, a legendary capo whose seat of power was in Caquetá, near the border with Ecuador.

One of my father's men approached and told me that Vargas had a message for us: we needed to pay him a million dollars that my father owed him. I doubted it, but a number of the prisoners vouched for the close relationship between my father and Don Leo. One of them added, "Juancho, you all need to figure out how to pay that man. He's honest, but he's brutal too. So it would be best to smooth things over with him so you don't have any trouble."

The debt was real, but there was a problem: we didn't have any money.

Around that time, we'd gotten word that the attorney general had finally arranged to return one of my father's planes that they'd confiscated almost ten years earlier. We had it appraised and found out it was worth close to a million dollars, the amount we owed Vargas. In the end he actually came out ahead: in an abandoned hangar in Medellín's Olaya Herrera Airport, we found three hundred thousand dollars' worth of plane parts that would work only for that specific aircraft. So we offered him the luxurious plane and the parts as a gift. Once his pilots confirmed that the aircraft was in good flying condition, he accepted.

And so we paid off one more of my father's debts and got another potential enemy off our backs. We had no appetite for more war. We needed to neutralize any possibility of violence, and we could only do so with money or other assets.

Once we'd made our rounds through a few prisons, it was time to visit Iván Urdinola in La Modelo. My mother had already gone to speak with him, but he'd insisted that I join too. I was pale when

I left Residencias Tequendama that morning in early 1994, as must have been apparent to the bodyguards and driver accompanying me in the attorney general's office's armored SUV. When we arrived at the prison and I started to get out of the vehicle, the driver took my arm and gave me a little white-and-gold keychain with an image of the baby Jesus on it.

"Juan Pablo, I want to give you this image to protect you because I know you're going through one of the hardest moments of your life," the man said, and I looked him in the eyes and thanked him, deeply touched.

I was wearing large, dark sunglasses so none of the prisoners could recognize me as the guards led me into the maximum-security wing. Otto and Popeye said that Urdinola was expecting me. The courtyard was full of men who had once served my father, old acquaintances such as José Fernando Posada and Sergio Alfonso Ortiz, known as "the Bird."

"Don't worry, Juancho, Don Iván is a good person. Nothing's going to happen to you. He's my son's godfather," Popeye assured me after a string of laudatory descriptions of Urdinola.

I entered the cell to find Urdinola with two men I didn't recognize. Then five more appeared, one of them noticeably tall with an air of mystery about him.

"Well, brother, you know who won the war, and you know that the new head capo, the one who runs everything now, is Don Gilberto [Rodríguez Orejuela]. So you're going to have to go to Cali to work out your problems with them, but first we need a show of good faith," he said.

What did I need to do to get on their good side? I had to retract a statement I'd made to the attorney general's office accusing the Cali capos of being responsible for the bombing of the Mónaco building on January 13, 1988. Even though that had been one of the most terrifying moments of my life, I knew I had no choice. Urdinola told me a lawyer would come see me in the next few days.

Backing out of an old accusation in exchange for staying alive seemed simple enough, but when I looked into Urdinola's eyes, I felt nothing but fear.

"Don Iván, I'm very sorry, but I'm really scared to go to Cali. Nobody in their right mind would go just so he could be killed. This goes against my most natural instinct. I know a lot of people have gone and come back, but it's not the same thing if I go and come back in a body bag. After all, I'm Pablo's son," I said.

"Who do you think you are, saying you won't go to Cali?" Urdinola replied testily. "The very agents looking after you are the ones who are ready to kill you; they're just waiting for us to call them up and give the order. Do you think killing you would cost them a lot of money? You think the thugs are charging a lot these days? Killing you would cost three hundred million pesos, and if you want I can call the boys who are going to do it right now. Now get out of here, assholes," Urdinola said as his wife, Lorena Henao, walked in. "I'm going to screw my wife."

Urdinola's words had left me dazed. I walked out of his cell racked by an indescribable unease. I was barely seventeen, and death seemed to be staring me in the face. Lost in thought, I was surprised to feel two gentle pats on my shoulder. It was the tall, mysterious man I'd noticed a few minutes earlier. He pulled me aside and told me to follow him. He wanted to talk to me.

"Juan Pablo, I know you're scared to go to that meeting, and I understand your fear. It's perfectly valid. But keep in mind that the Cali people are tired of violence, so you should take advantage of this opportunity to work out your problems once and for all. Urdinola just told you that your death has already been decided, so if you don't go, they're going to kill you anyway. You don't have many options, and it'll be easier to save yourself if you go and show your face," the man said, his words striking me as sincere.

"I appreciate the advice, but I don't know who you are. What's your role in all of this?" I asked.

"I'm Jairo Correa Alzate, and I was one of your father's enemies starting back when Henry Pérez was head of the Magdalena Medio paramilitary group. I own the El Japón estate in La Dorada, Caldas, and I had a lot of problems with your father. I'm in prison while we fight over whether they're going to extradite me to the U.S."

My short chat with Jairo Correa was eye-opening. At last, I saw a light at the end of the tunnel. I realized if I went to Cali, there was a slight possibility of coming out of this mess alive.

Popeye offered to accompany me to the exit, and as we walked down a long, narrow hallway, he said he had something to tell me.

"Juancho, I need you to know that Otto forced me to help him steal the La Pesebrera estate from your family. If I hadn't, I would have ended up on the outs with him."

My father's men didn't see us as the family of the boss who'd made them immensely wealthy, but as spoils of war. Of the men who were still alive after my father's death, I can say with certainty that only one of them remained loyal. The others exhibited only ingratitude and greed.

Just as Urdinola and I had agreed, a couple of days after my visit to La Modelo, a lawyer met with me in an empty room at Residencias Tequendama, where the agents from SIJIN and the attorney general's office couldn't hear us.

The lawyer got right to the point and instructed me to say that my father had forced me to finger the Cali Cartel capos for the Mónaco explosion in 1988 and that I had no definitive proof that they'd been responsible. A few minutes later, the prosecutor on the case and his secretary arrived to take my new statement on the first floor while the lawyer waited upstairs. From their expressions, it was clear that the two government workers realized I was acting under tremendous pressure. Their faces reflected their frustration at seeing one of their few solid cases against the Cali capos fall apart.

But there was nothing they could do, and once we were finished, they handed me a copy of the statement, and I took it up to the lawyer. After reading the retraction, she took her cell phone from her purse, dialed, and said, "No need to worry, sir, everything's settled."

Jairo Correa's counsel had been so helpful that I visited him in prison on three other occasions, since I felt like he was honest with me. We spent hours talking about life, reflecting on the things that had happened in an extremely respectful and cordial manner, and I had the chance to apologize for the damage my father had caused him and his family. I was amazed that we got along so well when he and my father had not, and I expressed regret that they hadn't been able to diplomatically work out their differences and live in peace. His response was that my father had always been surrounded by very bad advisers.

On one of those trips I found Urdinola, very drunk, in the company of an Italian man who was selling him industrial machinery. When Urdinola saw me, he gave me a cheerful greeting—probably because he was liquored up—and opened a box that contained at least fifty high-end watches.

"Pick whichever one you want," he said to me.

"No, Don Iván, why would you do such a thing? I'm very grateful, but there's no need," I said three times, but he was insistent.

"Take this one. It cost me a hundred thousand dollars." He made me put one on even though it was a little small for my wrist. It was a Philippe Charriol watch with a circle of diamonds around the face and solid gold hands.

My trips to La Modelo had one significant outcome: our first direct contact with my father's enemies. Just as Urdinola had demanded the first time I'd visited him, we arranged an initial meeting with the Cali Cartel. Ángela—Popeye's girlfriend—and Ismael Mancera—my uncle Roberto Escobar's lawyer—were to meet with Miguel and Gilberto Rodríguez Orejuela, the Cali capos. Urdinola had known that Popeye wasn't important within the cartel, and he'd wanted Vicky, Otto's wife, to travel to Cali instead, but Vicky was afraid, so he had no choice but to send Ángela.

The two emissaries traveled to Medellín and communicated the intention of my family and the men who'd comprised my father's criminal operation: to call off the war once and for all and find a way out that ensured we'd all live. When they returned, Ángela and Ismael Mancera told us that although the Rodríguez brothers had said little, they had seemed willing to negotiate.

The meeting must have been somewhat successful, because a few days later we got a call from a gruff man instructing us to let him into our apartment; he had a message from the Rodríguezes. And so we ended up having lunch with one of my father's old enemies, whom I will not name for security reasons. He was stern, though he occasionally displayed compassion. The Cali capos' message was clear and straightforward: it was going to cost us a lot to be allowed to stay alive. They needed to recover the money they'd invested in the war against my father and more.

"Juan Pablo, I spent more than eight million dollars fighting your father, and I have every intention of getting that money back," the man said. He didn't raise his voice, but it was clear he was determined to collect on his debt.

We were trapped, and we knew it. The security detail assigned to "protect" us at Residencias Tequendama hadn't even searched our unexpected visitor. There was no longer any doubt that our survival depended entirely on handing over all of my father's assets.

The flurry of messages, threats, and uncertainty came to a head in the last week of January 1994, when Alfredo Astado, my mother's distant relative, stopped by without warning. He'd just returned from the United States to speak with us about an urgent matter. He'd been living in the States for a number of years, having emigrated to escape the war and protect his family, even though he'd never been involved in shady business dealings or had run-ins with the law in Colombia.

Alfredo told us that he'd been at home when he received a call on his cell phone from none other than Cali Cartel capo Miguel Rodríguez Orejuela.

"Alfredo, it's Miguel Rodríguez . . . We need you to come to Cali. We want to talk to you," the capo had said brusquely, without even a hello.

"Sir, I have a number of matters to tend to here and won't be able to go to Colombia for another two or three months," Alfredo had said.

"I'll give you four days. And if you try to disappear, I'll track you down, but with another purpose in mind."

Alfredo's story was unsettling. Only a few people knew his phone number, and he'd been in a medium-sized city in the United States where he rarely encountered other Colombians. He'd traveled to Bogotá to see us before he would head to Cali.

Though we begged him to skip the meeting, Alfredo replied that he didn't have a choice. The Rodríguezes had already located him once. They'd be able to track him down anywhere on the planet.

The Cali capos had obviously dismissed the overtures of Ismael Mancera and Ángela and had elected to seek direct contact with us. Alfredo traveled to Cali immediately, staying at the InterContinental Hotel. A man picked him up the next day and drove him to a luxurious house south of Cali where the Rodríguez Orejuela brothers and three others he'd never seen before were waiting.

"Señor Astado, we've looked into you; we know all about you. You have a lot of ties with the Henao family in Palmira, and you're one of the people who can resolve a problem for us. The war with Pablo got out of hand, and a lot of innocent people died. We want to deal with the root causes of the situation, and that's why we need to talk to Pablo's widow," Miguel Rodríguez explained, acting as the group's spokesman.

Alfredo relaxed at this: apparently he wasn't in any danger. He not only offered his services for whatever was needed but suggested that my mother and I travel to Cali to meet with them.

The response, from Gilberto Rodríguez this time, was firm.

"We'll meet with her, fine, but not with Juan Pablo Escobar. That boy eats like a duck, walks like a duck, is a duck—he's just like Pablo. He's a little kid who should be hiding beneath his mother's skirts."

Despite the capos' harsh message and visceral hatred for my father, Alfredo headed back to Bogotá full of reassurance, determined to return to Cali at once with my mother.

With no other way out, we didn't spend much time debating whether or not it was in our best interest. Instead, we set about organizing a plan for sneaking out of Residencias Tequendama without the attorney general's office finding out. We approached the psychologist who did therapy with us all day once a week, and it wasn't hard to make her understand the difficult position we were in and persuade her to help us. My mother pretended to shut herself in with the psychologist all day, claiming that she was undergoing a special treatment to combat depression. None of the men charged with looking after us suspected a thing. My mother took the fire stairs down twenty-nine flights to the street, where Alfredo was waiting for her in a rented van.

It was a relatively unremarkable journey, if suffused with anxiety about meeting with violent people with such enormous economic, political, and military power. We were dealing with the all-powerful heads of the country's Mafia, who could do as they pleased now that they'd gotten rid of my father, the only one who'd challenged them for several years.

Once they made it to Cali, Alfredo called Miguel Rodríguez, who was surprised by how quickly my mother had arrived. The capo told them to wait in a hotel he owned in downtown Cali while he gathered everyone.

Twenty hours later, they were astonished when Miguel Rodríguez himself picked them up and took them to a farm in Cascajal,
where Cali's América soccer team practiced.

My mother, dressed in mourning clothes, and Alfredo entered
a large room to find nearly forty people representing the cream of
Colombia's narco crop—the Pepe kingpins—already seated.

They'd left an empty chair for my mother at the center of the
table, to the left of Miguel Rodríguez and diagonal from Gilberto
Rodríguez, who eyed her with disdain. Also at the table were the
Cali capos Hélmer "Pacho" Herrera and José "Chepe" Santacruz,
paramilitary leader Carlos Castaño, and three representatives from
the families of Gerardo "Kiko" Moncada and Fernando Galeano,
who had been murdered on my father's orders in the La Catedral
prison. Alfredo sat down at one end of the table. The place was full
of heavily armed bodyguards, and the atmosphere was extremely
tense from beginning to end.

"Say what you have to say," Gilberto said to open the meeting in
an aloof, recriminatory tone.

"Look, gentlemen, the war is over. We've come here to reach an
agreement with you to save the lives of my children and me, the
Escobar family, our lawyers, and Pablo Escobar's people in general," my mother said, clutching a bottle of mineral water.

Miguel then launched into a tirade against my father, accusing
him of having robbed a large sum of money from everybody and
noting that the war had cost each of them ten million dollars and
they expected to get that money back.

"And don't ask for anything for the siblings of that fucking
husband of yours," he said. "Not Roberto, Alba Marina, Argemiro,
Gloria, or that bitch mother of his, because they're the ones who
have it in for you. We listened to all the tapes we recorded during
the war, and almost all of the Escobars were demanding more and
more violence against us."

The capo's rant lasted ten minutes. Finally, he explained that the primary motivation for the meeting was to find out whether the Escobar family truly wished to pursue peace. Then he allowed the other attendees the floor. They spoke quite insultingly of my father, making a sort of inventory of what we would need to pay our debt and keep our lives.

"That bastard killed two of my brothers. How much is that worth, in addition to the money I spent to kill him?" one of them taunted, referring to my father.

"He kidnapped me, and I had to pay more than two million dollars and give him some of my real estate holdings for him to let me go. And as if that weren't enough, I had to flee with my whole family," said another, visibly furious.

"He burned down one of my farms and tried to kidnap me, but I escaped and had to leave the country for years. How much will you compensate us for that?" added another.

The list of claims was endless.

"I want to know, I want you to answer me this: if it was our wives who were sitting here with your bastard husband, what would he be doing to them? Something horrible, because he was a terrible man. Answer me!" demanded one of those who had been most affected by the war.

"God's ways are wise, gentlemen, and only He knows why I'm the one sitting here and not your wives," my mother responded.

After ranting about my father, Carlos Castaño told my mother, "Ma'am, I want you and Manuela to know that we searched high and low for you two because we planned to chop you up into tiny pieces and send them to Pablo in a burlap sack."

And Gilberto Rodríguez again spoke out, repeating what he'd already said to Alfredo:

"Look, those of us here are prepared to make peace with everybody except your son."

My mother burst into tears that became anger as she replied fiercely, "What? Peace without my son is not peace. I will answer to you for his actions, even if it costs me my life. I promise I won't let him stray from the path. If you want, we'll leave Colombia forever. I guarantee that he'll stay on the straight and narrow."

"Ma'am, you have to understand there's warranted concern that Juan Pablo might end up with a lot of money and go crazy one day, arm a paramilitary group, and go to war against us. That's why we agree only to let the women live. There will be peace, but we're going to kill your son," Gilberto insisted.

To tone things down a bit, Miguel Rodríguez explained why they'd allowed my mother to meet with them:

"You're sitting here now because we listened in on your conversations, and you were always trying to resolve matters; you never told your husband to expand the war or try to kill us. In fact, you were always asking him to try to make peace with us. But how could you have supported such a brute unconditionally? How did you write that bastard love letters, especially when he was always cheating on you? We've made our wives listen to the things you said on those tapes so they can hear how a wife should support her husband."

Eventually, he cut to the chase: "We need you to talk to Roberto Escobar and the men who are in prison and make them pay. Roberto owes us two or three million dollars, and the prisoners about the same. You owe all of us something like one hundred twenty million dollars—go ahead and start thinking about how you're going to get it to us, but it has to be in cash. We'll give you ten days, and then we expect you to bring us a concrete, feasible proposal."

A long silence spread through the room.

My mother and Alfredo headed back to Bogotá immediately. During that ten-hour journey, she wept inconsolably, unable to utter a word. She was dispirited, battered. Now, all by herself, she had to face the pack of wolves that weeks earlier had hunted down her husband and were now threatening to kill her son and seize all she had left.

When they got to Bogotá, she slipped back into Residencias Tequendama the way she'd left, without anyone having noticed her absence. At least that was one less thing she had to contend with.

Once they'd rested, Alfredo and my mother gave me a full account of the meeting, including the capos' decision to have me killed. In passing, my mother remarked that Pacho Herrera, one of the Cali Cartel capos, hadn't been rude during the meeting or demanded monetary compensation.

Over the next few days, we set about compiling a list of my father's properties and the few artworks that had been salvaged, their current physical and legal condition, and their approximate value. My mother and I, along with seven lawyers and other advisers, spent hours gathering information. We had to consult the prisoners and a few of my father's associates, as we were only aware of about thirty percent of the assets that he had scattered around the country. We drew up spreadsheets and sent them to Cali so each capo could choose which asset he wanted as "compensation."

The most important point to make to the capos was that we didn't have any cash—the hidden money had disappeared, and my uncle Roberto had pilfered three million more that my father had entrusted to him for my mother, sister, and me.

On the appointed day, Alfredo and my mother returned to Cali and met with the same narcos as the first time. They didn't insist about the cash, since they personally had spent years attempting to undermine my father's economic power and knew full well the state of his finances. They also knew my father had abandoned drug trafficking years before as the war had pulled him away from his business, and he'd devoted himself (and all of his money) to fighting. They knew my father had ordered the extortionate kidnappings precisely because he lacked liquidity and needed the ransom money.

Diego "Berna" Murillo Bejarano, in his September 2014 book *How We Killed the Boss*, best describes my father's situation at the end of his life: "Pablo was alone, completely hemmed in. Of his power and fortune, almost nothing remained. The man who at one time had been one of the richest in the world now could have headed up an Association of Impoverished Narcos."

This second meeting in Cali was much longer, as they went over each asset on my mother's list one by one. The capos agreed to accept fifty percent of the debt in assets that had been confiscated by the attorney general's office and the remaining half in properties that were not tangled up in legal proceedings and could be liquidated easily. They were willing to receive confiscated goods, which sounds like a stupid move, but the fight against my father had brought together a wide assortment of drug traffickers, government agents, and high-ranking officials in the Colombian government and other countries, so they had the connections they needed to "legally" acquire those assets—properties that would never have been returned to us anyway.

Included in the long list of properties was a twenty-two-acre parcel of land that was worth a fortune and that Fidel Castaño requested through his brother Carlos. It was right beside Montecasino, his mansion, so he could expand his already massive property. We also handed over other valuable lots in Medellín that today are the sites of hotels and other lucrative commercial enterprises.

In addition to the meetings my mother attended in Cali, there were also many held in Bogotá. She'd hand over paintings by the likes of Fernando Botero along with their appraisal documents. Little by little, she paid my father's enemies with the art she had so cherished. In the end, the only thing left was unremarkable art that didn't interest them.

The Miravalle apartment highrise in El Poblado, which my father had built in the 1980s, didn't survive the chopping block either. Though many of the units had been sold, we'd still owned more than ten of them, including the penthouse where my grandmother Hermilda had lived for years. There was also a farm that I'd never heard of before in the Orinoquía region. When I saw on the list how large it was, I thought it must be a typo: 250,000 acres.

The list included airplanes, helicopters, all kinds of personal vehicles—Mercedes-Benzes, BMWs, Jaguars, new and old models of high-end motorcycles—boats, and Jet Skis. We gave them everything. Everything. We couldn't risk lying or hiding assets. We knew that Los Pepes had all of that information since many of them had once been my father's friends.

Though we'd handed over a large number of properties, we knew it still wasn't enough to cover the exorbitant sum the capos demanded. But inexplicably Carlos Castaño intervened and threw my mother a small life preserver:

"Ma'am, I have one of your Dalí paintings, *Rock and Roll,* which is worth more than three million dollars. I'll return it to you so you can pay these people back," he said, almost certainly on the instructions of his brother, Fidel, who'd already promised to give back the artwork.

"No, Carlos, don't worry about returning that painting. Keep it. I'll have the original certificates of authenticity sent to you," my mother replied without hesitation, to the capos' great surprise. She didn't want to dig us in deeper.

The meeting had taken on a different tone this time. The massive table looked like a notary's office in which the property owners—advised by lawyers—selected properties as if they were collectible action figures.

Three hours later, to wrap things up, Miguel Rodríguez said:

"Whatever happens from here on out, a monster like Pablo Escobar will never again be born in Colombia."

On the way back from Cali, once again all my mother did was cry. This time, halfway to Bogotá, Alfredo received a phone call from Miguel Rodríguez.

"Pablo's widow is no fool. She scored a huge win today," he said.

"With that Dalí business, she's got none other than Carlos Castaño in her corner."

There were fewer capos at the next meeting, ten days later in the same location, as several of them had deemed their debt repaid with the assets we'd already given them. This meeting involved an additional matter: me.

"Ma'am, don't worry. There will be peace after this. But we're going to kill your son," Gilberto Rodríguez said once more.

Even though they'd already vowed to kill her son, my mother swore over and over again that she'd make sure I had no intention of continuing my father's war. At last, the capos agreed to let her bring me to the next meeting. There, my future would be decided.

MY MOTHER, ANDREA, AND I HAD STARTED TO ACCEPT THAT sooner or later I was going to have to make the trip to Cali. We didn't include my little sister in what was happening and told her instead that everything was fine.

I analyzed the situation over and over again. Should I flee and risk dying in the attempt? I could survive in hiding in Colombia for a while and then abroad. After all, I'd observed while my father spent more than a decade in hiding. Yet avoiding the meeting could lead to great suffering for my mother and little sister. Los Pepes wielded a huge amount of power and could track me down anywhere in the world. Hiding would only perpetuate a war I hadn't started or led, but had instead suffered through and sought to escape all my life. In the end, when I made my decision, I gave the most weight to my deepest emotions, the ones that told me that if I wanted real peace, I had to make peace, honor it, guarantee it. I had to shake the hands of my father's enemies.

In the cold solitude of the balcony of our rented Santa Ana apartment, which we'd moved to after our unpleasant stay in Residencias Tequendama, I reflected on the fact that I'd been on the run since before I was born, for as long as I could remember. Ever since I was a little boy, I'd been treated as if I were the perpetrator of my father's crimes. Only God knows that in my prayers I never asked for death, or prison, or ruin, or illness, or persecution, or revenge against the enemies I inherited from my father—which is not the same thing as saying *my* enemies, as I didn't earn them. I've only asked God to keep them busy, to keep them from focusing on me or seeing me as a threat, because I'm not.

Here I was at yet another crossroads. I had to go to the meeting in Cali, and I was terrified because I was sure I wouldn't be coming back.

The atmosphere in the Santa Ana apartment was gloomy, and we were all on edge. Overcome by the sensation that my days might be numbered, I wrote a last will and testament in which I left Andrea and my mother's family the two or three possessions I had managed to hang on to.

I hoped that if I offered myself up voluntarily, the vengeance of my father's enemies would fall only on me and not reach Manuela or my mother. I went into a sort of shock that numbed me to the possibility that my fingernails, teeth, and eyes would be pulled out and my body chopped up the way those of many friends had been during the vicious war between the cartels.

At four in the morning, while the bodyguards were asleep, my mother and I headed off to Cali with my uncle Fernando Henao. It was a peaceful journey, and we spent most of it discussing how to handle the meeting. There wasn't much for me to think about beyond that. I figured I was a dead man.

We arrived at a hotel in Cali at about six in the evening, entering through the basement and going straight up to a large room on the eighth floor. We didn't check in because the cartel owned the hotel. We took the precaution of keeping our voices low, as we thought the rooms might be bugged. We didn't order food either, for fear they might poison me, and I drank only water from the faucet.

WE KNEW THAT NOTHING WOULD HAPPEN TILL THE NEXT morning, so we decided to visit some of my mother's relatives in Palmira. We ate there, and a little after ten at night, my mother got a call from Pacho Herrera, who asked her to arrange a meeting with my father's family to talk about the inheritance and distribution of his assets.

"Don Pacho," my mother responded, "don't worry about that. Pablo left a will, so we'll work that out on our own as a family. We're here because Don Miguel Rodríguez called us to talk about establishing peace, and he just needed Juan Pablo, my son, to come with me to resolve the situation."

That night I got down on my knees and cried and prayed for a long time, begging God to save my life, to soften my executioners' hearts and give me a new chance.

At about ten the next morning, a man came to pick us up in a white Renault 18 with tinted windows.

I had gotten up at seven, an unusual hour for me since, like my father, I normally went to bed at dawn and started my day at about noon. As always, I took an hour-long bath, this time filled with dread. I took a deep breath, cleared my throat, and told myself several times, "Today this will all be over. I'm not going to have to run away from anything or anybody ever again."

My mother couldn't hide her distress either. She was very quiet, and my uncle tried unsuccessfully to reassure her.

"Don't worry, it's going to be OK," he repeated, but failed to conceal his own concern.

We got in the car, and in less than ten minutes the driver reached the basement of a building near the Caracol radio station offices. Nobody else realized it, but at that moment I was seized by an awful anguish, the unease of a person moving toward death. The driver escorted us up to the top floor and said he'd wait in a room down the hall. I was surprised to notice that there weren't any armed men present and that nobody had searched me.

As we headed into the waiting room, we were startled to find my grandmother Hermilda; my aunt Luz María and her husband, Leonardo; my uncle Argemiro; and my cousin Nicolás already seated. The room's darkened windows gave this unexpected meeting with my relatives a foreboding air. Up to that point we'd imagined that only my mother was in contact with my father's enemies. And for her it was solely in order to secure peace for the extended family.

How had they gotten here? Who had brought them before us? It was very strange and suspicious that while we had been updating my relatives on our efforts to negotiate peace, they had never mentioned that they already had direct access to the Cali capos. It was like a knife in the heart to witness how at home they appeared in our enemies' domain. We even saw Nicolás help himself to food from the refrigerator.

Our greeting was cool and distant, and during the few minutes in the waiting room, we exchanged only a couple of stiff words. Dumbfounded, I couldn't believe that the meeting at which I'd be sentenced to death had been postponed—at my own grandmother's request!—to discuss her son Pablo's inheritance first.

A black-clad servant ushered us into a larger room with two couches, armchairs beside them, and a glass table in the middle.

We'd hardly sat down when Miguel Rodríguez entered, followed by Pacho Herrera and José Santacruz Londoño. Gilberto Rodríguez was noticeably absent.

My mother, Uncle Fernando, and I sat on one couch, and a few seconds later my paternal relatives came in and occupied the other one. The Escobar Gavirias stared at the floor, avoiding our eyes, as they knew that today would mark the end of our ties with them. There was no longer any doubt that they'd betrayed us.

I recalled my mother's comment that at previous meetings, when she'd offered to pay to save my father's family, Miguel Rodríguez had said to her, "Ma'am, don't spend your money on those worthless people. It's a waste. Don't you see they're the very ones who are going to destroy you and your children? Let them pay their part, they have the money for it. They don't deserve your generosity. Believe me." He had insisted this to my mother several times, and until that day, like me, she had been unaware of the duplicitous game being played by those who shared our blood.

Pacho Herrera was clearly on the side of my father's family.

Miguel Rodríguez sat down in one of the chairs next to Pacho Herrera and Chepe Santacruz. He looked very solemn, I'd even say sour, judging by his furrowed brow.

At last he began to speak.

"We're going to talk about Pablo's inheritance," he said without preamble. "I've heard the demands of his mother and siblings, who want the assets he gave his children while he was alive to be included among the assets to be distributed."

My grandmother spoke next. "Yes, Don Miguel, we're talking about the Mónaco, Dallas, and Ovni buildings. Pablo put them in Manuela's and Juan Pablo's names to prevent them from being seized by the authorities, but they belonged to him, not to his children. That's why we're calling for them to be included in the inheritance."

I was struck by the absurdity of the situation: my grandmother and aunts and uncles had gone to the Cali Cartel to resolve a problem regarding the family of the cartel's most hated enemy. I thought my father must be rolling in his grave at the way his own mother and siblings were attempting to undermine his children.

Then it was my mother's turn:

"Doña Hermilda, from the beginning when Pablo built those buildings, it was very clear that they were for his children. He left lots of other assets to the family. You know that's the case, even though you've come here, with all due respect, to say things that aren't true."

Miguel Rodríguez intervened. "Look, I myself have corporations set up in my children's names, and those corporations have assets that I, in life, decided were for them. Pablo did exactly the same thing. So the assets he wanted his children to have will not be touched. End of discussion. The assets for my children belong to them, and the assets that Pablo chose for his children belong to them. Divide up the rest of it among yourselves in accordance with the will."

A long silence followed Miguel Rodríguez's speech until finally my cousin Nicolás piped up, thankfully bringing the bizarre meeting to a close.

"Hang on, what about the ten million dollars that my uncle owed my father? We all know my father was the one who supported Pablo."

At my cousin's foolish comment, the capos of the Cali Cartel laughed and looked at each other in disbelief. I had no choice but to speak up.

"Just listen to this guy. Nobody believes that one, Nicolás. You say the birds are shooting at the hunters now, huh? Turns out your father took care of mine? You've got to be kidding me."

Smiling, Miguel Rodríguez, Pacho Herrera, and Chepe Santacruz got up and headed toward the door without a good-bye.

Anxious, I motioned to my mother to get back to the real reason for our visit to Cali. My life was in the balance. She understood immediately and followed the capos, asking for five minutes more of their time. They agreed, and my mother signaled for me to join them.

They sat in another room, arms crossed, and I realized it was time to give it everything I had.

"Gentlemen, I came here because I want to tell you I have no intention of avenging my father's death. What I want to do, as you know, is leave the country to pursue an education and seek opportunities that aren't available to me here. I don't want to stay in Colombia so I don't bother anybody, but I feel unable to leave. We have no way out. I understand full well that if I want to stay alive, I have to go."

"Kid, what you have to do is not get involved in drug trafficking or paramilitary groups or things like that. I understand what you must be feeling, but you must know, as we all do, that a thug like your father will never be born again," Santacruz told me.

"Don't worry, sir, I've learned a lesson in life. Drug trafficking is a curse."

"Just a minute, young man," replied Miguel Rodríguez, his voice rising. "What do you mean, drug trafficking is a curse? Look, I have a good life, my family lives well, I have a big house, tennis courts, I go for a walk every day . . ."

"Don Miguel, please understand, life has shown me something very different. Because of drug trafficking, I lost my father, family members, and friends, my peace and freedom, and all of our worldly possessions. Please forgive me if I've offended you, but I can't see it any other way. That's why I want to take this opportunity to tell you that I am not going to create any kind of trouble. I realize revenge isn't going to bring my father back. Please help us leave the country. I feel absolutely helpless in finding a way out. I don't want you to think I don't want to leave. The airlines won't even sell me a ticket."

Carried along by momentum and now much more relaxed, I even made a suggestion: "How about instead of loading a hundred kilos of cocaine onto your planes, you take me along—I weigh the same—and fly me out of the country?"

My sincere delivery must have gotten through to them, because Miguel Rodríguez's hard, cutting tone changed as he gave his verdict once more.

"Ma'am, we've decided we're going to give your son a chance. We understand he's just a boy and should continue being that. You will have to answer for his actions from now on with your life. You have to promise you won't allow him to go astray. We'll leave you the three buildings so your children can get by. We'll help you get them back. To do that, you'll have to contribute some money to the presidential campaigns. Whoever wins, we'll ask him to help us, and we'll tell him that you contributed to his cause."

Then Pacho Herrera, who had been quiet so far, spoke up.

"Don't worry, man, as long as you don't get involved in drug trafficking, nothing's going to happen to you. You don't have anything to be afraid of. We wanted you to come to us so we could make sure you had good intentions. The only thing we can't allow is for you to have a lot of money, so you don't go crazy out there where we can't control you."

"Don't worry anymore," Miguel Rodríguez broke in again. "You can even stay and live here in Cali if you want. Nobody's going to do anything to you. Go visit my wife's clothing store. Wait to see what happens now with the new president who's coming, and we'll help you."

The conversation was over. It had lasted twenty minutes.

I didn't dwell further on Miguel Rodríguez's reference to "the new president who's coming," but a few weeks later we'd understand.

After saying a fairly friendly good-bye, Miguel summoned the driver and told him to take us to the shop run by his wife. As we exited, I'd never felt such emotional turmoil. I had to process the undeniable two-headed reality staring me in the face: the confirmation that my paternal family had betrayed us, and the permission to live granted to me by the Cali capos. I'd always expected the worst from them, but now I feel obligated to gratefully acknowl-edge Don Miguel and all of Los Pepes, who agreed to allow my mother, my sister, and me to live.

It didn't take long to reach a high-end shopping district in Cali. The driver pointed to a clothing store, and my mother entered. I opted to walk around the area and stopped in front of a men's clothing store with a terry-cloth robe in the window. I bought it.

It was a strange sensation: I felt alive. I had gone to meet death, and suddenly I found myself in the territory of the all-powerful Cali Mafia dons, without a scratch.

A couple of hours later, the driver dropped us at the hotel, and that same night we went back to Bogotá.

For the first time in a long time, we felt a profound peace. I could live. Over the past few months, we had given a large number of properties to the Cali capos and Los Pepes, but there were still vari-ous capos waiting for their payout. As I got undressed, Andrea asked if I'd read the note she'd put in my pants pocket for my ren-dezvous with death. In it, she'd reiterated her love for me and her conviction that everything was going to turn out all right.

WE HAD TO TAKE THE BULL BY THE HORNS, SO MY MOTHER QUICKLY met with Diego "Berna" Murillo Bejarano at Carlos Castaño's urging. Castaño arranged for them to meet in a house in Los Balsos in Medellín. But that first meeting didn't go well. Berna insulted her for marrying Pablo, and she, fed up with the constant threats, slurs, and accusations from mafiosos, responded vehemently.

"Sir, I am a lady, and you're not going to insult or attack me any-more. I don't have to take your rudeness when I've earned the re-spect of the rest of your friends. Please do me the favor of being respectful, not insolent and abusive," my mother said firmly.

They ended the meeting there.

Castaño called her that night and made it clear that Berna was extremely displeased, and she was going to have to placate him.

"Doña Victoria, the man's furious," Castaño said. "I understand that he provoked you. But please understand he's a very bad man, and you've got to give him something extra to calm him down."

The incident turned out to be very expensive. At a subsequent meeting, also organized by Castaño, my mother had to apologize and give Berna a pricy apartment. That was the only way to continue the negotiation of the other assets.

During our time in Santa Ana, it became the norm to see someone come pick up my mother to take her to meetings with capos who lived in or were passing through Bogotá. Sometimes those meetings were held in nearby houses in the very same neighborhood where we lived. The capos would invite my mother to drink whiskey with them, and when she'd refuse, they'd always get angry. They were exploiting the fact that she was alone, demanding more money, more paintings, more assets. Luckily, my uncle Fernando was close by at those times and wisely intervened to prevent further abuse.

Perhaps the most complicated negotiation at the time was with "Chaparro," a powerful leader of the Magdalena Medio paramilitary group, drug trafficker, and my father's mortal enemy.

With the permission of the attorney general's office, Carlos Castaño took my mother in an armored Mercedes-Benz to the Guayamaral Airport, north of Bogotá, where they boarded a chopper and flew to an estate on the border between the Caldas and Antioquia regions.

During the trip, Castaño revealed some details about my father's death that we hadn't known.

"The Pepes were already demoralized," he said. "We had killed ninety-nine percent of Pablo's people on the street, but we could never get to him. We almost threw in the towel because December was approaching and things are always harder around that time. Some prominent Pepes even started saying that if they didn't get results, they'd give up the hunt in December. And as if that weren't enough, the colonels in the Search Bloc had given Los Pepes an ultimatum."

My mother patiently listened to Castaño's account.

"To find Pablo, we had to get the most advanced phone call interception technology shipped in from France because the gringos' tech wasn't good enough."

"Who really killed Pablo?" my mother finally asked.

"I personally participated in the final operation. The police always sent us ahead during operations. This time they waited behind at the Obelisco shopping center. Once we'd killed Pablo, we called them. Pablo heard the first blow from the sledgehammer we used to try to break down the door and ran barefoot up a staircase to the second floor. He got off a number of shots with his Sig Sauer pistol, two of which hit my bulletproof vest, and I fell on my back. By then, Lemon was already dead in the front yard. Pablo took advantage of that moment when there was nobody coming after him to open a window and climb down a metal ladder that he must have set up earlier for his escape. With the ladder he made it down onto the roof of the house next door. But he hadn't realized that some of my men were already there. When he tried to turn back, he was shot in the shoulder. Another bullet caught him in the leg. By the time I reached the window he'd climbed out of and looked out, he was already dead."

My mother didn't get the chance to comment, as just then the helicopter landed in a field where two hundred men armed with rifles waited with the commander Chaparro, who greeted Castaño warmly and then addressed my mother:

"Good morning, ma'am, I'm Commander Chaparro, and this is my son. Your husband killed another of my sons and made thirteen attempts on my life. It was a miracle I survived."

"Sir," my mother replied, "I understand the situation, but please know that I had nothing to do with the war. I was just Pablo's wife and the mother of his children. Tell me, what do I have to do to make peace with you?"

Chaparro had actually caused my father a lot of trouble. I remember my father even laughed when his men informed him that they'd failed in yet another attempt to kill Chaparro. On two occasions, they'd blown up a car and a boat with powerful bombs, but he didn't die then, either. My father said resignedly that the man had more lives than a cat.

Chaparro came from a peasant family. Back in the late 1970s, he and my father had grown apart for reasons I'm not clear on, and he ended up joining up with Henry Pérez, one of the first leaders of the Magdalena Medio paramilitary group. My father had declared war on Pérez for failing to give him money to finance his fight against extradition and on Chaparro for his alliance with Pérez. Pérez was ultimately killed by some of my father's men, but to the day he died, Pablo never managed to take out Chaparro.

After several hours of negotiation, my mother and Chaparro reached an agreement and resolved their differences. We gave him several assets, including two thousand-acre parcels of land that were used for mining and livestock raising. Chaparro also got to keep the power plant at Nápoles, which he had seized a while back and which was powerful enough to provide light for an entire village. My mother told him to take whatever he wanted from the estate, since we no longer considered it ours.

As a favor, my mother asked Carlos Castaño to locate the bodies of at least five of her employees, including a teacher and Manuela's nanny, whom Los Pepes had killed and disappeared in the final stages of the war, when my father was practically alone and we were all confined in an apartment in the Altos building. Castaño said that it wouldn't be easy to find them. Los Pepes had disappeared more than one hundred people, and he didn't remember exactly where they'd buried them.

At the end of the meeting, my mother and Chaparro shook hands, and he authorized her to return to Nápoles, which was still in the possession of the attorney general's office, whenever she wanted.

My mother returned to Bogotá with one fewer enemy, and we finally had a few days of peace.

Occasionally the quiet was punctuated by unexpected visitors, such as the lawyer who came to the Santa Ana apartment and told us he'd been sent by the Rodríguez Orejuela brothers.

As we listened to his message, it became clear that the Cali capos had just included us—whether we agreed or not—in a plan to obtain legal benefits through bribery. They demanded that we contribute fifty thousand dollars so they could incorporate their own amendment in a bill currently moving through Congress to protect the Mafia's assets during confiscation hearings. The lawyer's threatening tone gave us no choice but to borrow that money.

The matter didn't end there. In May 1994, we received another visit from a Cali go-between, this time not a lawyer but a man known to be a mafioso. We reluctantly invited him in, and he told us that a large group of narcos in southwestern Colombia wanted us to contribute a substantial sum of money to finance Ernesto Samper's presidential campaign, with the idea that we, too, would benefit from the future government's aid, both in recovering our lost properties and in seeking refuge in another country. All at once we understood that when, in a previous conversation, Miguel Rodríguez had mentioned the "new president who's coming," he'd been talking about having the leader who would replace César Gaviria in his pocket.

We couldn't refuse this time either and delivered the money in a number of installments without really knowing where it was going. And despite our contribution, we never recovered our assets or had any help leaving Colombia. In other words, that money was squandered.

The worst part was that the Mafia still saw us as cash machines: we constantly received requests for money, and for the most implausible reasons. But how could we refuse given the circumstances? It was pointless to report them to the attorney general, as at the time its relationship with the Cali capos was so brazen that the cartel even had its own office on the same floor of the same building as Attorney General Gustavo De Greiff. For anybody who wanted to travel to Cali to resolve a problem with the capos, the attorney general's office was the first stop. I'm not making this up. It was normal to see Los Pepes coming and going as if they lived there. Every time we visited the head prosecutor, we had to ask if the Cali people were in agreement—and we didn't even have to leave the building to make the necessary inquiries.

Attorney General De Greiff knew all about my mother's secret negotiations. Even if the security detail didn't notice her leaving, Cali made sure to alert him. Several times De Greiff even joked about it to us.

In mid-August 1994, we accepted Chaparro's offer and traveled to the Nápoles estate accompanied by two CTI agents from the attorney general's office and one from the police's SIJIN criminal investigation unit. He said not to worry, that he would guarantee our safety in the region. It was like a mini-vacation. My mother, Andrea, Manuela, Fernando, and I traveled from Bogotá, and part of the extended family came from Medellín to see us, including my grandmother Nora.

We arrived at night to find Octavio, our long-time estate manager, waiting for us. He had made up the beds in four small cabins. Though they had bathrooms, only one of the cabins had working air conditioning. This part of Nápoles had been known as "the other side," as the only things there were a health clinic, an operating room, a pharmacy, and El Tablazo, a bar where my father housed a large collection of LPs and music memorabilia hung on the walls à la the Hard Rock Café.

But we felt like strangers during our short stay at Nápoles. We hadn't been back in a couple of years, and almost none of the luxuries and ostentations of the 1980s, when the estate had 1,700 employees, remained. We drove around the estate and were sad to note that the jungle had taken over the main house so that you couldn't even see the walls. The eyes of a number of bored hippopotamuses were visible at the surfaces of the lakes.

On our second night at Nápoles, I woke up suffocated with heat and was startled to see two men armed with AK-47s outside. They didn't seem hostile, so I went out to speak with them. They told me Chaparro had sent them to protect us, as a few days earlier they'd had a confrontation with the ELN guerrilla group in an area of Nápoles known as Panadería, where my father had one of his hideouts. They said not to worry because they had plenty of men patrolling the area.

They were thirsty and dripping with sweat, so I offered them *guarapo,* a drink made with water, sugarcane syrup, and lemon. Life's a funny thing: all that old hatred had vanished after the frank conversation between my mother and Chaparro.

By the end of August 1994, we'd been depleted of all my father's assets except for the Dallas, Mónaco, and Ovni buildings, which, it had been agreed, belonged to my sister and me. Even so, some doubt remained regarding the ownership of an airplane and a helicopter that had belonged to my father, so the Cali capos summoned my mother to yet another meeting in their city. There were nearly thirty people at the meeting, most of whom had been at the initial meetings at the beginning of the year. At the end, when the issue of the aircrafts had been settled, Miguel Rodríguez asked my mother why she hadn't approached them earlier, since they might have been able to avoid war with my father all together.

"I wanted to," she said, "but Pablo wouldn't listen to me. If you recall, gentlemen, I once located the brother-in-law of one of my cousins in Palmira who was working for you as a bodyguard and asked him to request a meeting with you. You said yes, so I told Pablo that I'd been seeking contact with the Cali people for a while because I was worried about my children and had a meeting pretty much set up. But he told me I was crazy, that he'd never let me go to Cali. 'Over my dead body,' he'd said, and added that I was naive, that I was too nice, that I didn't understand how the world worked, that his enemies would send me back wrapped in barbed wire."

In the end, my father was right about one thing: it was over his dead body that my mother was able to approach his enemies and live to tell the tale.

Epilogue

Two Decades in Exile

Getting out of Colombia was a matter of life or death. It was just that simple. Manuela, my mother, and I had been rejected by most of the diplomatic representations in Bogotá: Costa Rica, Germany, Israel, Australia, Argentina, Brazil, Canada, Venezuela, El Salvador, Italy, Peru, Ecuador, Chile, France, England, and the United States. The Catholic Church also shut its doors to us, though we had met with Apostolic Nuncio Paolo Romeo and Monsignor Darío Castrillón to ask them to intervene so we might have somewhere on the planet to live.

We turned to the International Committee of the Red Cross and the United Nations. We met with then-ombudsman Jaime Córdova and with the inspector general, Carlos Gustavo Arrieta. Though they received us cordially, they didn't offer us any aid. We tried Rigoberta Menchú, who had recently won the Nobel Peace Prize, but she responded that it wasn't her problem.

Desperate and with nowhere else to turn, my mother called former president Julio César Turbay, who told her, "Remember Diana, ma'am. You're well aware of everything your husband did; you know he killed my daughter. I can't help you." We said it wasn't fair to blame us for that incident. We might have been Pablo Escobar's family, but we weren't kidnappers or killers.

Our options for leaving the country had run out. Our lawyer, Francisco Fernández, came up with the strategy of invoking an old law that allowed people to correct errors in names or change names through a document executed before a public official. We made an appointment with Attorney General De Greiff to propose the idea. At first De Greiff saw no legal objection, though he refused to help us. All we asked was that the paperwork be done through the Office of Victim and Witness Protection to guarantee that our new identities would remain secret. The meeting became strained, and our lawyer stepped in:

"Look, Mr. Attorney General, this situation is becoming untenable. You can't protect the lives of the whole family, and they can't stay locked up in an apartment forever. There are two minors involved here. Every five minutes you tell them you're going to take away their protection, so if you don't help them obtain new lives and new identities, they'll have no choice but to go to the press and reveal everything they know and everything they've seen in this office. And you and I know perfectly well that it won't be good for the country or for you. If you continue to keep them in limbo, I will advise them to talk about everything they know. You see what you can do for them. You're the attorney general of the nation. You can't tell me there's nothing you can do to help. You helped them get kicked out of every country, so you can make sure they are welcomed too."

"No, no, please. Look, calm down. I'll see how I can help," De Greiff said. "Please understand, they aren't considered victims or witnesses, so that office won't be able to process their identity change. But let me see what I can do."

"I'm leaving you a copy of the law. It's all legal—all we need is your discretion and collaboration. It won't do any good to change their names only to have them published in the press the next day. This family has already paid a very high price, and you know it."

In the end, not only were we given new identities but also, through De Greiff, in February 1994 we met Isabel. She was a tall, blond Frenchwoman of around sixty-five, dressed in all black and wearing an extravagant hat adorned with ostrich feathers. She was said to be a countess. Isabel was accompanied by two men of African descent in suits and ties who claimed to be diplomats from Mozambique living in New York. They had brought the news we were waiting for: after hearing our pleas in the media, as a humanitarian gesture, the president of Mozambique wanted to offer his country as a place to start a new life. The countess acted as the intermediary and told us she had a foundation through which she sought aid for the countries that most needed it. If we were willing to contribute to that cause, she said, she could use her influence to get that country to take us in. We were overjoyed.

What we didn't know was that the so-called president was only a candidate. Mozambique was a turbulent country currently engaged in negotiations to end a civil war that had left close to a million dead over the past fifteen years. United Nations peacekeeping troops were maintaining order, and the population was experiencing a tremendous famine.

We only knew that for us, their offer meant freedom.

As soon as Francisco Fernández found out, he met with the intermediaries. Right from the start, he said, "The family is very grateful for the humanitarian aid you wish to offer them. As the family's lawyer, I want to know how much that aid is going to cost them."

They were evasive, saying there was no need to discuss a number so soon. Not wanting to make them uncomfortable, I blushed and told Fernández not to push so hard. We couldn't risk driving away our only shot at leaving Colombia.

Over the next few months, our lawyer stayed in contact with the intermediaries, who ended up requesting a substantial amount to help us reach a country that we couldn't even identify on a map.

My mother's family gave us money so we could make deposits in official government accounts—specifically, for Mozambique's Nut Ministry—to finalize part of the agreement. The idea was to finish negotiations with them once we were in their territory, giving them a work of art and some jewels as partial payment for the remaining amount.

Luis Camilo Osorio, who was the national registrar at the time, finally issued the passports, driver's licenses, and identity cards with our new names. It was already November 1994, and we immediately started planning our departure.

My name change was recorded in document 4673 at notary office 12 in Medellín, dated June 4, 1994, and executed before the civil-law notary Marta Inés Alzate de Restrepo. Juan Pablo Escobar Henao's birth certificate was now in the name of Juan Sebastián Marroquín Santos. In addition, my mother's document stated that, as my sole guardian and parental authority, she was changing her identity not to evade penal or civil responsibilities but to preserve her own life and those of her two children in the face of the death threats the family was receiving. The witness protection office processed a military reservist card in my new name to keep the army from learning my new identity. It cost the family twenty million pesos.

December 14, 1994, arrived. We would be saying good-bye forever to my maternal family—the only people who had offered us real support after my father's death. The other side of the family, my father's side, it seemed now had other priorities.

The Henao Vallejos spent that last week with us in the Santa Ana apartment. They didn't know where we were going or our new names. They wouldn't hear from us again for a decade, or us from them. At 5:45 A.M., everything was ready to go: the luggage in the van, all of us showered and dressed. We gathered in the living room for the final time and took a photo of that moment, the last family photo, most members in pajamas and filled with sadness.

We said good-bye. The last person I hugged was my grandmother Nora.

"Abuelita, tell me the truth, is everything going to be OK?"

"Yes, sweetie, I know that this time it's going to be OK, and nothing's going to happen to you. I don't sense any danger for you all. So go in peace, and don't worry, darling," she encouraged me.

We left the building in Alfredo Astado's van, and at the edge of the neighborhood I asked him to stop and got out to talk to "Puma," a particularly capable CTI agent who'd protected us in the Altos building.

"Brother, I want to thank you for having looked after us during such a difficult time for our family. Thank you for your decency toward us, for having risked your life so many times," I said. "It's time for the family to find its own path, so I have to ask you not to protect us anymore. We're leaving the country. I'm sure you understand that for security reasons I can't give you any details. Please don't follow us."

"Thank you for treating your bodyguards so well and for doing your best to make taking care of you an enjoyable duty," he replied. "I'm sorry for all the bad things you've gone through. Having freed me of my responsibility to protect you, you are not under arrest and are free to go wherever you wish."

Puma's cordiality would cost him his job. De Greiff was furious when he discovered Puma had lost track of us and that we were on our way out of the country. The officer responded that we weren't prisoners, but it was no use.

That trip was like a race, our own painful past in hot pursuit. Heading toward the border with Ecuador, we hadn't had much time to practice with our new names—we hadn't yet had the chance to try them on.

We were scheduled to cross the border on our third day of travel, as we had to make a flight we'd reserved in Lima for Buenos Aires. But first we had to get the immigration officials to stamp our passports without examining our identities or photos. Alfredo bribed a DAS agent, and we departed the country at last.

In the meantime, Andrea was preparing to leave the country on a direct flight from Bogotá to Buenos Aires. Nobody knew who she was, her face protected by anonymity.

The identity change seemed to be working: we made it out of Ecuador and Peru and arrived in Argentina without a hitch. In Buenos Aires they stamped our passports and granted us tourist visas for three months. During our twenty-four-hour stopover before beginning our trip to Mozambique, the other side of the world, I was captivated by Buenos Aires. It was summer, and the streets were cloaked in the green and purple of the jacaranda trees.

"Don't get emotional on me, Juanchito, don't get emotional on me—you all are moving on. We're here for twenty-four hours, that's it," said our lawyer, Fernández, who was accompanying us to Mozambique with his wife.

The next morning, Buenos Aires seemed even more lovely, but our path had already been set.

At Ezeiza Airport, a close call with customs officials made me feel I might never see my family again. An official stopped me, wondering why a sixteen-year-old boy had pockets full of jewelry. They took me to a small room and forced me to empty them. The Argentine official said that he'd have to call the Colombian consulate to report the situation.

"Look, maybe you want to avoid all this and catch that plane of yours. Whatever you want. Otherwise, you'll have to wait for the Colombian consul to come out here, and that complicates things, so think about what you want to do."

I thought I understood what he was getting at, but I didn't dare offer him anything.

"Look, kid, put three hundred dollars in that magazine you're carrying and pretend to forget it on the table, and I'll let you through. Does three hundred work for you?" he said.

I stuck five hundred dollars between the pages of the magazine and "forgot" it on the table. I put the jewelry back in my pockets and went out to the boarding area. Everybody was waiting for me, pale with worry.

We traveled in luxury to Johannesburg, South Africa, but the unsanitary conditions, odors, and discomfort we experienced on the journey from there to Maputo, Mozambique, foreshadowed what awaited us. We landed in an old airport that was stuck in time, without any commercial jets, just four United Nations Hercules planes from which sacks of grains and flour bearing the UN logo were being unloaded. Soldiers in blue helmets were guarding the food, which was sent as humanitarian aid.

The same men we'd met in Colombia with the countess were waiting for us at the gate. They led us to the airport's presidential lounge, a room that seemed to have been shuttered for decades, with a thick layer of dust on the red carpet and the presidential chair.

As we were leaving the airport, the car they'd hired to pick us up got into an accident with another vehicle. The drivers got out, examined the damage, waved, and got back in their cars. I asked our driver why he hadn't written down the other vehicle's information for the insurance paperwork and so on.

"Nobody has insurance here," he explained. "It doesn't exist. Nobody has the money to repair anything. People don't argue about money here. We just get out to look at the damage out of curiosity."

On the way to the place they'd rented for us, our new life began to unfold before my eyes, and I didn't like what I saw. Maputo was a city half in ruins after years of civil war. There were no streetlights, no sidewalks, no stores, and you could see the holes from tanks and rockets in the walls of the buildings, which families covered with pieces of plastic. The countess or the men accompanying her had conveniently omitted mentioning this state of affairs.

We arrived at our new home in the diplomats' neighborhood, a simple house with four bedrooms and a large combination living and dining room. It stank unbearably of sewage. The cupboards were almost bare, and Marleny, the housekeeper we'd brought with us from Colombia, had to go out to buy the essentials. She returned an hour later, her hands empty and the money unspent.

"Money is useless here. The supermarket was open, but there was no food or water or soda or fruit. Nothing," she reported.

It was December 21, 1994, and in four days we would be celebrating Christmas in a poverty-stricken country. We had traveled for nearly a week only to face an overwhelming reality. As usual, though, my mother insisted on seeing the glass as half full. She found potatoes and eggs in the pantry and cooked dinner, telling us that everything was going to be fine, that we would be able to study, go to college, escape from the burden of our last name. We could learn English in South Africa or bring South African professors here to teach us.

Our luggage had gotten delayed, so Andrea and I went to a small shopping center. But there were only empty stores, except for one souvenir shop with low-quality T-shirts that said "Maputo"—and cost a hundred dollars each!

Nothing, nothing at all gave us any indication that we might be able to build a life there. In fact, when we looked into the universities, we were informed that the only higher education available was a few medicine classes at the city morgue. There were no classrooms, desks, or libraries, much less a bachelor's degree in advertising or industrial design, the fields Andrea and I were dreaming of.

A few hours after we had arrived, we left the house that the government had given us for our lawyer's hotel, a spectacular mansion whose guests were mostly UN peacekeepers. Though it had televisions, they were never turned on; none of the channels had a signal.

The hours went by, and I became more depressed with every minute that passed.

At that point, I would rather have lived in confinement in a room in Bogotá, even if it meant risking my life. In a moment of total despair, I held up the dog leash to my mother and said: "If we don't get out of here, I'm going to hang myself with this. I'd rather be killed in Colombia, Mamá. I don't want this. I'm dying here."

Frightened by my resolve, my mother asked our lawyer, Fernández, to look into flights out of Mozambique. The destination didn't matter.

"The only plane out of the country leaves in two hours. The next one after that is in two weeks," he informed her.

In seconds, we packed everything, even sopping-wet blue jeans that had been soaking in the washtub. Fernández was furious.

"You're throwing away a year and a half of effort! This is irresponsible, it's madness. You can't listen to your son, who thinks he's a little prince!"

"It's very easy for *you* to come to that conclusion," my mother said. "Your daughter isn't telling you she's going to commit suicide. It's easy to tell us to stay when you're leaving tomorrow to spend Christmas in Paris with your entire family. Please help us get out of here. We'll wander around the world as long as it takes until we find a good place for this family."

The Mozambique government officials weren't scheduled to meet with us until the beginning of the new year. They never imagined that, having arrived with plans to live there ten years, we would last only three days.

We left Maputo for Rio de Janeiro. We tried to see something of the city, but the language barrier and the chaotic traffic were too much. Brazil wasn't for us. So we bought tickets to Buenos Aires, since we'd loved the city and already had a three-month tourist visa approved.

Once again, Alfredo Astado was there for us in a critical moment. We'd managed to send him an emergency message through a secret channel: we were heading to Buenos Aires and needed him to oversee every detail of our arrival to avoid any unpleasant surprises. Despite the holiday, he left his family and arrived in Buenos Aires on December 24, a few hours before us.

Buenos Aires was an avalanche of new experiences for me. I learned to enjoy the privilege of being anonymous. I rode a bus for the first time. Still, the challenge of normal daily life awoke myriad fears and insecurities in me. I found something as simple as going up to the counter at McDonald's to order a hamburger terrifying. I'd always had somebody to take care of everything for me. I realized how isolated I'd been from the world.

It was still difficult to trust people. I'd become an unwilling expert at living in hiding, and for months I wore sunglasses so people wouldn't notice me. Bothered by my behavior, my mother and Andrea said there was nothing to be afraid of; we were in a city of twelve million people, and I shouldn't think I was so famous that I had to keep living my life hidden behind large sunglasses.

Maybe they were right. I indulged them once and removed my sunglasses before going out to buy some concert tickets. I hailed a taxi a block from our building, but before the driver even asked where I was headed, he asked, "Are you Pablo Escobar's son?"

"No, man! That's crazy!" I said. "Those people are still there in Colombia and aren't allowed to leave the country. Nobody wants to take them in."

The taxi driver, who was no idiot, kept studying me in the rearview mirror until I gave him a stern look and told him to head to the Alto Palermo shopping center. I bought the tickets and returned to the apartment feeling like the whole world was after me. I really lit into my mother and Andrea, telling them not to be naive, that I'd been even stupider than they because I'd heeded their advice. I ranted on and on.

In contrast to Maputo, Buenos Aires had all the educational

opportunities we ever could have wanted. Within two months of arriving, we'd taken several computer courses. Andrea started studying advertising at the University of Belgrano and ended up graduating with honors. In March I enrolled in the industrial design program at the ORT technical schools. I, too, earned good grades, an average of 8.8 out of 10. I threw my whole being into my studies. My professors even offered me a job as an assistant in two classes.

Manuela was in high school now, and my mother spent her time walking through Buenos Aires, collecting and scouring pamphlets for information on real estate projects, which was her forte.

In Buenos Aires we rented apartments and changed our residence and telephone numbers every two years to prevent anyone from tracking us down. We were also very careful about who we would associate with, fearing that someone might find us.

In early 1997, Argentina granted us temporary residency. My mother went through the process of applying for permanent residency, presenting herself as an investor with capital. For that purpose, she hired an accountant. And so Juan Carlos Zacarías Lobos came into our lives.

After we purchased a parcel of land near Puerto Madero as an investment, we began to suspect that Zacarías might not be all that trustworthy. We got the feeling he'd quoted an inflated price and skimmed off a large amount of money. But one day a sudden offer from Shell salvaged his reputation: the company offered more than double what we'd paid for the land. The sale never materialized, but it made us commit the error of believing in him again.

During that year, 1998, I started working in 3D design and visual representation in 3D. My salary from my work at a design studio, the first one I'd earned in my life, was one thousand dollars a month. In years past I'd spent that much money on two restaurant tips, and now it covered a month's rent and utilities.

But life surprised us again. Using press releases, billboards, posters at bus stops, signs on public transport, and of course TV commercials, the Discovery Channel started advertising a special program about the life of Pablo Escobar Gaviria. Terrified, we decided to leave Buenos Aires for Cariló, on the Argentine coast.

Zacarías, who had learned of our former identities when he spotted us in an old issue of *Caras* magazine, recommended that we transfer to him the assets of Inversora Galestar, S.A.—a Uruguayan company with a Buenos Aires branch that we'd acquired to get into the real estate business. He promised to return them once the commotion over the documentary had quieted down.

His good intentions were short-lived. He showed up at our hideout a few days later to demand an increase in his fees because of the "danger" that providing his services to a family like ours entailed.

"María Isabel," he said, addressing my mother by her new name, "in order to work for you I'm going to need you to pay me twenty thousand dollars a month."

"Twenty thousand dollars? Good God, Zacarías! There's no way I can pay you twenty thousand dollars. I wish I had twenty thousand for myself. If you can keep your promise to earn this family sixty thousand dollars a month, I have no problem giving you twenty out of that. But I can't pay such an amount out of nothing."

"No, María Isabel, I don't need the money for me. I have to pay my associates Óscar Lupia and Carlos Marcelo Gil Novoa to take care of you all."

The fever around the documentary died down, so we dropped the matter for a while and returned to Buenos Aires, where we spent an uneventful Christmas and New Year's. We were living in apartment 17N at Calle Jaramillo 2010, which Zacarías had rented for my mother and Manuela. Andrea and I were staying there temporarily while Zacarías helped us rent an apartment of our own.

By the first week of February 1999, Zacarías was nowhere to be found, and my mother was growing suspicious. Still concerned about possible fallout from the Discovery Channel documentary and wary of Zacarías's intentions, we put our house at the Las Praderas de Luján golf club up for sale. We'd bought it a few months earlier as an investment.

After a few days, Luis Dobniewski, a respected lawyer, contacted us to express his interest in buying the house. But Zacarías got in touch with him and charged him a deposit of one hundred thousand dollars. He never gave us that money.

"My God, the man is nowhere to be found, and he's got all my money. What am I going to do?" my mother would say.

Zacarías wasn't answering the phone, wasn't returning calls, wasn't responding to messages. My mother went to his office, and they told her he was in the hospital after a stress-induced breakdown. Before she left, she asked to use the office's landline to make a call. She dialed Zacarías's cell phone, and of course he answered.

"Why, hello, Juan Carlos, didn't they tell me you're in intensive care and basically at death's door? Where are you, what are you doing?"

"I don't want to talk to you. I will communicate with you only through Tomás Lichtmann as an intermediary," Zacarías replied, referring to our former lawyer.

"I have no problem with communicating through whatever intermediary you wish, but have some shame. What are you up to? You have my money! You have my property!"

"No, you tricked me! You didn't tell me who you really are!"

"I didn't trick you! My name is my name—I have to be careful about my identity. But let's not get sidetracked here. Return my money. You say I'm the one who tricked you, but you're the one who's got my money!"

After the argument, Zacarías promised to return everything, but through Lichtmann. My mother called Lichtmann, who told her he wasn't interested in helping or having anything to do with us.

"I didn't deceive anybody. I couldn't tell anybody my true identity. It's a matter of life and death for me and my children. Please help me out, give me a hand. Zacarías is stealing from me, and you, as my lawyer, recommended him to me. Please help," she said.

Lichtmann ignored her pleas, and Zacarías became even more confident in swindling us: he used the powers signed over by my mother to transfer ownership of a piece of land and two apartments we'd acquired cheaply at auctions, intending to refurbish and sell them. He even used a blank document my mother had naively signed to execute a surrender of accounts that we never requested.

But Zacarías never imagined that we would challenge him using the only weapon available to us: the law. And so in October 1999, my mother sued him along with his accomplices, Lupia and Gil. In response to the lawsuit, Zacarías hired Víctor Stinfale, one of the most high-profile lawyers in Argentina at the time, known for having defended Carlos Telleldín, the first person charged in the 1994 bombing of AMIA, a Jewish community center, that killed eighty-five people.

In a typical move, Stinfale asked Telleldín, who was incarcerated at the time, to leak to a journalist the news that Pablo Escobar's family was in Argentina. If we kept demanding what was ours— as Stinfale himself threatened my mother several times—the plan was to frame us for a crime or plant drugs on us to "take us off the table." The goal of such maneuvers was to force us to flee the country and leave them the assets we had earned honestly. What Stinfale and Zacarías didn't know was that we'd become experts in dealing with these high-pressure situations and attacks. Still, the toughest part was yet to come.

One day I came home earlier than usual from ORT, where I was now teaching evening classes. As I was parking, a Renault 19 with four men inside pulled up. Two of them walked up to my window, dressed in civilian clothing. I looked in the rearview mirror and found that I'd been blocked in by a white truck without police markings. I had no idea what was happening.

"Get out of the car!"

I grabbed the pepper spray I always carried with me and got out of the car. One of the men, obviously inebriated, shouted for me to follow him. I was about to use the pepper spray when they started walking toward the main entrance of the building. As we went up to the apartment, they introduced themselves as agents of Argentina's Federal Police. Three men were waiting at the apartment door, and another five had managed to get in after Andrea had demanded that they slide the warrant under the door. She'd let them know that there were two young girls and an old woman in the apartment, so they couldn't all come in, much less display their weapons. They'd obeyed.

I remained in the dining room, where two of the agents kept an eye on me. Snowflake, Cottonball, Beethoven, and Da Vinci were hysterical and barked incessantly. My grandmother Nora, who was visiting us at the time, was crying. At one point Andrea noticed that an agent had stayed in one of the bedrooms with Manuela and her schoolmate, who were doing homework, and even tried to question them.

My greatest fear was that they would plant drugs on us. That corrupt practice was all too common in Argentina. It had happened to Guillermo Cóppola, soccer player Diego Maradona's former manager, who was arrested and prosecuted after the authorities discovered drugs in his house that in fact had been planted by the police. He was eventually exonerated.

The intruders poked indifferently through the apartment, and it was clear they didn't know what they were searching for. Andrea practically instructed them on where they could look and where they couldn't. When they rifled through a drawer that contained some of my mother's documents, she told them not to look there because the papers were from Manuela's school. They complied and immediately closed the drawer.

At that moment, Snowflake heard my mother's footsteps in the hall outside the apartment and raced toward the door. Olga, the maid, managed to open the door and gesture to my mother to turn around and go, but the dog ran out after her. When she'd almost reached the building's side door that led out to Calle Crisólogo Larralde, ten armed men in civilian dress blocked her way.

"Freeze! Drop your weapons!"

"Relax, gentlemen. What weapons? This is just a little white dog," my mother answered.

Back in the apartment, the agents couldn't get my mother to sit still. She told them, "Go ahead, this apartment is my home. Search it as much as you like." She took a shower, changed her clothes, managed to slip some papers into an envelope and hide it in the bathroom, and surreptitiously made a few phone calls to alert the lawyers and notaries who knew about Zacarías's scam. The police might have had control of the apartment, but Andrea and my mother were controlling the police.

At about three in the morning, Jorge Palacios, commissioner of the Federal Police, arrived and announced that we were under arrest.

As we were being taken to the headquarters of the Federal Police's antiterrorist unit, Channel 9 was broadcasting the operation live on its program *Memoria*. The host was Samuel "Chiche" Gelblung, a veteran journalist with a famous appetite for scandal and sensationalism.

According to the case file, our supposed problems with the law began with a report from a police officer, Roberto Ontivero. Ontivero claimed he'd been standing on a random street corner in Buenos Aires when he saw a woman resembling Pablo Escobar's widow driving a green Chrysler pickup with tinted windows. He claimed to have recognized my mother from photographs he'd seen at the Federal Police's Superintendency of Dangerous Drugs, photographs that were twenty years old, making it implausible that he'd recognized her—and especially through tinted windows in the brief period before the stoplights changed. Because of his "commitment to justice," though, he'd written down the license plate number and run it through their system.

The pickup truck was registered as having been purchased through a lease-to-own agreement, its papers were up-to-date, and it was in the name of Galestar, S.A, our real estate company. That was enough evidence for the judge, who issued arrest warrants for us, accusing us of laundering drug money.

The media went into a frenzy. Over the next several days, we would be the top headline: "Pablo Escobar's widow" had been arrested in Argentina. The day after our arrest, a Federal Police convoy took me and my mother to the courthouse on Avenida Comodoro Py, near the Buenos Aires port. They filled out forms to book us at the Federal Penitentiary Service, but upon noticing that they'd written Juan Pablo Escobar, I told them that wasn't my name.

"Do you think we're idiots? We know what your name is! You can't lie to us!" they shouted.

I knew that if I identified myself as Juan Pablo before any legal authority, I would be accused of having fake papers.

"I'm sorry, gentlemen, but no matter how much you don't like it and yell at me, that's my name. That's what my identity card says, and that's what my name is. That document is legal. There's nothing funny going on here. Period. End of discussion."

"Sign it! That's an order!" they demanded.

"I'll sign, but my name is Juan Sebastián Marroquín Santos. I'm not going to sign as Juan Pablo Escobar." In the end, they gave in. They booked us in separate cells, and I didn't see my mother after that, didn't know whether they'd arrested Andrea, didn't know what was going on outside or what was going on with my little sister and grandmother. The cells were very small, about five feet deep and three feet across, with a little cement bench. There wasn't enough room to lie down—you could only sit or stand. I spent three days in isolation there, not eating for fear they might poison me.

Judge Gabriel Cavallo had our case. Famous for striking down Argentina's Law of Due Obedience and Full-Stop Law, he was ambitious and currently angling for a spot on the Federal Appeals Court. Declaring those laws void had given him the reputation of a saint, so I initially believed he'd see our case as an obvious setup. But I was wrong.

While my mother and I were waiting in our cells, he held press conferences in which he announced that, after a careful pursuit, he'd managed to capture the narco's family. What he conveniently omitted was that when he'd had the civil-law notary's offices raided, he'd found the evidence that absolved us. My mother had registered seven declarations in sealed envelopes with the notary, detailing the extortion attempts and threats by the accountant Zacarías, his lawyer, and his other accomplices. It was all thoroughly documented through our statements and the recorded phone calls with their threats. Each envelope had an authenticated date, and each notary could certify when they'd been registered, the first of them six months earlier.

But that evidence didn't matter. Absurdly, the judge decided that I'd committed the high crime of traveling to Uruguay and designing a piece of furniture. Yes, I'd traveled to Uruguay on vacation using my identity card, and yes, I'd designed a piece of furniture because that's what I'd studied in school and how I made my living. Every statement we gave was altered and rewritten in the form of a confession. Of course we refused to sign them.

The prosecutors Eduardo Freiler and Federico Delgado, who had ended up on our case, presented no formal charges. Their inquiries with Colombian authorities made it clear that our new identities were legitimate and had been supplied by the justice department. They also concluded that our company, Galestar, S.A., had been legally acquired. The other assets—the house in Praderas and the two cars—had been purchased through honest work. In addition, we were making payments on the Chrysler pickup truck and a Mazda 121 that I drove.

Even without an indictment, with our explanations, with the evidence of the legality of our identities, with the proof of the threats and extortion attempts we'd been subject to, Judge Cavallo pushed on with the trial. He convinced the public that he firmly supported the (clearly fantastical) statement made by the police officer who worked for commissioner Jorge Palacios. And when the prosecutors refused to present formal charges, the judge arranged to have them removed from the process.

On the fourth day of our incarceration, they sent us to Detention Unit 28, right in downtown Buenos Aires. They let me take a shower and settle down on a mattress that was soiled with urine and excrement. Though I'd been confined and in hiding many times before, in that cell I truly discovered what it meant to have one's freedom snatched away.

We were waiting for an indictment from the attorney general's office, but it wasn't coming. Cavallo had to decide where to hold us in the meantime, so my mother took the opportunity to talk to him about the danger we would face if they sent us to a standard detention center.

"Your Honor, you are responsible for what happens to me, my son, and the rest of my family. As long as we're being held, you have to answer for it, and you have to answer to the Colombian government."

So Cavallo sent us to the Superintendency of Dangerous Drugs. There, we could receive calls from Colombia and have visitors every afternoon.

At around that time, Zacarías was arrested and sent to the Devoto Penitentiary. According to his own statements at trial, the other prisoners, angry that he had dared to steal from Pablo Escobar's widow, almost lynched him when he arrived. Because of the widespread animosity toward Zacarías in the prison, he was moved to the same building we were in, but one floor up.

At the Superintendency of Dangerous Drugs, my mother and I were able to visit each other's cells, so we spent many hours together. She, who had always suffered from claustrophobia, made up any excuse she could to get out of the cell. She even suggested to the commissioner that she paint all the cells, bars, and doors in the detention center. After that, she offered to clean the offices and the bathrooms every day just so she could stay active.

The guards had been ordered never to turn off the lights in our cells, and my mother took the opportunity to read everything she could get her hands on. I read the Bible and recited Psalm 91, about God as a place of refuge, which I'd learned by heart in Medellín during the war. Because of our behavior, the guards grew less and less resentful of us. You could say that we'd earned their respect.

In the meantime, Judge Cavallo decided to confiscate our assets. He demanded that my mother pay ten million dollars; Andrea, three million; I, two million; and Stinfale, who was included in the legal action, three thousand five hundred.

Cavallo pressured my mother, always insisting that if she helped him out, she would see certain benefits. If she gave him the password to an encrypted disk found in the raid on our apartment, he would release me; if she made statements against former Argentine president Carlos Menem, he would release her. He wanted us to say that we had negotiated with Carlos Menem to come to Argentina.

In a very short time, seven different prosecutors were put on our case, one after another, and none of them found reasons to hold us: Freiler, Delgado, Stornelli, Recchini, Cearras, Panelo, and Aguilar. In one document, Aguilar requested that Cavallo be investigated for breach of public duties, abuse of authority, and unlawful deprivation of liberty: "The judge, in a clear abuse of authority, orders the arrest of María Isabel Santos Caballero (the new identity that

Colombia gave Henao Vallejo to protect her safety) merely for being Escobar's widow."

MY LOVE AND APPRECIATION FOR ANDREA ARE LIMITLESS. SHE chose to climb into my plane when my engines were failing and my fuel was running out. It had been the worst moment in the history of the Escobar Henao family, and she'd risked everything to be with me. I thought about her all the time while I was in prison. To be at my side, she'd abandoned her studies, her family, her friends, her identity, her country; she'd left it all for me.

In that first month of my incarceration I decided it was time to take a step forward. I'd been wanting to propose to her for some time now, but I hadn't been able to find "the right moment." As soon as I told her I wanted to spend the rest of my life with her, Andrea started crying and hugged me, overcome with emotion. After accepting, she said, "My love, I have faith that everything's going to be better. We've already fallen so far down into the muck, so I am positive everything's going to be better from here. I love you unconditionally."

My mother, who was in the cell with us, hugged us and said everything was going to be OK. One day, all we were living through now would just be an experience.

But we didn't want to get married in a prison, so we agreed to wait.

On December 29, 1999, they took my mother and me, handcuffed and in bulletproof vests, to a new hearing in Comodoro Py. It was the last day that court would be in session before the January judicial recess. All at once, I realized the guards had left the keys in my handcuffs. I didn't know what to do. I thought it might be a trap to see if I would attempt to escape. I concluded that even though I had a real opportunity to make a break for it, it was better not to. I didn't want to spend my life on the run the way my father had. I called a guard over.

"Look, you forgot these."

Surprised, the woman removed the keys and thanked me. She said I'd saved her her job.

Once the proceedings were over, they locked us in a cell in the basement of the building to wait for a vehicle that would take us back to prison. As evening fell, our lawyers Ricardo Solomonoff and Ezequiel Klainer arrived and gave us the good news that Judge Cavallo had ordered my release that afternoon, though with several restrictions: I couldn't leave the city limits, and I had to report twice a month to confirm that I was still in Buenos Aires.

Rather than being excited, though, I felt enormously sad to think that I would be leaving my mother alone in that place. With my release order in hand, we began the exit process. That's what I was doing when I spotted Zacarías in a nearby cell and approached him.

"Sebas, Sebas, did they release you?"

"Yes."

"You're a good kid, a good person. All of this has been a huge mix-up, a mistake. I didn't say all the things you think I said. I never lied. Stinfale is the one who's responsible for all this. Look at me here—I'm in prison too."

"You know what, Juan Carlos, you still think we're stupid, but there's no way I'm getting tangled up with you. The person who took things to such extremes and ended up getting us here was you."

"No, I swear, Sebi, I'm telling the truth. There have been mix-ups, lots of lies, and the judge promised things that he never came through on."

My talk with Zacarías was fruitless, and I headed back to my cell to pray with my mother and thank God, because I had my freedom and things were finally getting cleared up.

"Be brave, son. I know you'll fight to get me out of here. They couldn't have released both of us. I am sure you won't let them hold me here a day longer."

We cried together, and I clung to her, not wanting to say good-bye. The guards were telling me, "You can leave now," and I replied, "Let me stay a little longer, please." I felt indescribable pain at leaving my mother there, locked up in a cell, under the constant gaze of security cameras, artificial lights blazing twenty-four hours a day—knowing that she was innocent.

My mother walked me to the elevator, and we hugged again. Even the guards were tearing up. I promised I'd spend my days fighting for her release, whatever it took.

On the suggestion of a good friend of ours, the singer-songwriter Piero, I met with Adolfo Pérez Esquivel, winner of the Nobel Peace Prize, and explained our case.

"Everything you've told me seems to be true," he said. "But I can't risk intervening in the case through SERPAJ (Service for Peace and Justice) until a lawyer reviews the whole thing and sends me a detailed report of possible violations of your human rights and those of your family. She'll be in touch with you."

That process seemed to take forever, but at last I received a copy of the letter that Pérez Esquivel wrote to Judge Cavallo:

The SERPAJ is writing to inform Your Honor that we have received in our office a declaration from the Marroquín Santos family regarding the case under your charge that is being pursued against them in the Court, which we consider to constitute a veridical account of possible human rights violations.

According to the abovementioned report, legal proceedings are currently moving forward based on a serious accusation—unlawful association and money laundering—whose fundamental basis is family kinship with Pablo Escobar Gaviria.

It is our intention to put ourselves at the disposal of the

Court to clarify the points referred to as violating inalienable human rights, motivated only by a policy of good offices whose aim is to safeguard the not-insignificant circumstance that a foreigner in Argentina has the same rights as any citizen.

Adolfo Pérez Esquivel

At last, someone had seen beyond the smokescreen created by those forces that were out to get us.

But the harassment didn't stop. We discovered that a police officer had attempted to infiltrate the family, passing himself off as a friend of my sister's. Manuela, who was fifteen at the time, was still paying a high price for our father's misdeeds. She studied at the Jean Piaget School, until one day the headmaster called me up to say that some of the teachers were refusing to have her in their classes because of her family history.

"I appreciate your candor," I replied. "I will be withdrawing her from this school, which clearly does not take care of or respect its students. My sister isn't going learn anything from ignorant people anyway."

Manuela had to endure yet more discrimination at another high school in Buenos Aires after the TV host Chiche Gelblung, apathetic to the fact that he was breaking the law, published her photo. Many parents at the school complained, and some students bullied her, even spraying graffiti about her.

For his part, Judge Cavallo was still obsessed with keeping my mother locked up. One time he even argued that the mere fact of being Colombian made her guiltier. Her arbitrary detention was ultimately a kidnapping that would last a year and eight months.

On one occasion during her incarceration, my mother almost lost her life. A sharp pain began to form in one of her molars, and the lawyers requested permission to take her to the dentist. The judge denied them. They asked again because the infection was getting worse, and again he rejected them. When they petitioned him a third time, Cavallo's response was incredibly unjust and heartless: he sent her a pair of pliers so she could extract the tooth herself.

The swelling wasn't going down, and she'd had the infection for more than a week. Only when Cavallo was told that the situation was now dangerous did he finally authorize the dentist appointment. The diagnosis: my mother was three or four hours away from suffering septic shock—that is, having the infection invade the rest of her body.

Once this scare was over, I decided it was time to be straight with my colleagues at ORT, where I taught classes. I wanted to give them my version of the facts, so I invited all the professors to an informal meeting. As soon as I started speaking, one of them interrupted:

"Hang on, hang on, Sebastián. You don't have to explain anything. We've known you for four years. You come every day and are one of our best students. You're also the employee and neighbor of Alan, our colleague. If it's possible to launder money at three in the morning, which is when you'd have a bit of free time, then you'll have to give us some sort of explanation. But we've already talked about that here with the ORT administration, and everybody agrees on what we all know about you. Use this meeting to talk about something else if you want, but we don't need you to explain anything. We're well aware of the pack of lies they've cooked up on you."

In July or August 2000—the end of winter in the southern hemisphere—posters advertising the University of Palermo were up around the city. I'd been rehired at the same design studio where I'd previously been working, with permission to work from home so I could continue my efforts to defend my mother. I told my mother I wanted to study architecture at the university—the tuition wasn't too expensive, and I would be able to take only a few classes at a time so I could focus on her case. So that's what I did, and it went well at first. I passed many of my classes thanks to my knowledge of design concepts. But between my work and my studies, I had almost no time for my efforts to free my mother. Around May 2001, I decided to quit school and was on my way to the office to withdraw officially when I got a call from Solomonoff, one of our lawyers, with wonderful news: my mother was going to be released.

In the end, the judge had found no more excuses for keeping her in custody. His last-ditch effort was to level an unfounded accusation of criminal conspiracy against her. His claim? My mother was the head of an international criminal organization because she'd hired two Colombian lawyers, Francisco Fernández and Francisco Salazar, to handle her legal affairs in Colombia. This new determination by Cavallo began to fall apart, but when our lawyers presented an appeal, the federal judge Riva Aramayo—a friend of Cavallo—didn't address the fundamental questions and beat around the bush.

It was a critical day in the proceedings, and we would finally know whether my mother would go to trial while still in custody or once she'd been released. We were waiting for the verdict when Judge Cavallo stormed out, his face red with rage. His displeasure was the result of the attorney general's office's finding that there was no evidence against my mother beyond our family kinship with Pablo Escobar.

One of our lawyers emerged after the judge left and gave us the happy news that they'd set bail to secure my mother's release. We had no money, but I was ready to try to borrow it. But Solomonoff said he'd pay for my mother's bail that same day in case Cavallo tried to come up with a new charge to keep her in custody.

"I am profoundly grateful to you for resolving this for me and my mother. But I have to clarify one thing: not only do I not have the money, but I don't really know when or how I will be able to pay you back. You know better than anyone that Zacarías cleaned us out," I told Solomonoff.

"No, Sebastián, don't worry. Forget about it. Your mother is being released today. Cavallo has to set her free. They've notified him already, and they have to release her."

Over the next two hours, there was a serious conflict between Cavallo and our lawyers regarding the payment of the bail bond. Finally Cecilia Amil, the judge's secretary, went to the national bank to count the money.

It was after ten in the evening when Judge Cavallo reluctantly signed the release order, and we went to get my mother out of prison.

She wanted to return to normal, but she was sunk in a deep silence for several months. She had a hard time reintegrating into everyday life and recovering her vigor, but eventually she got back into the swing of things and continued pursuing education at several prestigious institutions. It was a relief to know that we were all home again.

The judicial proceedings finally moved on to their final stage: the Supreme Court of Justice. That court ordered an exhaustive review of our accounts, which showed that the supposed money-laundering schemes had never existed. And so the investigation was shut down. We were completely cleared of all charges by the Federal Oral Criminal Tribunal No. 5. The media reporting on the topic was now muted, in contrast to the blaring headlines that had followed the news of our capture all those years before.

As our nightmare was finally ending, I graduated with my degree in architecture from the University of Palermo. I slowly made advances in the profession and opened my first studio, Box Arquitectura Latinoamericana. I was part of the team of architects—along with Estudio AFRa, LGR, and Fernández Prieto—that won the competition to design the mausoleum of Juan Domingo and Eva Perón. I also designed a fourteen-story building and won other competitions in the Puerto Madero area with the president of the

Central Society of Architects at the time, Daniel Silberfaden, and renowned architect Roberto Busnelli.

In December 2002, I kept my word and married Andrea. We wanted to hold the ceremony outside at a hotel, but the Argentine Catholic Church required that weddings take place inside churches. As always, my mother stepped in and achieved the impossible: the bishop of Buenos Aires, Jorge Mario Bergoglio, authorized the wedding. Against all odds, my mother managed to secure an audience with the man who would become Pope Francis.

In the meantime, I also designed and built two large houses for private clients in Colombia. The first, a weekend getaway home, was challenging, as I had to do the work long-distance through blueprints, photos, and videos alone. The second project, in Medellín, was praised for the purity of its forms and the warmth of its design.

It hasn't been easy to find this kind of work, since very few people dare to employ the professional services of a person who bears the stigma of being Pablo Escobar's son. In 2005, I received a call from the Argentine film director Nicolás Entel, who proposed—as many others had before him—making a documentary about my father. I told him I was interested as long as it wouldn't be more of the same depictions we'd been seeing for years.

We developed a general concept, and filming took four years. During that process, I wrote a letter to the sons of the politicians Luis Carlos Galán and Rodrigo Lara Bonilla, asking their forgiveness for the harm my father had inflicted upon them. We were able to engage in a dialogue of reconciliation.

I was forced to interrupt the fulfilling experience of making the documentary in early 2009, when I filed a criminal complaint against a despicable person in the United States who was pretending to be me. My uncle Roberto had devised this scheme after my repeated refusals to participate in a project with U.S. companies interested in making a movie about my father's story. My uncle decided to clone his nephew instead with the help of José Pablo Rodríguez, a thirty-year-old man weighing three hundred pounds, an American of Costa Rican descent who lived in New Jersey.

On Roberto's instructions, the impostor managed to find my professional e-mail address and wrote me a message brazenly stating that he'd been using the name Pablo Escobar, Jr., since 2001. Thanks to this appropriation of my identity, he'd been approached by major corporations such as Nike and Red Bull with deals worth millions of dollars, and he also said that rappers such as Nas and 50 Cent had helped make him famous. If I collaborated with him in making his deception credible, he said, both of us would be millionaires.

Indignant, I asked my lawyer to file a lengthy criminal complaint against the man in Colombia. In the document, we described the full timeline of contact with this person. In my accusation, I also noted, "I have no doubt that in addition to José Pablo Rodríguez, my uncle Roberto de Jesús Escobar Gaviria is also behind these threats, since in the past, for unknown reasons, he has tried to do me harm, seeking the complicity of all of my father's closest collaborators in making statements against me and cooking up a criminal trial in Colombia in an effort to rob me of my freedom."

The impostor was infuriated by my response to his proposal. In a message dated March 10, 2009, and titled "Letter to a Clone," I suggested that he seek his own path, as I was doing, and encouraged him to reflect on the situation, trying to make him realize that there was no need to appropriate a story that wasn't his.

I thought he'd accept my arguments, but he reacted violently, with threats and insults: "I'm only going to tell you this once. I tried to go about this nicely, but you ignored me. If you want your future children or your family members who are still alive to grow old and not be reunited with your father before their time, you'd better not get in my way. Believe me, we can speed up the process to make sure that reunion happens sooner rather than later. There are plenty of people who would pay good money to know where you and your family live. You'll never sleep easy again."

We were amazed when the impostor didn't stop. He gave interviews to media outlets in Colombia, Central America, and the United States, where he even appeared with Cristina Saralegui on her television program *The Cristina Show*. My uncle Roberto allowed him to upload videos to YouTube in which the two of them appeared as if they were family members and he acknowledged him as "my nephew Pablo."

I learned of the interview with Cristina a week before it aired, and after protesting, I managed to secure the right to respond. Imagine the surprise of my uncle, who'd probably invited lots of people to watch the spectacle he'd organized. On the program, I exposed the impostor, presented the complaints filed against him, and made it clear on the air that he was a fraud.

With the exasperating incident behind us, the documentary *Sins of My Father* finally had its premiere at the Mar del Plata International Film Festival. Since then, it's been featured at the world's most important film festivals, including Sundance in the United States and festivals in the Netherlands, Japan, Cuba, Ecuador, France, Poland, Germany, Mexico, and others. The United Nations also screened it in 2010 to celebrate the International Day of Peace.

That documentary literally reopened the doors of the world to me when it won seven prizes and other important recognitions. The countries where it was shown granted me entry visas, including the United States, which gave me a visa good for five years. Three days later, though, I received a call from the U.S. embassy saying there had been a mistake with the visa. The mistake was being Pablo Escobar's son. They canceled the visa.

I was astounded. After all, John Cohen, head of the DEA in Argentina, had told the American consul and a representative from the U.S. State Department, "The DEA has investigated Sebastián for years and found that he has no relationship whatsoever with his father's activities or with drugs. As such, the DEA does not oppose his entry to the United States because he no longer represents a threat to the country." It's been twenty-two years now that because of my father's actions—not mine—I haven't been allowed to enter the United States.

The following year, I founded Escobar Henao, a clothing company that sold pieces inspired by unpublished documents and images from my father's life, like his birth certificate. All of the apparel was printed with unambiguous messages of peace, urging people not to repeat his history.

Several individuals rushed to denounce the idea, including, sadly, Colombian Senator Juan Manuel Galán, who judged the project "an insult, an aggression." He added, "I'm not against it if they want to make TV shows and write books," but claimed that the only message my business was sending was "a cult of personality for a criminal and murderer." Some manufacturers refused to work with us, and a bank even closed our accounts.

Many people think that we've lived off a large inheritance from my father all these years. That's not true. We have survived thanks to the assistance of my maternal family, my mother's business acumen in dealing art and real estate, and our own salaried jobs. Nobody knows better than we do that dirty money brings only tragedy, and we have no desire to relive that past.

My family and I have learned to live and work with dignity, always in accordance with the law and with the aid of our education. We have the right to live our lives in peace, as we have always strived to do.

I have asked forgiveness for events that occurred before I was even born, and I will continue to share that message for the rest of my life. But my family and I deserve the opportunity to live without hatred and scorn. My father's history robbed us of our friends, our siblings, our cousins, half of our family, and our country. In exchange, it left us with exile and the burden of fear and persecution.

I spent years rejecting the prospect of becoming a father, as I thought it was irrational and selfish to encumber a child with a cruel legacy that he or she would have to carry around forever. Today my views have changed. I want to have the opportunity to show my children the value of honest work, commitment, education, and respect for life and the law. I want the chance to raise them to be upstanding people. The best legacy I can leave them at the end of my days is this: make sure every step you take leads you toward peace.

Acknowledgments

To my father, who showed me what path not to take.